American Work-Sports

ALSO BY FRANK ZARNOWSKI
AND FROM MCFARLAND

The Pentathlon of the Ancient World (2013)

*American Decathletes: A 20th Century
Who's Who* (2002; paperback 2011)

American Work-Sports

A History of Competitions for Cornhuskers, Lumberjacks, Firemen and Others

FRANK ZARNOWSKI

Foreword by Bil Gilbert

McFarland & Company, Inc., Publishers
Jefferson, North Carolina, and London

LIBRARY OF CONGRESS CATALOGUING-IN-PUBLICATION DATA

Zarnowski, Frank.
    American work-sports : a history of competitions for cornhusters, lumberjacks, firemen and others / Frank Zarnowski ; foreword by Bil Gilbert.
       p.   cm.
    Includes bibliographical references and index.

    ISBN 978-0-7864-6784-6
    softcover : acid free paper ∞

    1. Contests—United States—History. 2. Sports—United States—History. 3. Employees—United States—Competitions. 4. Agricultural laborers—United States—Competitions. 5. Blue collar workers—United States—Competitions. I. Title.
GV1201.6.Z37 2013
790.1'34—dc23   2013028908

BRITISH LIBRARY CATALOGUING DATA ARE AVAILABLE

© 2013 Frank Zarnowski. All rights reserved

No part of this book may be reproduced or transmitted in any form or by any means, electronic or mechanical, including photocopying or recording, or by any information storage and retrieval system, without permission in writing from the publisher.

Front cover image: Postcard showing a man riding a bucking bronco with spectators in the background, 1910 (Library of Congress, Prints and Photographs Division, LC-DIG-ppmsca-19089)

Manufactured in the United States of America

McFarland & Company, Inc., Publishers
  Box 611, Jefferson, North Carolina 28640
    www.mcfarlandpub.com

For Sarah, Rachel and the Wallin family,
and to the memory of Bil Gilbert

Table of Contents

Foreword by Bil Gilbert — 1
Preface — 7
Introduction: The Emergence of American Work-Sports — 13

PART ONE: WORKER COMPETITIONS IN THE 19TH CENTURY, 1840–1900

1. Rock Breaking and Other Early Work-Sports — 23
2. "Put Out That Fire" — Firemen's Musters — 31
3. Worker Games for Slaves — 48
4. Setting Type, the Story of the Swifts — 55
5. Circus Leapers — 66
6. Ten Miles of Track in a Day — 74

PART TWO: WORKER COMPETITIONS IN THE 20TH CENTURY, 1900–1940

7. Rodeo — 83
8. Lumberjacks — 96
9. Rock Drilling and Steel Drivin' Men — 105
10. Office Games — 117
11. Corn Husking and Other Agricultural Contests — 127

PART THREE: WHAT HAPPENED TO WORKER COMPETITIONS, 1940 TO THE PRESENT

12. Obsolete Work-Sports — 145
13. Modern Work-Sports — 160

14. Work-Sports in Popular Culture	170
15. Why Work-Sports?	178

Appendices
1 — U.S. Workers in Common Work-Sports Occupations, 1900	193
2 — Sample Muster News Account	194
3 — Numbers of U.S. Work-Sports Athletes, 2010	195
4 — U.S. Occupational Sports, 2010	196
5 — Wall Street Journal *Front Page Work-Sports Stories, 1995–2005*	198
Chapter Notes	201
Bibliography	213
Index	221

Foreword
by Bil Gilbert

Bil Gilbert wrote this foreword in September 2011, four months before his unexpected death in January 2012.

Among other things, *American Work-Sports* is a very aptly named book. It represents an impressive amount of work and it is a serious book which illuminates important aspects of American history and culture which have previously been much and unfortunately neglected.

But it is also a book which was born out of sport and playfulness. I think I am uniquely qualified to comment on its origin since, from the time it was only a gleam, so to speak, in the author's eye, I have been involved with it as, if not a godfather, at least as a doting uncle.

To support this immodest claim: Dr. Frank Zarnowski and I met by accident some fifty years ago. He was a young economics instructor at Mount St. Mary's College — now a university in central Maryland, just south of the Mason-Dixon line. I was a bit older, beginning to be a published journalist and essayist living a few miles north in Pennsylvania. It is surprising that the two of us have been such close friends for so long because temperamentally and vocationally we are a fairly odd couple.

As an economist, specifics and statistics greatly engage Zeke. (After all of these years I cannot reprogram myself to think, write or speak about "Dr. Frank Zarnowski.") As for myself, as a writer whose subjects often have to do with American social and natural history, I lean toward the general and speculative. Also, our lifestyles have always been quite different. Zeke was, as he has remained, a bachelor with — how shall we put it — a large and varied social agenda. Ann, still my wife, and I were preoccupied with four young children and the always-changing but present menagerie which has traditionally been part of our household: dogs, cats, horses, burros, foxes, raccoons, ferrets, crows, hawks, owls, etc., etc., etc. When he came to dinner as young bachelors want and need to do, Zeke was politely tolerant of the kids and other creatures, but was obviously outside of his comfort zone. On the other hand we did and still do share a common, and in some respects, uncommon interest in sports. We have both played and coached a variety of more or less organized games, sometimes together, sometimes as competitive rivals. We are conventional followers and fans of our athletic superiors: e.g., we have spent a lot of time arguing about the relative merits of Zeke's St. Louis Cardinals and my Detroit Tigers. But most important, we are both fascinated by what might be called the sporting culture. The last word is used in its largest sense, i.e., to describe the ancient memory bank or source of what Richard Dawkins called *memes*, which have been accumulating for many centuries.

Zeke and I have been meeting for a two- or three-hour, almost weekly, lunch for about 30 years. (Inexactitudes annoy him. The above one may drive him to the files where he keeps old expense records, and keep him there until he is certain we started these meetings thirty-one years, seven months and eleven days ago.) Whenever they began, food has always been incidental to conversations. Sometimes we gabbed about ordinary things, war, peace, politics, money, sore backs, good and bad colleagues. But much of the time we have talked about current and historic athletic events — underrecognized and overrated ones; comic and suspect performers. We were always alert for unique sporting happenings. And those we found were brought back to entertain at the lunch table.

During the 1980s many of these athletic tidbits which I thought were lunch-worthy came from the early and mid–19th century because I was working on books which had to do with this period. Among others there were the goose pull, a competition between men on horseback who in a full gallop tried to pull down geese with greased necks who had been hung from limbs; oyster swallowing, through the nose; and contests between laborers who were breaking up rocks for the bed of the first national highway.

As Zeke and I pondered these seemingly disparate entertainments we began to think that, in fact, there was a connection. Many of them were ad hoc, on-the-job games which made use of the materials, tools and skills of working men and — less often — women. The more we talked, joked and generally considered the phenomenon the more significant it seemed to be in regards to American culture, past and present.

In, say, arbitrarily 1850, athletic recreation of the sort we now think of as true sport was largely restricted in this country to a very small group of affluent and leisured people who lived within a few hundred miles of the Atlantic Ocean. Then and there the gentility genteelly punted and paddled, croqueted, lawn bowled, sailed, skated, and sometimes ran and swam a bit. However, for the great majority of Americans the sporting menu was minuscule in comparison with the present one.

Foreword by Bil Gilbert

When Abraham Lincoln was first elected president of the United States, baseball was in its infancy. Basketball, football, softball and the modern Olympic games had not been invented; nor had roller skates, sneakers, ski lifts, etc. Golf, tennis, soccer and a good many other amusements would not be imported from Europe until later. There were a few professional boxers, runners and strong men. But by contemporary measure they were not paid much, attracted small crowds, and were not invited to White House dinners. And 24/7 sports radio and TV were more than a century away.

Beyond the obvious technological reasons, there were good social — in the broadest sense of that word — reasons for this apparent lack of interest in what is now thought of as sporting activity. In 1850 the majority of adult Americans were manual laborers. Typically they worked longer and harder days and weeks than we do now. And when they got off the job they were not inclined to spend their free time vigorously running, jumping, throwing, catching, lifting, pounding, hitting. Even if there had been such things it seems unlikely that our sporting ancestors would have joined an after-work softball league or exercise club. Taking off your shoes, sitting in a rocking chair — if you had one — on the porch with a refreshing beverage was, understandably, more the style of the times.

Furthermore, games playing and recreational sporting then had a fairly bad reputation; they were generally regarded as certainly feckless, time-wasting activities, and quite possible sinful ones. The common wisdom in this matter was neatly summarized by Cotton Mather, the prominent 17th century divine. He puritanically thundered, "That which is not useful is vicious."

Yet despite attempts at moral repression, and a lack of facilities and venues, what might be called the sporting spirit remained strong. Throughout the 19th century it repeatedly burst out in surprising ways and places. Very often Americans playfully competed where, when and as they were supposed to be doing useful work. Sometimes they were encouraged to do so by their employers; at other times they were not.

Again, Zeke may have a different take on it, but it seems to me the seminal moment for *American Work-Sports* occurred in Fairfield, Pennsylvania, late in the 20th century. Fairfield is a village southwest of Gettysburg near which Ann, I, and the ever-changing community of children and beasts lived for nearly 50 years. A longtime resident of Fairfield was the late Percy Polley, who during the time we knew him became a nonagenarian.

One warm afternoon we got to talking about the decline of the Fourth of July—from the free-form, satisfyingly risky Walpurgis day for youths to the present tame civic and smarmy political affair. Mr. Polley said that, once, a big part of the Fourth celebration in Fairfield was the mile-long brick pull.

I naturally said, "The what?" Mr. Polley explained this happening as follows:

> I don't know who thought it up, was before my time. But not much was necessary to get ready. A lot of us young fellows worked baling hay. So there was big spools of binder twine around. And where the train tracks crossed the road was just a mile from Main Street in Fairfield. And there used to be brick factories. So this is what we did. The ones who wanted to take part in the contest took their binder twine and a brick out to the train tracks. Then you'd tie the end of your twine around a brick with a good, firm knot. Then you'd start unrolling the twine while you were walking back to Main Street. Depending on the size of the spool it would take 3 or 4 of these spliced together to reach back to Fairfield. When everybody got set there, somebody would shoot off a gun and we'd start pulling in our brick from the railroad crossing. It wasn't an easy thing to do as you'd see if you ever were to try it.

On the Saturday following our weekly lunch Zeke drove up to our house and said he was ready. For what? For the Experimental Brick Pull.

In the trunk of his car Zeke had a couple of bricks and a huge spool of binder twine. (Since circa 1900 haying has become much more mechanized but there was still demand for binder twine.) The road from the rail tracks to the center of town had long before been paved, and would have made a smoother pulling surface than it was in Mr. Polley's youth. But we decided there was too much traffic on it for our purposes. Not having enough local clout to get the road closed for a few hours we settled on a stretch of empty parking lot and driveway at the local high school. This gave us a straight quarter of a mile pull which was how much binder twine we calculated we had. This would, we thought, provide a decent trial.

I will leave the details of this event to Zeke. But even this puny, quarter-of-a-mile test was enough to convince us that the Great Fourth of July Brick Pull had not been an easy event. Dragging a brick and a great gob of binder twine was much more strenuous than we had thought it would be. As we pulled — in relays — the bricks would skid off at off angles and the twine would break. And the more we pulled the more apt we were to get tangled up in snarls of twine which collected around our feet. When he heard about our attempt, Mr. Polley asked with a straight face if he had not mentioned that the brick pull was a team contest. He had not.

"Well, there was a kicker. He followed the brick in from the tracks, kicked it out of the weeds, kept it on a straight course, and tied the broken ends of the twine. The winder wrapped the twine around a big stick to keep it out of the way of the puller. The puller was supposed to be the strongest, the winder the handiest, and the kicker the quickest. But it didn't always work out that way."

Foreword by Bil Gilbert

Not long after the Experimental Brick Pull, the idea of a book on work-sports came to be. For a time we thought to make it a joint project. But shortly we agreed that this would not be good for us or the subject. Zeke is a scholarly researcher while I am an itinerant ruminator. This subject clearly had more need for the former than it did the latter; i.e., work-sports require and deserve the specifics and stats which they have previously lacked and which Zeke has so industriously collected and cogently presents in this book.

A number of once-were work-sports which Frank Zarnowski describes here have, like the Fairfield Brick Pull, disappeared. Some are preserved as museum displays in civic celebrations, Chamber of Commerce promotions and performances staged by enthusiastic re-enactors; e.g., fireman musters, jousting, cornhusking bees. Some have evolved into what we now think of as "real" competitive sports, for which the contestants train seriously, and are given material rewards and, now and then, time on late-night cable TV. Included in this category are such things as rodeo, lumberjack contests, dog mushing, horseshoes and the modern pentathlon. And new ones keep coming. Now we have races for urban bike couriers, and driving bootleg whiskey from still to market has morphed into NASCAR.

In historical perspective it can be plausibly argued that few if any present sports commenced as recreational pursuits. Rather it seems they evolved from imperative activities, from things people had to do for economic or even basic survival reasons: from lifting, pulling, throwing, catching, hunting, gathering, and, of course, fleeing and fighting. (An inordinate number of "real" sports memorialize and tamely duplicate the skills and behavior of ancient warriors.)

As the in-house ruminator here it seems to me that *American Work-Sports* smartly emphasizes a great mystery concerning our kind which has been too often and too skittishly ignored. It is: according to both historical and archeological records, we—for as long as we know anything about ourselves—have been inventing games and contests and participating in them with considerable seriousness. We have done so in hard times and places, and in dangerous and disastrous ones. Why? An atavistic flaw? Original sin? An adaption of critical survival value? It's worth exploring.

The late Bil Gilbert was the author of ten books and several hundred articles and essays in major American periodicals including Audubon, Discover, Life, *the* New York Times, Smithsonian, Sports Illustrated *and* Time.

Preface

There was an awkward silence in the immediate moments after the truck windshield shattered. It had been smashed by a wood and steel missile traveling more than 50 miles per hour. The brawny assailant was Carl Wallin, 30, a newly hired construction worker who, from more than 70 yards away, had just taken out a dump truck windshield with his four-foot shovel. Then quickly, among a roar and whoops of wonder and disbelief, came the comments. "Who's gonna tell the boss?" cried one co-worker. "At least you could have hit your own truck," wisecracked a second. But most of the comments like "Helluva throw" or "Nice going Carl," were a mixture of congratulations and incredulity.

Each Friday afternoon in the summer of 1971, a road construction crew working near Fairlee, Vermont, could be found straining, huffing and grunting in tests of strength, spring and agility. Beers in hand, eight to ten non-union employees of the Milt Jewell Construction firm would kick back by using their construction equipment — barrels, shovels, and the like — in competitive contests. Their primary project was building Interstate 91, a north-south artery through Vermont and New Hampshire. But the secondary goal was to have some fun at week's end. After participants parked their 10-wheel Ford dump trucks, the very first event of this construction mini–Olympics was a drum-jump, where participants would take a running leap over prone barrels, two, three, and four at a time, as ice skaters do. From there the games usually moved to the empty barrel leap, where contestants, with a running bound, landed, feet first, into a 3 foot, 6 inch standing empty drum with a four-foot diameter. Enough said.

The ultimate Fairlee game was the shovel toss, where four-foot shovels weighing five to six pounds were wheeled and tossed from behind a foul line. The primary organizer of these worker competitions was Wallin himself, a summer employee and the newly hired track and field coach at nearby Dartmouth College. Wallin stood 6 foot 4 and weighed in at somewhere near 260 pounds. Had his co-workers known of his track and field background, they might have parked the trucks much farther from the throwing area. Wallin had been a world class shotputter who placed fifth in the event at the 1964 U.S. Olympic Trials. His versatility was surpassed only by his desire to make a contest of everything. He was an addicted competitor.

"I could throw the shovel a freakin' mile," he recalls. "Well over 200 feet. No one knew my track background and I developed my own technique, throwing it like the modern hammer event, with a spin. After two turns I let the shovel handle slip out of my hands." When pressed further about the incident, he recalled, "We played those games at week's end because we had a case of beer and a lot of testosterone to work off." The company, incidentally, put an end to Wallin's frolics, but not to his employment. He is still noncommittal about whether his pay was docked for the cost of a windshield.

Wallin has since retired as the Dartmouth track coach and one of his prize athletes tells his own work-game story. Sean Furey, an "04" as they say at Dartmouth, and a world-class javelin thrower (2010 national U.S. champion) was a high school student in 1997 when he found himself on a summer landscaping job for R&N Construction, Inc., of Methuen, Massachusetts. "My first job was to rake up rocks at a residential site. We'd rake them into piles, and then use shovels to carry them into a wooded area behind the house, about 35 yards away," recalled Furey. "Our job was simply to get all the rocks into the woods. My co-worker Adam Wright and I got bored just of walking the full shovels into the woods, so we started tossing them. From there it was pretty easy to advance to a contest in which we'd throw the entire shovel full from where we stood. The rocks were golf ball size and a shovel full weighed in the neighborhood of 15 pounds."

Furey, also a star prep quarterback, quickly invented a one-turn technique for the square shovels, which had four-foot handles. "Usually no one was home in the middle of the afternoon, so we just had rock throwing and shovel tossing contests for a couple of hours. In all honesty, we did it because we were bored."

Unfortunately, while experimenting with a two-turn technique one warm summer day, Furey lost a shovel full of rocks, which took off at a 90-degree angle. "I just lost control and the rocks went over a neighbor's fence. It was about five feet high. When Adam and I looked," Sean continued, "we found the rocks at the bottom of an above-ground swimming pool. The rocks had torn the pool's liner in half a dozen places and water was flooding out. It took us all summer to earn enough money to buy the owner a new pool liner."

Neither the 1970s Vermont shovel throw nor the 1990s Massachusetts rock/shovel toss evolved into popular pastimes. Not because they resulted in property damage, but because they were functional only at the moment and, like many ad hoc competitions, had a brief and exciting tenure. When the job was completed the games vanished, usually recalled only when there was a dramatic outcome, like a shattered windshield. They were reminiscent of many early 19th century worker competitions: impromptu, local and without the standard characteristics of modern sports. But playing at work, especially in 19th and early 20th century America, was no coincidence, no fluke. In many cases these contests were a normal part of the workday. They may have emerged as friendly challenges, or a way to blow off steam or to win a wager, or just to entertain. But, in fact, playing at work was quite normal and we know this because some of the more popular worker competitions eventually became formalized as popular pastimes. Rodeo, lumberjacking, firemen's musters, cornhusking, harvesting, brick laying, blacksmithing and sheep shearing are a few notable examples of such sports that are still popular one to two centuries later. Yet there were many, many more, and when one steps back one can observe an entire sporting/labor trend. Each work-sport was but a small piece of a much bigger picture. An overview of the work-sports movement, a description of the conditions which set the stage in the 19th century, and an ideological framework are all presented in the introduction.

My intention was to make this book entertaining while raising the reader's curiosity about a trend that has slipped past most historians. There is no attempt to be comprehensive here. Not *every* work-sport can be documented, so I have chosen a notable dozen, popular ones during their own heyday, and assigned a chapter to each. The first part covers work-sports that initially became modish in the 19th century, generally from 1840 to 1900. Some fizzled and faded away while others continue to this day. Chapter 1 tells the story of rock breaking, an occupation which became a contest during the construction of roads. Chapter 2 deals with the first major team sport in America, the firemen's muster. Chapters 3, 4 and 5 demonstrate that worker competitions ran the gamut of working situations. Chapter 3 covers common contests, notably cotton picking, held by slaves on Southern plantations. Chapter 4 offers a description of unionized employees, newspaper typesetters or "swifts," who demonstrated their occupational skills by competing with one another. Chapter 5 is about traveling circus performers, acrobats and leapers, who wowed crowds under the big tent.

Many worker competitions arose from wagers. Perhaps the biggest stake of the century, $10,000, matched the teams laying track for the Union Pacific and Central Pacific railroads in 1869. Chapter 6 offers details on how the Central Pacific won the bet.

Part Two contains five additional chapters on worker competitions which generally became prominent in the 20th century. Chapter 7 focuses on rodeo, initially through the accomplishments of one of its earliest stars, dusky Bulldoggin' Bill Pickett. Chapter 8 covers the lumberjack and how his day-to-day work tasks became a popular spectator sport.

Chapter 9 deals with a mining contest, rock drilling. Necessary for the excavation of many minerals and the construction of tunnels, rock drillers conducted their own national championships in the earliest days of the 20th century. Chapter 10 illustrates the changing nature of American occupations in the new century, from production to service. New forms of office tasks—typing, shorthand, Morse codes—provided an opportunity for many office workers to compete.

Chapter 11 covers farming and harvesting competitions and could very well have been placed at the beginning of the book, since plowing competitions were the earliest standardized and nationally reported work-sports, dating to the second decade of the 19th century. But it comes last because it features the story of corn husking, which was enthusiastically embraced by the farm population and which conducted nationally broadcast (radio) events right up to the outbreak of World War II.

Part Three provides four additional chapters which put into perspective, from the standpoint of both labor and sporting history, America's century of worker competitions. Chapter 12 offers a dozen examples of worker competitions that were popular for a brief period, but which sputtered and died out. Chapter 13 tells the story of what has happened to work-sports contests, that is, the location of work-sports today, from ESPN2 to the vocational school curriculum. Chapter 14 tells how popular U.S. culture has influenced and has been influenced by work-sports. Finally, Chapter 15 answers some common questions about the work-sports movement, including why it occurred and what it has meant.

In the appendices documentation is offered for, among other things: the dozens of modern occupations in which Americans choose an annual national champion; an estimate of the current number of U.S. work-sports athletes (now over one and one-half million), and a decade-long list of worker-competitions which have shown up on the front page of the *Wall Street Journal*.

For the past 15 years I have gathered work-sport related material. The preparation of the text spanned 40 months. My indebtedness to colleagues and friends has become so vast that it is impossible to list all of those who deserve credit. First, I should mention the late Bil Gilbert, with whom I often discussed the origin and nature of games. We even tried a local occupational game, brick pulling. Bil was a contributing editor at *Sports Illustrated* and magazine writer of note and our discussions led to a summer research grant from my employer at the time, Mount St. Mary's College in Maryland. I used the grant at the best historical journal research library I could find, at the University of Wisconsin in Madison. As I gathered material, I realized that an entire sporting/labor movement had been overlooked by historians, and I applied for a visiting scholar position at Dartmouth College. I found a sympathetic ear in Bill Fischel, the Economics Department chairman, and I spent a fall term in Hanover, New Hampshire, preparing a journal article. I found a good deal of resistance to my idea but eventually "Working at Play: The Phenomenon of 19th Century Worker Competitions" was published in the *Journal of Leisure Research* in 2004.

I am grateful to some of my colleagues at Mount St. Mary's, in particular Carol Hinds, Peter Dorsey, John Larrivee and Curt Johnson, who encouraged the project. The librarians at the National Sporting Library in Middleburg, Virginia, made available the original copies of 19th century newspapers like the *Spirit of the Times*. And the Library of Congress, Washington, D.C., the Library at Hood College, Frederick, Maryland; and the Dartmouth libraries were consulted for much of the newspaper research. Abby Markwyn, a University of Wisconsin graduate student, was very helpful in searching historical journals. The Hagely Museum in Wilmington, Delaware, provided company histories and the Circus World Museum in Baraboo, Wisconsin, proved invaluable in rummaging circus history.

I am indebted to my students and colleagues at Dartmouth College, in particular Carl Wallin and Sean Furey, who shared their work-sports experiences, and to Patsy Carter of Dartmouth's Baker-Berry Library, a splendid and obliging librarian who effortlessly obtained 19th century inter-library loan materials, documents and manuscripts. I am appreciative to Denton Kreitz, Kory Hirak and Pete Coe who kept my computer working and to Jennie Knox of Gettysburg, Pennsylvania, who did an admirable job with all of the illustrations. And again, I owe a debt of gratitude to Bil Gilbert, who started all of this with a brick.

In American history the basic structure of society has been constant — free enterprise and capitalism — an economic system based on private property and profit. This system has dominated from the Colonial period to the present day. The system has not changed, but the push for profit and cost saving devices has led to a revolution in the nature of work over 200+ years. In the 20th century, for example, U.S. employment patterns shifted rapidly, especially to service industries. As general employment grew, it stagnated in mining, manufacturing and agriculture, not only eliminating jobs but also the work-sports which these pursuits had spawned. This is one explanation for both the decline in U.S. worker competitions after World War II and for our lack of recognition of the work-sports movement in the first place. Few of us have ever seen someone hand drilling rocks, nor setting type, nor husking corn. Further, virtually none of us realize that, for over a century, those who did these and dozens of other hard, physical jobs, fashioned contests while at it. The purpose of this book is to remember those American workers who did the work and who had some fun while at it.

Introduction

The Emergence of American Work-Sports

This is a book about competitive work games, what I have termed work-sports, which became a regular part of America's economic and cultural life beginning in the 19th century. For nearly a century American work-sports champions performed feats of strength, dexterity and endurance at or after work. So common were these contests that, by 1900, more than 45 percent of the American workforce found itself in occupations in which worker-competitions were widespread.[1] These competitions (work-sports) were physical contests derived from a laborer's occupation. In fact, there were two distinct types. The first included games reflective of a service provided by laborers and included, among others, firemen's musters, rodeos and office games. The second, in which resources were retrieved or products manufactured, involved competitions such as harvesting and construction, lumber and rock drilling, and many more.

This is a study of a cultural phenomenon in the American workplace. These competitions were an outgrowth of work based on achievement. The view that sports and work are contrarily structured systems of behavior has no validity here.[2] Initially, and at times on some job sites, it may have been difficult to differentiate between work and play, so informal were the contests. Yet worker competitions went through the very same stages of development as other sports and so many became popular and institutionalized that the entire experience can be classified as a sporting movement.

What Are Work-Sports?

The heyday of American work-sports was a century long, stretching from the latter two-thirds of the 19th to the first third of the 20th century. Worker competitions were both common and popular and took place on many fronts—in farms and factories, and on the frontier. They occurred in so many different settings that they represent both a labor and a sporting movement. The evi-

v

Norman Rockwell's' *Blacksmith Boy* now resides at the Berkshire Museum of Pittsfield, Massachusetts. It originally accompanied a 1940 *Saturday Evening Post* fictional account of an early 20th century blacksmith contest and may be the best representation of the concept of individuals fashioning a contest from their occupation: a work-sport (used by permission of the Norman Rockwell Family Agency, Book Rights Copyright © 1940 The Norman Family Entities).

dence of work-sports is scattered among trade and historical journals, diaries, occupational and folklore histories, trade union journals, and local and sporting newspapers. When this evidence is pieced together what emerges is a picture of a nation at work *and* play. These competitions were seen as true sporting events at the time but were initially restricted to local reports. The very first work-sport to be reported in a non-local newspaper was an 1828 Maryland plowing match, although, the report asserted, such contests had been common in New England for years.[3]

Derived from occupational functions, work-sports were productive physical exercises. As the games developed, the productive character was often lost. Initially these competitions were practical exercises, local in scope and played without standardized rules. Many were arranged ad hoc and the distinction between the spectators and the players was, at times, not clear cut. And there was no need to distinguish between amateurs and professionals because most contests were demonstrations of a profession. Some of the contests were initially part of a larger pattern of folk recreation. As defined here, worker-competitions or work-sports should not be confused with what sports historians often refer to as "worker's sports," the amusements and recreations of the laboring class.[4] Nor should work-sports be confused with the work situation in which laborers compete with one another for better materials (especially in piece-rate jobs) or work space.[5]

Taking a long-range view, work-sports may be seen as an aggregate of dissimilar activities and movements which are, at first glance, unrelated. Yet they are tied together by their attachment to the workplace, the job, the occupation. In structure, work-sports most closely resemble the sport of track and field, which itself is a collection of diverse events (jumping, sprinting, race walking, hurdling, throwing, relays, marathons). Each was initially practiced separately, and was, itself, a distinct, unrelated game that eventually made up a small portion of the sport. So too were on-the-job games. Yet worker competitions were just too diverse to be collected under one roof the way the 19th century Scots (not the British, incidentally) took diverse games of strength, leaping and pedestrian contests and fashioned the sport of track and field. This may be one reason why work-sports have, until now, been unrecognized as a sporting movement.

Incidentally, there has been a modern attempt to fuse many worker competitions into a single sporting affair. Competitions in as many as 80 occupations are contested simultaneously by vocational students each June at the Kansas City, Missouri, Convention Center and the nearby Kemper arena. More of this later.

Three broad social changes lie beneath this narrative. First, unlike many other forms of American sports, work-sports *did not follow the lead* of the mother country in the Colonial period or afterwards. Three thousand miles removed from Britain, Americans in the 19th century had the formidable task of creating a nation, of forging a civilization out of a substantial wilderness. They cleared forests, harvested crops, built towns, roads and canals, industrialized and came to terms with the frontier. Geographical isolation created an opportunity for work-sports. Although a few games and forms of recreation may have been borrowed from the Old World, Americans created many new ones, often organizing play as an extension of their more fundamental work. It is no coincidences that work tools, like hammers and wheelbarrows, and work products, like horseshoes, became the foundation for games in the Colonial period.

For instance, the factory work-sports experiences of the United States and the motherland were vastly different. Faced with industrialization and the problem of boredom, U.K. workers created a day of escape and absenteeism from work, the holiday culturally known as "St. Monday." Americans, on the other hand, played. Their invented games were fast-moving, dynamic and powerful. Gentlemanly sports were just too slow to become popular with the U.S. working class. In the antebellum period, British–exported sports like rowing, cricket, and sailing never became popular with the American masses. The American working class found boxing, blood sports and worker competitions more to their liking.

A second common feature is that the competitions *initially took place in*

The earliest American worker competitions occurred on the farm. Mowing matches using long-handled scythes were not uncommon on individual farms or at agricultural fairs. This 1872 wood engraving appeared in the September 18, 1875, issue of *Harper's Weekly* (Library of Congress, Prints and Photographs Division, LCUSZ62-100538).

the workplace. At the turn of the 19th century, the workplace was the farm. In 1800, 90 percent of Americans lived and worked on farms, and by 1820 only a dozen U.S. towns had populations exceeding 10,000. By the outbreak of the Civil War, 93 towns exceeded 10,000 inhabitants and eight exceeded the 100,000 mark.[6] By 1860 the vast majority of Americans still lived in rural regions, but as the new nation urbanized, industrialized and heeded Mr. Greeley's suggestion, work-sports spread to the cities, factories and the frontier. By the end of the century occupational competitions were so numerous that they should be aggregated by historians and seen as a national happening.

Third, the workplace gave its language to the playing fields. That is, the language of work and play commingled. By the end of the 19th century the term "work," for example, had become an integral part of athletic terminology. The jargon of sports makes explicit use of the term "work," and in doing so, makes the connection between sports and work. Consider the terms "workout," "weight-work," "speed-work," "hurdling work," "strength work."[7] Decathlon–like athletes were known for their "all-around work."[8] So too other words connect sports and work. The term "technique," for example, suggests a basic procedure for how to get something done, and refers to actions as varied as movements on an assembly line to clearing a crossbar. The fact is that work-sports, like other sports, represented a struggle for achievement and success and demanded hard work.

Many early occupations were unquestionably skilled, requiring strength, speed, dexterity and eye-hand coordination.[9] In most cases we are talking

Introduction

about hard, physical labor. Examples of contests where these skills were vital include plowing and mowing, breaking or drilling rocks, logrolling and tree cutting, and laying rails or bricks. The examples are so numerous, that, for purposes of this book, some delimitation is necessary.[10] The author has eliminated from his definition of work-sports all competitions in which machines play the major role in deciding the outcome (e.g., tractor pulls); all marksmanship contests (with pistols, rifles, or bows and arrows) because it is difficult to differentiate between hunting for necessity and hunting for sport; all food preparation games; all consumption games (such as pie eating); and all contests of personal appearance (such as cosmetology). What we are left with are, in the main, physical contests: rock breaking, rail laying, rock drilling, timber games, corn husking, rodeo, fire engine pumping (musters), brick making, plowing, shearing, stitching, typesetting and butchering. Even physical contests by slaves (like cotton picking) are included. It should be noted that worker competitions as described here have little to do with work structured as a consent-producing game as described by Michael Burawoy.[11]

Rationale for Worker Competitions

Although they are not comprehensively recognized (nor reported), an explanation for the emergence of work-sports is essential. One possible explanation for the surfacing of worker-competitions may have been worker alienation. Marx argued that in a modern capitalist society, the worker lives in an alienated and dehumanizing existence. Alienation was the historical product of the division of labor and capitalism. Weber extended Marx's argument, contending that, in modern work, men could no longer engage in socially significant action unless they joined large scale organizations in which they were allocated specific tasks and to which they were admitted only upon condition that they sacrificed their personal desires and predilections to the impersonal goals and procedures that governed the whole. By doing so they would be cut off from a part of themselves, they would become alienated. It is possible that one push toward 19th century worker-competitions may have been the alienation described by Marx and Weber. But, given the voluntary nature of most of the contests, this line of reasoning is unconvincing.

The immediate justification for the American worker to engage in such spirited activity may have been to have some fun, relieve boredom or win a monetary sum. Because much work was impersonal and tedious, games emerged as a way to relieve boredom and flex some muscle. There may have been deeper reasons. For example, implicit in both labor and worker competitions is the demand that they continually raise the level of achievement. It may have been the Industrial Revolution and the advent of capitalism which made workers compete with one another in the market place. Striving for achievement became institutionalized in a world of work and professions. "Achievement has thus become a socially sanctioned model of behavior related to high productivity, economic competition, material rewards, vocational practice, and social mobility."[12]

In the world of work the demand for success manifested itself in establishing goals that are continually corrected upwards. In the world of sports this is called breaking records. The results of labor can be expressed quantitatively, as output, sales, costs, revenues, profits. It is this same quantification and measurement of achievement that is the very substance of sports. What will be noticeable in this book is that all the worker games resulted in measurable performances, the concern for establishing 'firsts' and with breaking records. And by the time of the Civil War the *New York Clipper* began to collect and publish work-sports records.

Both work and sports accomplishments result in gains in personal prestige and in the recognition which follows. Successful performance at work, or at games, or at work-games, to some degree, leads to a cause-effect relationship between achievement and social mobility.[13] A well known 19th century rail splitter, for example, found his way to the White House.

Regardless of the reasons for participation, successful work-athletes won bets, set records and enhanced their own local reputations. And since worker competitions amounted to de facto on-the-job training programs, productivity was advanced in many occupations. Not only did the games demonstrate the capability of workers and develop new tools and techniques, but they served as early efficiency training.[14]

The American Work-Sports Experience

An expanding nation set the stage for work-sports. In the post–Civil War era the United States was transformed from a primarily agricultural and rural society to an industrial and urban machine. America's industrial explosion is attributed to many factors: an expanding labor force fueled by immigration, abundant natural resources and advances in technology. Heavy industry developed and a network of railroads delivered both resources and products to a nationwide market. The industrialization of America pushed cost minimization to the forefront and set the stage for many worker competitions. The average work week was nearly 70 hours in 1860 and many factory and farming jobs were repetitive and mind-numbing.

Many managers not only tolerated competitions among within their workforce, they actually welcomed them, because they resulted in faster production and less boredom. Rock breakers, typesetters, track layers, lumberjacks, rock drillers, cowboys, and the work forces of dozens of other occupations routinely held impromptu contests while floor managers, trail bosses, camp supervisors, and assorted other superiors gave their blessing. Worker productivity was enhanced. It is difficult to gauge the economic impact of worker-competitions, especially on 19th century labor productivity.[15] Work-sports were in a similar situation to that of the Industrial Recreation (IR) movement, which was legitimized during World War II. The concept is well understood both at the local and national levels.[16] Hundreds of plants and factories provided recreational programs, facilities and equipment to wartime workers, emphasizing the importance of teamwork for the war effort. A mid–20th century journal made repeated claims that IR directly contributed in increased levels of productivity during wartime.[17] Although the inferences appear reasonable, no measurable evidence supports this contention.

Labor historians will eventually treat worker-competitions in the same vein and as a subset of education and training. For much of the 20th century, education and training accounted for about 12 percent of U.S. growth.[18] What data we do have for 19th century industries, in which work-sports were frequent, is notable. Mining, for example, experienced a 29.2 percent increase in productivity between 1880 and 1900.[19] Productivity improvements in manufacturing approached 50 percent in the same period.[20] Productivity increases in the building of railroads were even more impressive, improving 29.4 percent in just ten years, 1889 to 1899. The Census Bureau tells us that gains in agriculture were equally significant. For example we find that in 1800 it took 373 man-hours to produce 100 bushels of wheat. By 1840 that figure was reduced to 233 man-hours, and by 1900 it took but 108 man-hours. The data on corn are equally impressive. The significant savings in time could be devoted to other tasks (or more wheat).

Worker competitions played a small part in these impressive productivity gains. First, work-sports demonstrated to participants and non-participants alike both the quality and quantity of work that could be accomplished. When Secretary of Agriculture Henry A. Wallace formalized national corn husks, he felt they "would make an excellent sport for farm families." In addition, he predicted that "on-looking farmers could learn how to become better huskers themselves."[21]

Typesetting Swifts provide us with all the evidence necessary on the impact of worker competitions on productivity. Throughout 19th century history, production quotas were a recurrent issue that dominated the agenda of the International Typographical Union (ITU). By the mid–1880s, typesetting swifts had raised the productivity standard to such a high level that "on May 9, 1886, the Board of Delegates of New York's local [ITU] No. 6, officially condemned typeracing," fearing management would raise production quotas.[22]

Worker competitions also facilitated the refinement of equipment. Such labor-saving devices explain the bulk of the productivity gains. For example, champion drillers pioneered the shape of new hammers and the diameter of steel drills, resulting in an enhancement of industry-wide drilling performances.[23] Lastly, worker competitions verified the importance of planning and preparation as a means of increasing labor productivity. The Central Pacific's "Ten Mile Day" in 1869 demonstrated that substantial gains in laying rail could be produced when every worker movement was analyzed and supplies were within easy reach.

In summary, much of the productivity improvement in the late 19th and early 20th century is explained by standard factors: technological advances, more capital and economies of scale. A minor part is explained by the plethora of worker competitions. Etzioni reminds us that productivity is enhanced when people derive psychological, social and cultural rewards from work.[24] Labor historians normally interested in 19th century labor institutions could do well to focus on laborer or occupational activity.

The Historical Evidence and Rebuff by Historians

One wonders why the work-sports movement has gone virtually unrecognized by both labor and sporting historians. In part the answer lies in the misunderstanding of the nature of work and play. Some may have felt that a contest involving both work and play was a paradox, the terms being literal opposites. What they may have failed to comprehend is that work was simply the origin of the contests. Guttmann reminds us that "we have a marvelous ability to transform any tedious or unpleasant task into a game."[25] Work-sports began as utilitarian occupations. But in most instances, using a standard taxonomy, the transition from occupational play to organized game to competitive contest to work-sport occurred in a relatively short period of time.

As well, there was so much competition from the rise of other 19th century spectator sports that worker competitions, perhaps seen as random and disjointed, simply got lost in the undertow. It's more fun to describe the importance of baseball as part of the cultural landscape than to do the same for rock drilling. Most of the systematic reporting of sports in America, especially in the late 19th and early 20th century, has been restricted to those sports that are still popular today or which drew the largest number of participants or spectators.

Standard overviews of American sports history give scant to no attention to worker competitions.[26] Rader did identify that the roots of the American sporting tradition lie in the woodchopping, rail splitting, rock breaking and plowing of the colonial era. But he drops the notion.

For the most part, work-sports have been ignored. Yet it is obvious that many of the 19th century worker-competitions eventually met all the formal characteristics of modern sports: secularism, equality, bureaucratization, specialization, rationalization, quantification, and an obsession with records (Guttmann, 1988).[27] For example, as early as the 1850s in fire musters, *secular* "engine-playing" imposed the same rules on all competing companies *(equality)*. Regional *bureaucracies* administered musters and by 1858, even planned a "national championship" affair.[28] Competing firemen had *specialized* roles while musters had well-defined rules *(rationalization)*. Results were copiously recorded and reported *(quantification)* and records were kept by the national media *(obsession with records)*. Within a few years the *Clipper*, in its annual record book, had established and maintained records for a dozen work-sports, from butchering to typesetting. Yet, given the application of this useful typology as a heuristic device, modern sporting historians have all but overlooked this movement.

The nation's first sporting newspapers, the *American Turf Register* (1829), and the *Spirit of the Times* (1831) printed abundant reports on worker competitions sent by local enthusiasts.[29] By mid-century, worker competitions and challenges were frequently detailed in the national sporting media, and the *New York Clipper* annually published work-sports records. For example, from 1856 to 1858, the *Clipper* alone published 135 accounts of worker-competitions. These normally included the date and location of the contest, a short description of the event, the name(s) of the contestant(s) and frequently the size of the wager. Before the modern media of television, radio, the Internet and the sports page, the 19th century weekly sporting newspapers—of which there were many and which provided evidence that leisure, sports and pastimes were socially important—had a fundamental hold on reporting work-sports.

The sports that are most popular today in America were not in existence when American work-sports started and many were in their infancy during the work-sports heyday. These include such favorites as baseball, football, basketball, ice hockey and tennis. Track and field is not included in the list since it has (in America) an older tradition and experience than is commonly believed. The mid–to late 19th century was a time of athletic revolution. Eyler studied the origins of 98 sports and concluded that most were developed in the 19th century, and most of those in the latter half.[30]

It may be that the work-sports movement went unrecognized, in spite of the large number of early accounts, because worker competitions were often described and reported in a disjointed manner and without a formal structure. This may partially explain why, until now, they have been ignored by labor and sporting historians. Each may have believed that the issue was the other's responsibility. Or both may have seen individual work-sports as unconnected to a larger cultural movement and therefore paid little attention to them. Yet there is just too much evidence to ignore. The same, incidentally, can be said today. For example, from 1995 to 2005, the *Wall Street Journal* published 19 front-page stories about individual worker-sports, everything from window washing to rodeo, lumberjacking, fire fighting, courier racing and more. And still labor/sporting historians have not seen the broader picture.

The 19th and early 20th century was an age of hard, physical labor. Americans blended work and play by fashioning practical games like wood chopping and rail splitting contests, husking bees and plowing contests. As the century wore on they added many more. These contests, initially ad hoc but later very formal, provided entertainment, overcame boredom and provided a platform in which workers demonstrated speed, strength, dexterity and endurance, in essence, allowing them to become worker athletes.

PART ONE: WORKER COMPETITIONS
IN THE 19TH CENTURY, 1840–1900

1

Rock Breaking and Other Early Work-Sports

A Beginning for American Work-Sports

On a spring day in Southwestern Pennsylvania in 1848, a pair of popular laborers gave locals and co-workers a sporting treat. The antagonists were well known rock breakers and the spot was on the National Road, a few miles east of Uniontown, Pennsylvania, on what is today U.S. Route 40. This "Old Pike," often referred to as the Cumberland Pike (since it began in Cumberland, Maryland), was the nation's first federal road. From the time it was thrown open to the public in 1818 (at a cost of nearly $13,000 per mile) until the coming of the railroads west of the Allegheny Mountains after 1852, the Old Pike was the nation's main highway joining the East Coast with the interior. Countless travelers used the road in a seemingly endless parade of coaches, carriages, wagons, ox carts and other vehicles.

The early work on the road required that it be constructed of three strata or layers, a design as old as the Roman Empire. The road itself was crowned, was 20 feet wide and dug within a 66-foot right of way. The lowest layer was to be filled about 12 inches deep in the center with rocks which could pass through an iron ring 7 inches in diameter. The middle layer, about 6 inches deep in the center, had to contain rocks that could pass through a 3-inch iron ring. A layer of sand and gravel was placed on top. Coach, wagon and foot travel packed it down.[1] Although built to government specifications, the road saw heavy use, necessitating constant repair. Relentless use by stage coaches, Conestoga wagons (which hauled up to 12,000 pounds of cargo), other wagons and foot travel by individuals and livestock made the Cumberland Road the nation's most utilized infrastructure during the first half of the 19th century.

Actual construction began in Cumberland in 1815 and rarely stopped.

For those who lived along its route, the construction was indelibly etched in the mind: "a thousand strong they came," wrote a farmer near Uniontown, "with their carts, wheel-barrows, picks, shovels and blasting tools, grading those commons and climbing the mountainside, leaving behind them a roadway good enough for an emperor to travel over."[2]

Thousands of rock breakers were employed to both build and repair the road, and a few earned larger-than-life reputations. Alexander Campbell of Sommerfeld, Pennsylvania, was one of the speediest on the road. Robert Hogsett, later a well-known millionaire from Fayette County, Pennsylvania, who made his fortune coal mining, broke stones on the road as a boy. Peter Kelley was one of the best stone breakers on the road but spent his later life incarcerated after he killed a man in a drunken brawl.[3] In Western Pennsylvania in 1848, the two best stone breakers were Captain Elias Gilmore and Robert S. McDowell. Both were contractors engaged in road repair and, on a bet, squared off for a one-on-one, 7- and 3-inch ring contest. Because of their reputations, the challenge drew hundreds of spectators as work stopped for the day to watch these worker athletes.

The challengers were remarkably dissimilar. Gilmore was a stout bully who lived in Ohiopyle, about 8 miles north of the Pike. He was a wagoner and was employed mostly in hauling stones for road repair. An energetic contractor, he was broad-shouldered and generally affable but had a pugilistic streak when irritated or challenged. It was said that he could not nor would not lose a fight. When the Good Intent Line, a famous stage coach line, hired a famous fighter, reputed to be a "man-eater," to drive between Uniontown and Mount Washington, Pennsylvania, Gilmore went looking for him. He found the "man-eater "outside the Mount Washington Tavern, and, when introduced, said to him, "You are a pretty stout looking man but I can lick you." Without any additional pleasantries the two went at each other and tradition tells us that Gilmore had the better of it. On another occasion, while in Uniontown, Gilmore parked his wagon, ladened with lumber, and blocked the entire street. When the local constable, John P. Sturgis, asked him to move his wagon, Gilmore fell upon Sturgis and beat him senseless. On that occasion he was jailed and fined. But Gilmore was always up for a challenge.[4]

Robert S. McDowell, from Dunbar, Fayette County, Pennsylvania, was a "Pike boy," a name given to the sons of wagoners, stage drivers, tavern keepers, farmers and people in any other occupation of families who lived adjacent to the road. His father, known as "Gate Bob," was a toll taker, gatekeeper and local politician who ran as the Democratic Party candidate for county commissioner in 1854 but lost to the Know Nothing Party candidate. Two years later "Gate Bob" became a commissioner of the National Road. Robert S. McDowell inherited many traits from his father. He grew up tall, thin and

1. Rock Breaking and Other Early Work-Sports 25

During the construction and repair of the National Road (1811–184?) crews employed thousands of rock breakers to fill the roadbed. Road building the first half of the 19th century called for breaking stones to pass through a seven-inch ring for the lowest layer, a three-inch ring for the middle layer and sand, gravel and fine stone for the top layer. Most of the construction workers were Irish or English immigrants. This illustration dates to 1850 (National Archives).

muscular, a fighting man, and was known as the speediest stone breaker on the road.

In April, 1848 the stone-breaking reputations of Gilmore and McDowell clashed and a challenge ensued. The contest had political overtones since Gilmore had married into the local Rush family whose patriarch was Sebastian 'Boss' Rush, a tavern owner, wealthy land baron and influential Republican politician. The McDowells were active Democrats. There is no surviving report of the size of the wager. As a way to measure their endurance and strength both parties agreed to use the seven- and three-inch rings, even though contractors had generally discontinued their use for some time. They would, in essence, lay a road with the winner breaking the most rock by day's end. Word got out, all other construction work ceased and a large crowd appeared to watch the pair break rocks. As with most ante-bellum American sporting events, alcohol and gambling played a supportive role.

Early in the morning the stout Gilmore and the angular McDowell arrived, hammers in hand. For the bigger rocks both used large sledges (the type both Scots and Irish had used to invent a pastime by the same name) likely with 4-foot hickory handles. A much lighter hammer, utilizing a one-pound iron ball with a hole cut through the center for the insertion of a foot long handle, was employed for the smaller 3-inch rocks. Performance and pay for stone breakers was measured in *perches*. Two perches equaled one rod or 16½ feet of laid stones 20 feet wide. On average, a stone breaker covered four rods (or eight perches) a day. Typical pay was 12½ cents per perch and stone breakers normally made a dollar a day or six dollars a week.[5]

At the starter's signal they worked in opposite directions, pounding the bejesus out of large stones. For the stones that would pass through the seven-inch rings they stood and swung the large hammers. Using the smaller hammer they would sit on a rock pile, moving their position as the work advanced. To protect them from the rays of the sun they used a ready-made movable bower.

Reports indicate that the crowd of co-workers, farmers and other locals was considerable. The beverage of choice was hard. Beer and pop were unknown on the road at the time and so commercial or home-made spirits prevailed. So popular was hard liquor on the road that even some of the well known teams of stagecoach horses earned drinking reputations. Betting was lively.

Hour after hour Gilmore and McDowell moved away from one another, pounding, pushing the stones though the rings and then shoveling the broken pieces into the road bed. By noon, the stone-breakers were about 50 yards apart, having collectively laid 150 feet of road, 20 feet wide and 18 inches deep. McDowell had opened a noticeable lead and the betting odds changed. Spectators continually shifted from one camp to the other to watch the work.

By mid-afternoon (after approximately seven and one-half hours of relentless hammering) the vigorous Gilmore, finding himself hopelessly behind, dropped his sledge and "yielded the palm," signaling his defeat. A cheer went up: "Huzzah for McDowell."

Officials quickly got to work measuring the winning effort. McDowell's feat was so impressive that one chronicler recalled the record two generations later. His distance of 16 perches and 2 feet was more than twice what a normal laborer accomplished in a full day. One rod (16.5 feet) equaled 2 perches. In something less than a full day he managed to break enough stone to cover the 20-foot-wide and 18-inch-deep roadbed 134 feet long and 2,680 square feet on the surface, moving over 4000 cubic feet of stone. McDowell's crushing and shoveling rate amounted to approximately 360 square feet per hour or six square feet every minute for more than seven hours! At the finish the combatants were over 260 feet apart and, although there is no "official" dis-

1. Rock Breaking and Other Early Work-Sports   27

Three strata of road bed made up most roads in the United States. In the foreground rock breakers are using small hammers to crack stones which will pass through a three-inch ring, the road's middle layer. In the background two laborers rake the middle layer which will be topped with sand and gravel. The 1920s painting is by Carl Rakeman (1878–1965) and titled *1823—First American Macadam Road*. It was prepared for the Federal Highway Administration (Federal Highway Administration).

tance for Gilmore, it can be surmised that collectively the pair of worker athletes laid a road nearly the length of a modern football field.

It should be noted that in the same year a local contractor invented a machine for breaking stones. It was operated by horse power but proved a failure. It was abandoned and for many years lay by the side of the National Road on the summit of Laurel Hill, a few miles from the famous rock-breaking dual.

The Nature of Work-Sports

Although the *political* dimension is no longer significant, the Gilmore-McDowell battle is important for several other reasons. First, this was an *economic* issue since the contest was a demonstration of worker skills pitted against encroaching technology. The concern of labor vs. capital had been an issue since the beginning of the Industrial Revolution. The disgraced stone-breaking machine nearby served as a reminder of the economic controversy of worker vs. machine with all of its accompanying employment implications and hinted of a more famous future contest between a rock-drilling machine and the legendary steel driver, John Henry.

Time and time again in the 19th century worker skills and accomplishments would be surpassed as technology provided substitutable machinery. In harvesting, printing, rock drilling and numerous other occupations technology altered the nature of work yet American workers reacted differently than their foreign counterparts. In the face of advancing technology, British workers struck and the French demonstrated. But American workers fashioned contests from their occupations and *competed*.

Second, it should be remembered that competition between and among workers willing to exhibit their skills was neither a new nor unusual concept in the antebellum period.[6] This contest was neither a fluke nor a coincidence. It was rather likely. This was a *social* phenomenon already in place and fast moving toward formality. Before there was a tennis court, baseball diamond, golf course or basketball court in this country, Americans played at work. Along with boxing and horse racing, the numerous forms of worker competitions *were* sports in American in the antebellum period.

Sports of all types including those in the workplace blossomed in America after the Civil War. Work-sports composed a portion of what modern observers have described as an emerging 19th century "sporting male culture." The field encompassed both athletes and spectators. Not only did the work place, here a roadbed, offer the opportunity to compete or observe competitions, but the emergence of billiards rooms, barber shops, dance halls, saloons, Union halls and amusement parlors offered males an opportunity to discuss the sporting scene and make wagers. Work-sports were a collection of individual occupational games in various stages of development. Some developed faster than others and surprisingly, by or around 1848, some of these contests were well on their way to becoming modern sports with codified rules, regular schedules, standardized equipment and record keeping.

Stages of Development

Although some sporting historians offer criteria to judge when games become formal, they do little to explain the process of how these contests become modern sports.[7] Like all forms of sporting activity, the individual worker competitions went through a variety of stages in their development as individual sports. Worker competitions basically started as simple affairs. When workers stood elbow-to-elbow doing a task, the shared experience and inevitable competitiveness often resulted in a friendly challenge. If one worker thought he was faster, stronger or more skilled at a task than his colleague, it was natural to offer a challenge. Thereupon the workers selected equivalent portions of the job at hand, set a time limit, and raced. Most often the worker-athletes had no bone of contention except to prove who was better. The prize may have been a small wager or a beer at the local saloon after work hours.

If one worker was so superior to all others, his colleagues might offer a prize if he could accomplish an improbably large quantity of work within a limited amount of time. They then bet on his chances. At times each type of contest (mano-a-mano or timed work) may have become popular because the contest was spirited, entertaining or because a notable performance resulted. So the contest was repeated. The 19th century produced lots of tradesmen and working men with considerable skills, and they used these skills to demonstrate their productivity. Many gained a reputation for their prowess.

Although individual worker competitions progressed at different rates, frequency bred formality and a need for rules, respected referees, standardization of equipment and some elementary record keeping. Some of the contests broke out of the work place and were played in front of the general public instead of for co-workers only. For example, typesetting contests soon moved to dime museums in the 1880s. Labor historian Walter Rumble noted that the dime museums took type-racing off the shop floor and turned honest, mundane toil into entertainment.[8]

Often purses or prizes were offered. Team worker competitions appeared. In some cases Unions gave their blessing as a way to demonstrate the skills of their members. Challenges would appear in print as contests grew in popularity and became regional in scope. Numerous forms of worker competition made the final step to formal sports in the second half of the 19th century. Fireman musters, rodeo, hand drilling, typesetting, lumberjacking, blacksmithing, cornhusking and office contests all had attained, or nearly so, the characteristics of modern sports. And all began in the work place as a challenge of workman skills. The games became bureaucratic and a form of entertainment, had nationally accepted rules, formal scheduling and tours, large purses and large crowds of spectators, touring professional worker athletes, formal record keeping, media coverage, national championships, handicapping, and all the appropriate problems and scandals of modern sports including eligibility questions, equipment sabotaging and fixed events, referred to at the time as hippodroming.[9]

Early Work-Sports

These informal contests were essentially intramural affairs, impromptu in nature and at times it may have been difficult to distinguish between the contestants and the spectators, who occasionally switched places. The play may not have been distinct from the work itself as it occurred right at the job site, the shop floor, the farm, or the assembly line. Most of these ad hoc contests were local in nature and went unreported. The National Road rock breaking contest was an exception. Yet rock-breaking was only one of many worker activities that never progressed past this initial intramural stage.

But many other worker activities did. The earliest examples of formal American work-sports occurred at agricultural fairs, which provided an opportunity to demonstrate competence by displaying output and to win premiums in competitions. American farmers independently advanced their own schemes and technologies at the beginning of the 19th century by forming agricultural societies. The earliest agricultural fairs took place in New England in the first decade of the 19th century and were an attempt to display farming skills, for example, plowing and sheep shearing. These exhibitions quickly turned into contests. Agricultural fairs spread to the South and Midwest (then the West) by the 1820s.

By the outbreak of the Civil War, worker competitions with all of sports' accompanying trappings had arrived. At the same time the National Road was in decline. It eventually pushed to Vandalia, Illinois, before federal funding expired. But by the early 1850s technology changed the way people traveled. The steam locomotive was perfected and soon the railroads reached the Alleghenies and pushed into the nation's interior. Traffic quickly declined on the National Road and an 1879 *Harper's Weekly* article claimed that the Old Pike was left to die. The advent of the automobile returned the National Road to prominence and it became U.S. Route 40, serving as the major east-west artery until the Federal Highway Act of 1956.

As for the early heroes of American work sports, Elias Gilmore and Robert S. McDowell, their lives became much less lively after their 1848 clash. Gilmore had married Hilda Rush in 1833, the daughter of influential politician "Boss" Rush. Gilmore abandoned his pugilistic past and migrated to Illinois before eventually settling in York, Nebraska where he lived out his days as a farmer, livestock dealer and much-respected citizen. He died in 1898 leaving nine children.[10] McDowell remained in southwestern Pennsylvania and died about 1890, in Dunbar, Fayette County, PA.

2

"Put Out That Fire"— The Firemen's Musters

Firefighter William W. Bush was at the peak of his career. In 1858 the *New York Clipper* had named the 25-year-old Bush the national champion fireman and published his likeness and an extensive biography of the volunteer smoke-eater.[1] The 5'10", 170-pound Lockport, N.Y., native, impetuous and often acting without regard to consequences, was known to rush into danger with no regard to personal safety at fires in and around Rochester, New York.

For instance, at a Lockport fire on the Fourth of July 1856, Bush entered a burning building "and worked like a man of iron in the very fire, so much so that they played one stream of water upon him to keep him from being consumed; he worked away until the fire was conquered and came out as good as new with the exception of his hair being singed and burnt."[2] Bush once jumped off a steamer in the middle of Lake Erie and saved a man who had fallen overboard.

Although there is no evidence that Bush was known to his friends as "W," his membership in the volunteer fire company did exempt him from military service. And his notoriety provides us with evidence of the high esteem with which firemen were generally regarded by the public in the mid-19th century.

Volunteer firemen were much admired for their bravery and practical value. For most of the eighteenth and 19th centuries American buildings were constructed of wood and the risk of conflagrations was considerable. The number of reported building fires in U.S. cities in the 19th century alone exceeded five million.[3] In 1864, New York City had 84 fire companies which responded to 2000 alarms. In Philadelphia, the number of engine companies was 89 and the number of alarms similar.[4] The first recorded fire in America occurred just days after the founding of the colony at Jamestown in May 1607.

A brief explanation of U.S. firefighting will allow us to appreciate the role of musters in the mid-19th century. Organized American fire protection dates to 1647, when Peter Stuyvesant, the feisty, one-legged Dutch governor of New Amsterdam, issued guidelines to citizens on how to answer fire alarms. In 1736 in Philadelphia, Benjamin Franklin recommended starting the first volunteer fire company in the colonies. The introduction of hand-pumping fire engines required plenty of hands and gave rise to volunteer companies of men. By 1751 the city of brotherly love had six volunteer outfits with 225 men; eight engines, over 1000 buckets and 36 ladders.[5] Before and after he commanded the Colonial Army, George Washington was a keen volunteer fireman with the Friendship Company in Alexandria, Virginia.

Fire companies ordinarily selected their men (volunteer firewomen were a rarity) with great care, and it was a mark of distinction to belong to such a group. To its proud members a volunteer fire company was a civic responsibility, a social club, and an energy outlet. Members regarded their own group with a far from impartial eye.

Social and political value were attached to membership in a fire company. There were parades, meetings, musters and matches, picnics, even balls. For good reason many wives found themselves fiercely jealous of fire companies. At times membership provided the volunteer firemen with challenging choices. In one well-worn tale, it was between wedding bells and fire bells. It seems that a New York fireman left his bride at the altar to respond to a fire alarm and failed to return for three days. "What was a fellow to do?" he asked simply. "Let the engine get passed?"[6] Happily he was forgiven.

The political link with volunteer firemen has been well documented. Because of company loyalty, the firemen usually voted as a block and many politicians got started as by organizing firemen votes. A noteworthy example was William March "Boss" Tweed, the corrupt leader of Tammany Hall. His guile was less successful when he was the leader of a volunteer engine company.

> When Tweed was foreman of American Engine Company Number 6 in New York, his men participated in a spirited contest to see whether any pumper could project a stream of water above a tall new Liberty pole in front of Riley's saloon at Franklin Street and West Broadway. Tweed's boys may have been politically inspired, but they were just about as good a company of firemen as the city then had. Their stream reached higher than those of their competitors, but was still three feet from the top of the pole. Amidst heavy wagers Tweed promised to have his men shoot a stream over the pole on the following day. That night the boss hired a sailor to climb Riley's pole and saw off the top six feet; this was the day of the clipper ship, when seamen were familiar with lofty riggings. Tweed promised to pay ten dollars for the job, five dollars being paid on the spot. That night the

sailor surreptitiously climbed the pole, and on the next day the Americus Six again was able to wet the pole three feet from the top. The consistency was remarkable but Tweed's men lost their bets. In a towering rage he sought out the sailor, who calmly explained that, inasmuch as only half of the fee had been paid, only half of the pole had been severed.[7]

Volunteer companies took great pride in how swiftly they responded to fire alarms, and how well their men and engines performed at the conflagration. Rivalries were engendered in the process, so much so that extinguishing fires in many American towns and cities ended up being competitive events. If there were two or more companies, automatically there was someone else to beat. Interestingly it was fire insurance companies or town citizens who caused much of the rivalry by offering cash prizes to the first company to reach the scene or actually get a stream of water on the flames. Historian Robert Holzman tells us that "as early as 1740 Boston offered a premium of five pounds to the company who shall be brought to work at each fire."[8]

William W. Bush, Lockport, New York, was 25 years old when the *New York Clipper* published a short biography in 1858. Bush was a well-meaning and impulsive firefighter. He was styled by friends as the "Champion Fireman of America," for his derring-do at fires in the Rochester, New York, area. The *Clipper* frequently singled out workers and dubbed them "occupational champions" (*New York Clipper*, January 16, 1958, p. 312).

At the clang of a fire alarm, volunteers raced to the fire house, donned uniforms (often red shirts, black pants and leather helmets) and prepared their fire engines, commonly called pumpers, which were little more than wheeled water tubs with hand pumps called brakes. Then they were off, pulling their engine through the city streets, as were other companies, all headed in the same direction. In the days before hydrants, brigades of individuals carrying leather buckets raced with the engine. There was always the temptation to race the engines on the more smoothly surfaced sidewalks, scattering pedestrians.

Races ensued. If one company overtook another on the way to a fire, the first engine was said to have been "passed" and this was a dreadful humiliation. At times a flagging outfit would weave erratically on the street making passing difficult. Collisions would occur and brawls ensued. To avoid the shame of being passed, a foreman might shout to his men, "stop and fix that wheel." Technically his company was not "passed" (it had stopped for repairs), yet few were deceived.

The American Fireman Series: Facing the Enemy lithograph by Currier and Ives appeared in 1858 and idealized the life of a fireman. In fact both Nathaniel Currier and James Merritt Ives served as volunteer firemen themselves in New York City (Abraham and Julienne Krasnoff Collection, Library of Congress).

In order to prevent rival companies from getting water on a fire first, some companies employed plug guards, often "pedestrians" (noteworthy distance runners) who would dash to the scene, sometimes with a barrel, which they would place over the nearest hydrant. They would innocently sit on the barrel until their own firemen arrived with the engine.

If the hydrant was not reasonably close to the conflagration, the engines would be set up in tandem, that is, side by side, so that an engine at the hydrant or cistern would pump into a second engine nearer the blaze, then into a third and so on until water would be pumped onto the flames.

This positioning of the tubs/engines created yet another competitive situation. Water moved from tub to tub. If a company could absorb more water in its pumper than another outfit could pump into it, the latter outfit was said to be "sucked." Even more of a disgrace was being "washed," which took place when a company could pump more water into the next engine in line than the apparatus could pump out again, with the result that the excess water overflowed from the "washed" engine.

In their lifetimes, few engines could boast of having never been washed. In the volunteer days (before about 1860), one "virgin" pumper that could offer the boast belonged to Engine Company Number 15 in New York. No. 15 was widely known as "Old Maid." Outpumping a rival company was a source of great pride among volunteer firemen.

Another form of fireman's competition, which lasts until this day, was in decorating the engine with engraved woodwork and gold leaf painting. Scenes of battles, buildings, famous individuals, and mythological female figures or animals often engendered nicknames, a modern sporting feature.

One 1830s engine that sported a distinctive logo, a Bengal tiger, was the Americus No. 6, whose foreman was William March Tweed (later the "Boss"). The Tiger engine No. 6 was instantly recognized as she flew through the city streets. When Tweed left for Tammany Hall in 1851 he took the Tiger logo with him and it later became universally known as a symbol of corruption. Generations before the tigers were embraced by the Universities of Missouri, Clemson, LSU or the city of Detroit, they belonged to Americus engine No. 6.

Firefighters were also expected to rescue victims of burning buildings, and tales of bravery are legion. The gathered crowd would raise cheers when volunteer firemen carried women, children and the unconscious to safety. But sometimes the crowd was a problem. For example, on April 14, 1857, a terrifying fire hit a block of warehouses in Baltimore on Charles and Lombard streets. Interfering with the firemen's efforts were about a dozen persons intent on stealing boxes of cigars in one of the warehouses. Several times they were urged to leave the building before it collapsed in on them. The next day 13 bodies were removed from the smoldering ruins, including one charred body, with hands and feet entirely burned off, the skull severed from the trunk, and a box of cigars still intact under each arm.[9]

Occasionally the volunteers went beyond the call of duty. For instance, in March 1868, John Denham performed several remarkable feats at a fire at New York City's P.T. Barnum Museum on Broadway. He chased and killed the resident tiger with an axe when the beast rushed from the building into the street, then carried out the fat lady, who weighed in excess of 400 pounds. Not done, he rushed back into the burning building and emerged carrying the "wooly-headed" women.[10]

Although there may have been glamour and romance in 19th century

In the foreground two teams of hand pumpers throw streams of water on the Jennings Clothing Store fire of April 25, 1854. The hand pumping exercise was evolving at the time into team sport with rules, completion (muster) schedules, rule, records and standards. This 1854 lithograph appeared in the *New York Times* a few days after the fire and was later published in *The Volunteer Fire Department of Old New York: 1790– 1866* (*New York Times*).

firefighting, the profession had a rough edge. Initially volunteer firemen wanted to merely extinguish the fire; then they wanted to do so before rival companies could. Rivalries were natural, especially in the decades leading up to the Civil War. One author reminds us that in New York City "the struggle for precedence on the way to the scene of the conflagration was hot and vigorous. On the way to the fire two engines (#13 on Duane Street and # 12 on nearby Williams Street) usually met at the corner of Roosevelt and Pearl Streets, and when, as was often the case, the arrival at the hydrant or cistern was almost simultaneous, a fracas was the natural result. These rivals came to hate each other most cordially."[11] In like manner, New York Engines 5 and 14 carried rivals who, on the way to uptown fires to claim hydrants with superior speed, always seemed to encounter each other in front of the *New York Tribune* building, making newspaper reporting of their violent brawls both convenient and timely. Engines 40 and 15 always came together at the junction of Centre and Chatham streets (now Park Row). Engine 6 (with Boss Tweed as foreman) and Engine 8 had many a lusty tussle at Chatham Square. When police arrived to ascertain when the first punch was thrown, someone would always respond, "Oh, about 1798," the year of the first New York volunteer engine company. In vain did municipal authorities fine or suspend offenders.

The membership of many volunteer companies included accomplished brawlers. In New York City many had close connections to Tammany Hall. In the 1830s the Old Maid (Number 15) Engine Company employed a colorful (if not brutal) cast of characters which included Johnny McCleester, Country McCluskey, San Banta (a sidekick of boxer Yankee Sullivan who later would watch the pugilist hang at the hands of San Francisco vigilantes) and the four Chanfrau brothers — Frank, Peter, Joseph and Henry. Frank later became a famous actor who created the role Mose of the Bowery B'hoy in the long-running and often-imitated production *A Glance at New York*, initially produced at the old Olympic Theatre at 444 Broadway in 1848. The play was based on the shenanigans of Moses Humphreys, known as Old Mose, the famous leader of the Bowery B'hoys gang, and a fireman of the Lady Washington Engine Company Number 40, the bitterest enemy of the Old Maid.

In addition to Old Mose, the Lady Washingtons enlisted an aggregation of celebrated fighters that would have done the hockey movie *Slap Shot* proud. There was Jim Jeroloman, a 6'4" professional boxer and ship builder who sported earrings which dangled to his shoulders, and a notable slugger named Orange County whose boots bore studded nails, the better to stomp his opponents. One Jeroloman opponent complained that Big Jim was biting, and indeed, when he removed his shirt, half a dozen of Jeroloman's teeth imprints were found on his shoulder. Big Jim himself once complained that he could not make it in the world of professional boxing because biting, kicking and eye-gouging were forbidden by the rules.

But their leader was the vicious and huge bully Moses Humphreys (some say he was seven feet tall), whose stature and flaming red hair under a beaver skin cap made him the most recognizable individual in the city. When he wasn't marching at the head of the Bowery B'hoys gang looking for a fight with gangs like the Forty Thieves, the Roach Guards or the Dead Rabbits, or pulling the lead drag rope of the Lady Washington pumper, he was raising hell and beating the stuffing out of rival firemen.

One could not be ambivalent about Old Mose. On one hand he was heroic, rescuing many women and children from burning blazes. His bravery was admired. On the other hand his intimidating and terrorizing behavior to other firemen was appalling. Humphreys was either loved or despised and his public appearance drew both cheers and jeers. He was a 19th century Barry Bonds.

On a summer afternoon in 1836, at a time when the Lady Washington and Old Maid feud had reached a feverish pitch, Old Mose met his demise. It was surprising, swift and complete. The two companies, each containing about 500 firemen, runners, supporters and fighters, were returning from a Sunday afternoon fire near Wall Street. The Lady Washington outfit had recently enlisted even more fighters from other companies and rumors surfaced that its members would attack the Old Maid if the opportunity presented itself. A large crowd, more interested in a possible brawl than in the smoldering ruins, left the scene of the fire and trailed the two companies.

Instead of returning to their own fire house the Lady Washingtons followed the Old Maid to Chatham Square, where the two groups came face to face. Amid much trash talking, Jeroloman removed his earrings and punched McCluskey, while Old Mose let out a ferocious yell and leapt upon Henry Chanfrau. Soon, all down the line, men and boys were swinging, kicking, stamping (and biting) one another while the rewarded spectators roared. The brawl continued for more than an hour with no discernible victor. Hen Chanfrau barely held his own against Old Mose, while his brother Frank, then 12, watched the melee from atop a pole in front of the hat store where he was a part-time clerk. Hen's sweetheart, Julia, watched from a nearby window. Amid the din Frank was reported to yell, "Give it to him Hen! Julia is looking at you from the window!"

Reportedly the encouragement gave Hen renewed vigor and he, in a real-life David vs. Goliath effort, caught Old Mose with a blow to the windpipe. Before the stunned giant could regain his feet, Chanfrau stomped and unmercifully beat him silly. The firemen of Lady Washington, seeing their champion down, turned and fled, abandoning their engine. The Old Maids confiscated the beautifully decorated engine and "washed" off all of its elaborate white and gold painted decorations. It was then rolled through the streets to the Old Maid engine house, overturned and left in a gutter.

The Lady Washington Company never recovered from the humiliating defeat, and in 1843, it disbanded. As for the disgraced Old Mose, he hid for a week then took a ship to the Pacific. He disembarked in Honolulu and soon opened a saloon and billiard parlor. He later became friends with the king of the Sandwich Islands, who made him fire and police commissioner. The long-running success of the Broadway play *A Glance at New York*, with Frank Chanfrau playing Old Mose, transformed the giant, like later work heroes John Henry and Paul Bunyan, into an American folk legend.

The 1836 brawl represented a problem all too common among volunteer firemen. Melees beset many American cities. Historian Amy Greenberg has documented the violent brawls of Baltimore, St. Louis and San Francisco volunteer companies.[12] Other examples are abundant. For example, in Boston in 1837, rival engine companies battled each other for the better part of a day before police arrested 50, and a like number were hospitalized. A Philadelphia volunteer fireman was stabbed to death *during a fire* in a quarrel between two companies in 1856.

The impact of the firemen's brawls was twofold. First, city officials, demanding that firemen fight fires and not each other, began to replace the volunteer companies with professionally paid firefighters. Baltimore, as an example, had compiled the most disgraceful record for quarrelling among volunteer firemen. A pitched battle at Lexington Market in September 1856 in which combatants brought their pistols resulted in at least seven deaths. The *Baltimore Sun* highlighted the role of the New Market Fire Company, and shouted, "It was a most surprising spectacle for a civilized community."[13] City fathers soon disbanded the volunteers and formed a full-time, professional fire department.

This 1910 lithograph illustrates a hand pumping contest at a muster. Hand pumping a stream of water for either height or distance was a popular fireman's game in the second half of the 19th century (*Ye olde fire laddies*, New York: A.A. Knopf, 1930).

Cincinnati was the first city to establish an all-professional fire department in 1849, twenty years before it became the first city to establish an all-professional baseball team, the Red Stockings. By the 1850s every major city had begun to replace the volunteers.

For financial reasons the transformation from amateur to professional firefighters was never complete. Many volunteer companies survive in small communities and rural areas. Today there are 1.4 million authorized firemen in the U.S. Seventy-five percent are still volunteers.[14]

The second reaction to the brawls was also long-lasting. Many historians have noted that brawls were, in a sense, recreational. In the eclectic and competitive world of ante-bellum firefighting, a substitute or surrogate form of competition was necessary to uphold the traditional concept of honor at the fire house. Yes, there had been occasional streaming contests for firemen, often when a new hand-pump engine arrived in town. Existing companies would usually issue a challenge to the newcomer to see who could pump a stream of water the highest (flag poles or church steeples provided convenient benchmarks) or the longest distance. And racing engines, that is pulling them through city streets against time, was not uncommon. Yet these were informal affairs with usually drinks or a meal on the loser.

What resulted from the need of firemen to uphold the honor of their engines was the "muster," a recreational forum at which competitions were held in firemanship skills. City officials in Bath, Maine, conducted the first organized firemen's muster on July 4, 1849, and the concept in the years immediately before the Civil War, caught on like wildfire.[15] On that day firemen from five companies (two from Bath and three from other local communities) agreed upon a fairly accurate system to measure the length of streams of water. The Bath pumper of Kennbec #1 played 156 feet for the victory. Today, four of the five original engines are still in existence and two (16 decades later!) are in demonstration use. Later that summer, Ashland, Massachusetts, and Utica and Troy, New York, hosted firemen's musters.[16]

The number of musters doubled the following year, and then doubled again, and again. By mid-decade a conservative estimate would put the number of major, reported musters at 50–60 annually. The Grand Muster of Worcester, Massachusetts, in 1858 took three days to complete, as 52 engine companies and over 2,500 firemen took part.[17]

Although newspaper coverage of musters of the 1850s occurred mostly in local newspapers or later in trade journals like *The Fireman's Journal*, there were so many of them that they did achieve national attention. For example, The *New York Clipper*, from May through September 1857 reported on 36 major musters. Even though the reports were sent by local "correspondents," the *Clipper* was truly a national organ whose readership stretched from New England to the Deep South and to the Mississippi Valley. Many of the reports were extensive and always included the date, site, nature of the contest(s), participating engine teams, amount of wager/awards, team leaders, placing and distances. Some reports were so extensive that they would make modern sporting pages, with aggregate sections, pale by comparison.

The press treated firemen with the same adulation as other sporting heroes. It cannot be underestimated how important the press was in championing the cause of sports in mid-century. Betts reminds us that it was John

S. Skinner (*American Turf Register*, 1829) and William T. Porter (*Spirit of the Times*, 1831) who reported sporting activities in weeklies devoted primarily to horseracing.[18] Neither paid much attention to worker competitions, including musters. But it was Frank Queen's weekly *New York Clipper* that gave worker sports and especially musters an encouraging boost.

Improvements in the printing press and telegraph lines in this era enabled newspapers to more economically and speedily cover sporting contests. In the 1850s the *Spirit of the Times* and the *Clipper* shared nationwide readership with three other popular sporting weeklies: *New York Sportsman*, *Sporting Life* (published in Philadelphia) and the sometimes lurid and salacious *National Police Gazette* of Richard Fox. The latter occasionally ran biographies of popular firemen and offered medals as muster prizes. Fox's paper likely had the largest readership of the five, for it was a staple in every saloon, barbershop and billiards hall in America. The popular local sporting weekly *California Spirit of the Times* (1859) was an expansion of an earlier weekly, the *Firemen's Journal*, which, as one can imagine, offered extensive muster coverage.

A fairly typical example of 19th century newspaper coverage of a fireman's muster is offered in Appendix 2. It is reproduced from an 1857 edition of the *New York Clipper*. A final point should be made about the influence of America's newspapers on the evolution of musters. Initially individual musters kept their own records, for instance, for achievements like the highest or longest streams of water pumped. But it was the national newspapers, notably the *Clipper*, which provided *comparisons* of marks from muster to muster, in effect, establishing national records. At the time of the Civil War it was Queen who produced the *Annual Clipper Almanac* that listed records and notable performances in dozens of sports, including athletics, sailing and aquatic sports, baseball and musters, usually referred to as "fire engine playing." Queen's *Almanac* was a de facto *Guinness Book of World Records* and his paper took responsibility for maintaining records and notable performances. Only later would leagues and national federations take up record-keeping responsibility. For example, in 1859 the *Almanac* listed records for ten different categories of fire engine playing: permutations of streams for hand pumped or steam engines; length of hose; and whether the streams of water were horizontal or perpendicular. For example, the longest horizontal stream, hand pumped, through 100 feet of hose, one inch nozzle, was 228 feet by the Niagara of Dayton, Ohio. The highest stream on record by 1859 was 196 feet by Old Diligent engine of Philadelphia.[19]

Firemen's musters, like all other sports of the era, were also the beneficiaries of improved transportation networks. Participating teams of firemen would load their "masheens" on a flat railroad car in the early morning and

Top: 19th century fireman's musters were a nation-wide work sport that stretched to all ethnic groups and not just the prerogative of the Northeast. This 1888 rooftop photo by John C.H. Grabill captures the great Hub-and-Hub race at Deadwood, Dakota on July 4, between the only two Chinese hose teams in the United States (Library of Congress, Prints and Photographs Division, LC-USZ62-13397).

Bottom: Winning Chinese Hose team of the great Hub-and-Hub race at Deadwood, Dakota, July 4th, 1888 (Library of Congress, Prints and Photographs Division, LC-DIG-ppmsc-02679).

travel to the host town by rail, returning home usually on the same day. By 1860 there were 30,000 miles of track in America.[20] For a short time, as cricket declined in importance and baseball attempted to elbow its way into the public's consciousness, musters held sway as the nation's primary team sport, a fact unnoticed by most 19th century sports historians.

In 1857 musters were held in 21 states (there were 31 states at the time, California being the newest). In 1858 the *Clipper* reported an attempt to set up a national organization, the National Fireman's Musters Association (hereafter NFMA), to standardize tournaments, schedules, and rules and set up a national championship to include 100 engines, one from every substantial town in America. Canadian companies then lobbied to be included in this group.[21] It should be noted that firemen led the way in the codification of sport, and this occurred years before there were attempts to codify and standardize other sports at a national level. For instance, for baseball, this occurred with the National Association of BaseBall Players (NABA) in 1865, while track and field formalized rules with the founding of the North American United Caledonian Association (NAUCA) in 1870.

It may be believed that, although firemen were sporting actively, they *really were not* respectable athletes. Not real jocks. Perhaps the vision of a modern-day, overweight fireman, sloshing down the street at a muster on the way to coupling a hose nozzle is ingrained too deeply in our consciousness. But in the 19th century such was not the case. Likely, America's best athlete in the antebellum period, certainly its most versatile, was John Goldie, a volunteer fireman at New York's Mutual Engine Company. The Mutuals were frequent and successful muster participants.[22] In June 1857 the Mutual firemen also formed their own base-ball (before the Civil War it was *base-ball*, not baseball) club and annually challenged for the *pennant*, symbolic of the nation's top base-ball honors.

In April, 1869, the *Clipper* offered a description of John Goldie's baseball expertise and hasty temper.[23] The brawny and slugging first basemen played for five top teams in his career, and by 1868 was a leading hitter (first baseman) for the Unions of Morrisiana, the national champion team. In 1869 the Unions relinquished that title to the newly professional Cincinnati Red Stockings when the latter topped the Unions 13–12 in an early September game in which Goldie had 4 hits.[24]

Goldie, a Scot, was also an outstanding Caledonian "heavy" and "jumpist"[25] from 1858 thru 1869. He was a member (and later chieftain) of the New York Caledonian Club which sponsored the nation's *de facto* top track and field meet of the era. The annual meet of the Caledonian Club, drew anywhere from 5,000 to 25,000 spectators and Goldie was its star performer. He became noteworthy because he would contest virtually every event at the

Caledonian Games. In 1859, for instance, he entered twelve of the 13 running, leaping and throwing contests, winning five and placing in the top three in five more.

This was not uncommon for him. In 1865 he captured the club's third consecutive high jump title, won three other events and placed in several others. The club awarded him a silver cup, emblematic of being the meeting's top overall athlete.[26] He was a true "three-sport star," a term that would not be used until adopted by schools and colleges in the following century. But there is no doubt, in hind sight, that the nation's best athlete of the Civil War era was the amateur baseball and professional track star John Goldie, the fireman.

He was succeeded by his younger brother, George, who came from a circus and acrobat background. George became the first coach (of anything) at Princeton College, the first coach of the New York Athletic Club, and, among other things, the inventor of the rowing machine. His older brother, John, died unexpectedly in the summer of 1871 and his funeral was attended by every fireman, Scot and baseball fan in the city.[27]

A typical firemen's muster of the ante-bellum period would last 3 to 5 hours, include approximately a dozen engines and involve about 600 competing firemen. A reasonable estimate for the mid 1850s would be that approximately 150 companies nationwide participated in at least one muster, while some took part in as many as half a dozen annually. That would put the number of nationwide firemen/athletes at approximately 7,500, ten times the number of baseball players. By mid-century, the average attendance for musters reported in the *Clipper* was nearly 3000, making nationwide annual attendance well in excess of 100,000, an extraordinary figure given the size of the U.S. population at the time.[28] A well-known woodcut of the 1869 Fireman's Muster in Merrimack Square, Manchester, N.H., illustrates an attendance of approximately 8000 people.[29]

In the late 1860s, baseball caught fire, and became, both in participation and attendance, the national pastime. But it is fair to say that firemen's musters were the first nationwide team sport in America, and at one time (the 1850s), the most popular. There is little doubt of the importance of musters in U.S. sporting history. More than 160 years after the initial muster, hand engine streams of water are still played. The sustained popularity of firemen's musters is ably captured by Pulitzer Prize-winning author John. P. Marquand in his novel *Point of No Return*.[30]

Musters continued throughout the nineteenth and twentieth centuries, but were not without their own problems and bizarre incidents. A few early day examples:

- In 1855, in Lockport, New York, at a muster in which William W. Bush surely took part, organizers fixed the results so that the local company would win. A full scale riot resulted.
- In 1860, at a muster in Battle Creek, Michigan, 13 of 18 engines refused to pump after the wind had shifted from a favorable to a head wind, complaining that their efforts would be useless.
- At an 1860 muster in Springfield, Massachusetts, the local sheriff arrested one of the muster bands for playing too loudly and disturbing a judge presiding over a nearby trial. Infuriated firemen mobbed the judge.
- At the outset of the Civil War many fire companies were short handed. At the annual tournament in Newburyport, Massachusetts, only one company could field a team and won in a walkover.
- At a Portsmouth, N.H., muster in 1871, the town neglected to build a pumping platform, forcing all engines to pump in the street, which soon became a quagmire. The engines had to be dug out of the mud.
- A Massachusetts engine company took its case to court after winning a Providence, Rhode Island, muster in 1897 but being disqualified for using the wrong type of nozzle cap on its hose. The company won.
- On occasion, a temperance society sponsored a muster. Given the hard drinking reputation of firemen, perhaps the societies thought a captive audience would make converts.
- Although wearing ribbons proclaiming "STILL SOBER," news accounts claimed that a 1900 muster in Manchester, N.H., set an all-time record for most drunks. One pumper, from Gardner, Massachusetts, dropped dead during the contest.
- On Columbus Day 1898, in Cambridge, Mass., eleven of 26 handtubs registered "negative" distances for their efforts due to very strong headwinds, which blew their streams of water backward. Wind direction and strength has always been an issue at musters. When a gale helped the Defender Company of East Weymouth, Mass., record an incredible distance nearly the length of a football field, officials decided the mark was "wind-aided" and would not count it for the record books. It took other sports, notably track and field, another 70 years to segregate wind-aided performances.
- After an hour of trying, a Cranston, R.I., company was disqualified at an 1899 muster for being unable to couple a hose to its tub.
- In May 1900, the engine house in Arlington, R.I., burned to the ground while the company firemen were attending a muster.
- By 1902, the South Weymouth, Mass., fire department had an answer to the wind problem. It allowed each company to choose the direction of its stream when called to play.
- In August 1901, organizers of the Pan-American Exposition (World's Fair)

at Buffalo included a "World Championship Muster," yet only invited 4 handtubs. The winner, the Red Jacket Company of Cambridge, Mass., whose measured stream of 185 feet, 5 inches was so disappointing to the winners, left town without claiming the title or prize. Three weeks later President McKinley was assassinated on the fairgrounds.

- At times firemen's pride went too far. A Taunton, Mass., company, after taking over first place in a 1904 muster, went out and purchased 75 brooms to be used to signify a "clean sweep" in the succeeding victory parade. When another engine beat the company out at the last moment the brooms were put away for another day.
- Occasionally experience counted for little. To the chagrin of a dozen veteran companies, a spur-of-the-moment group of high school students led by their teacher won the 1907 Marblehead, Mass., muster.
- The crew of a Brockton, Mass., company left early for a 1910 muster in Rochester, N.H., and left orders for its tub to the shipped by rail later. On competition day the firemen learned that they had shipped the tub to Rochester, N.Y.
- At a 1914 muster in Athol, Mass., a company was disqualified when judges determined that its stream included a "foreign substance."
- 1911 was a hot, dry summer in New England. A Hillsgrove, R.I., muster had to be cancelled after only three engines had pumped. Organizers ran out of water.

Although it had emerged from a violent past, the highly charged and competitive world of ante-bellum firefighting, the muster was an innocent enough form of competition. It separated fighting from firefighting. Firemen just loved to pump. In this century of work sports, at a time when other forms of competition may have been regarded as unproductively wasteful, even immoral, the utilitarian nature of fire drills rescued this form of rivalry from public disapproval.

The popularity of firemen's musters did not wane in the second half of the 19th century. But they were now enjoyed by veteran firemen and active volunteer departments whose main source of fire protection was still the trusty hand engine. In fact, by 1890, a Veteran Fireman's League was organized with mostly New England members.

As the 19th century ended and twentieth began the muster adjusted to the changing nature of firefighting. Professionals as well as volunteers took part. Steam engines had replaced many hand engines, but the musters adapted to the new technology, and to the higher/longer streams of water.

International exhibits of firefighting techniques began in Paris in 1867, and American companies from then on could be counted to win far more than their share of prizes. At the international Fire Congress in Paris in 1900, conducted as part of the International Exposition and Olympic Games, the Kansas City Fire Department team of fourteen men won the professional title in a competition that included 20 nations and over 8,000 contestants. The Kansas City steam engine threw a 1¼ inch stream 180 feet vertically and 310 feet horizontally.[31] One writer reported a back-handed compliment from the Germans and the French who "say that we (Americans) ought to have the best fire departments in the world, because we have more fires than any other country, and consequently more experience in fighting them."[32]

Today firemen's musters are alive and well. They run the gamut from the old-time contests with hand pumpers to the extreme Firefighter Combat Challenge, normally televised on ESPN, in which teams of exceedingly fit firefighters take part in contests based on normal firefighting duties. One fast, strong and agile competitor from Ontario at recent challenges is Dave Steen, a University of California graduate who was the decathlon bronze medalist at the 1988 Seoul Olympic Games.

Someone traveling through New England and New York state at any of 20 or so major scheduled summer musters would see basically the same activity that his forbearers saw a century and half ago. One of the nation's largest musters is held annually in Salisbury, Maryland, where fire companies from seven states come to compete in more than 40 firemanship events. Thousand of spectators attend.

At least 400 fire companies participate in musters annually in the U.S. today continuing a tradition that began when there were few other sports. As sporting activity grew in the post Civil War era, musters remained important, especially in New England, but were pushed off the sports pages by the growth of other sports, namely professional baseball, college football, amateur track and field, and boxing. Yet their presence in the history of numerous towns and cities remained engrained in the public's consciousness. No better testimony of their fame and status can be found than the experience of American Expeditionary Forces (AEF) doughboys under General John B. Pershing in World War I. Upon finding old hand pumpers in an overrun French town behind the lines, in their spare time, the troops conducted musters.[33]

3

Worker Games for Slaves

Scholars have shown a distinct antipathy toward sports and the recreation of slaves. Between 1830 and 1860, two to four million African-American slaves from Maryland to Florida to Texas worked on plantations, farms and ranches in a period when cotton was king.[1] Although slavery was a dehumanizing and harsh system, slaves engaged in sport, including many versions of work-sport, with more passion and regularity than has been reported.

However loathsome, the plantation system never destroyed the creative or competitive instincts of slaves. Nor did it prevent them from establishing their own unique culture. Slaves played and competed on the job. Much of their work-sports activity was determined by the viewpoint and personality of the planter/owner. And each plantation was unique. Work sharings were events on Southern plantations where "work was turned into play. Many of the men's tasks turned seemingly dull tasks into competitions."[2]

David Wiggins tells us that "much of sport and popular pastimes of the slave" were "influenced by the type of work done on the plantation. For the slave corn shuckings, log rollings, hog killings, quiltings, and occasionally cotton pickings were joyous events."[3] In the day-to-day world of the slave, Wiggins may be overstating the "joyous" part, but slaves did look forward to many of the worker contests. Historian and civil rights activist W.E.B. Du Bois reminded us that slaves held a different work ethic than Euro-Americans and their attitude toward work and leisure undoubtedly arose from oppressive life on the plantation.[4] They were not lazy, but rarely worked to full capacity, making owners believe they were lazy.

Slaves could and did work hard. In many cases they also played hard. The autobiography of Josiah Henson, a slave born in Charles County, Maryland and the prototype of Harriet Beecher Stowe's Uncle Tom, first appeared in 1849. Henson offers an insight into how competitive slaves could be. "At fifteen years of age there were few who could compete with me in work or

3. Worker Games for Slaves

Top: "A veteran in a new field," from a painting by Winslow Homer. A slave's labor was often stringently defined, for example, in so much grain to be threshed. Often physical labor on the farm was turned into competitions. This wood engraving appeared in the July 13, 1867, edition of *Frank Leslie's Illustrated Newspaper* (Library of Congress: Prints and Photographs Division, LC-USZ62-92640).

Bottom: This plantation scene shows men cutting grain with cradle-scythes as women tie the stalks and children carry water to other workers. It appeared in *Harper's New Monthly Magazine*, 88, December 1893, p. 13.

sport ... (and I aspired) ... to out-hoe, out-reap, out-husk ... out everything every competitor."[5] The bottom line, at least in Henson's account, was that plantation work was not all misery and the nature of play and festivals could help make slave life tolerable.

In some cases the slave's daily routine was stringently defined: so many rows of rice to be sowed, so much grain to be threshed, or so many post holes to be dug. Slaves not meeting labor requirements faced hunger, the lash or a trip to the "workhouse."[6] There was a "spare the whip and spoil the slave" attitude among many planters.[7]

Some slave owners offered gifts as a work incentive, "and apportioned gifts according to their perceptions of the quality of slave labor over the course of the previous year. One slave owner distributed four Dutch ovens among his slaves as a reward for having picked more cotton to the hand than usual."[8] Thomas Dabney, owner of the Burlieghy cotton plantation in Hinds, Mississippi, annually gave a monetary prize to the slave who picked the most cotton. One year this amounted to seventeen dollars.[9]

Slave Work-Sports

Documented slave work-sports were of two types, both organized by the slave owner. First, resourceful slaveholders orchestrated social gatherings around a type of work, for example, corn shuckings, hog killings, log rollings, quiltings and occasionally cotton pickings, where work was transformed into contests which combined the elements of work and play. As a consequence many of these formidable tasks were completed without a sense of overwhelming exhaustion. Instead the slaves might find these activities to be a source of physical enjoyment and emotional emancipation.

As an example, corn shucking (the removal of the ear from its husk) required many hands. After harvest, as was common in America from Colonial days, the husks were placed in huge piles and slaves from nearby plantations were invited to participate in the work. Shucking was a nighttime activity, a sort of overtime for slaves. Food and drink were plentiful. The shucking was frequently conducted as a team competition, each with a captain, pitted against one another. Teams worked feverishly to finish their pile first. The best shuckers might get a small monetary sum or a suit of clothes. Those who found a red ear could expect a dollar or the opportunity to kiss the prettiest girl.

An extensive 1930s writing project gathered the recollections of many still-living ex-slaves.[10] The finished document, edited by George Rawick, filled 41 volumes and transcribed interviews provide dozens of references to plantation corn shucking contests. For example: "Next to our dances, de most fun was corn-shucking. Marsa would have the corn hauled up to de crib, and piled as a house. Den he would invite de hands 'round to come and hope shuck it. Us had two leaders or generals and choose up two sides. Den us see which side would win first and holler and sing.... Marsa would pass de jug around too. Den dey sho' could work and dat pile'd just vanish."[11]

Hog killings and log rollings (where timber had to be lifted and placed in piles for burning) were also competitive events on the plantation.[12] Neither have survived today as a sporting activity. Again, many hands were needed and slaves from other plantations participated with much anticipation since owners always supplied plenty of drink, food and music.

Harvests were busy times on plantations when the cotton, corn, wheat, sugar, rice and indigo had to be picked, gathered or brought in. Besides the harvest, plantations had many other "special" times when much work had to be accomplished in a short period of time. Corn-thinning, wheat-threshing, fodder-pulling, and ice-getting, says Wiggins, were fatiguing times for slaves but much anticipated since they were treated as festivals. The planter turned these tasks into social and competitive events to get the best results. Small cash prizes were often used as incentives. For example, "in Perry County, Alabama, plantation owner Hugh Davis divided his workers into rival teams and had them compete for prizes. He supplemented this collective competition with individual contests."[13]

Historian Weymouth T. Jordan relates that Davis "followed still another common practice of rewarding his slaves, namely: either to divide them into gangs and allow the gangs to compete for a prize, or to conduct a contest in which a prize was offered to an individual winner. Both practices were commonly pursued during the cotton picking months (usually September to December)."[14] The custom was mentioned in Davis's logs as early as the cotton picking season of 1851, when nine slaves were placed in each of two gangs. Davis kept copious records of his slaves' performances. By 1859 his slave gangs were picking exceptional amounts weekly, with one slave, Lucy, averaging virtually 400 pounds of picked cotton per day. Davis boasted of his top pickers. Jordan speculates that Davis "made wagers with his neighbors that his slaves could out pick theirs and took part in inter-plantation cotton picking contests, for such betting was not uncommon."[15]

By 1856, on his Beaver Bend plantation, Davis offered another type of contest, one that gave a hat to "that hand which picks the greatest excess this week over his or her Monday work provided that Monday's work was over 200 [pounds of cotton] & provided we get 24,000 [pounds] this week." Davis had eight qualifiers. During the week the elite 8 and 16 other hands picked 25,245 pounds, by far the best work ever done on his plantation. A typical week usually netted about 10,000 pounds. This was good cotton picking. And

Plantation frolic in the southern states. Frolics provided an opportunity for job sharings, and some, like corn shuckings, morphed into competitions. This wood engraving appeared in *Frank Leslie's Illustrated Newspaper*, December 26, 1857 (Library of Congress, Prints and Photographs Division, LC-USZ62–49857).

all this for a hat. Not surprisingly, Lucy, who possessed astonishing eye-hand coordination and consistently outworked the male slaves, won the hat easily and wore it constantly as a badge of honor for years to come.[16]

The harvest or picking season was a double-edged sword for slaves. On one hand they looked forward to the festivals, gaiety, food and drink. On the other hand there might be punishment for failure to meet quotas. During cotton picking season, many planters had expectations on acceptable work. In an 1854 letter to plantation owner George Noble Jones, D.N. Moxley, an overseer at a Florida plantation, noted that two negroes had to be whipped for "light cotton," not picking over 85 to 95 pounds of cotton per day.[17] Moxley noted that on average his slave hands picked about 110 pounds per day, and could frequently pick up to 130 pounds of cotton per day.

The second type of slave work-sports arose when plantation owners fashioned work-sports with the express intent of developing worker quotas. Cotton picking is a case in point. Solomon Northrup, in his 1854 autobiography, tells us that on Louisiana cotton plantations, each worker was tasked according to his or her picking ability. In his slave experience (he was a New York freeman who was captured and sold into slavery for a dozen years), an ordinary day's work was about 200 pounds of picked cotton. Some slaves, he claimed, had a natural knack, a quickness, that enabled them to achieve high standards. "Patsey was known as the most remarkable cotton picker on the Bayou Boeuf. She picked with both hands and with surprising rapidity, that five hundred pounds a day was not unusual for her."[18]

Picking standards varied geographically and over time, depending upon the strain of cotton. Swearigen maintains that in the first decades of the 19th century "an adult slave picked no more than 50 to 60 pounds a day, but as the years passed planters developed and used a cotton whose bolls opened wider and from which it was easier to pick the lint."[19] He claims that through acquired skill slaves could pick up to 200 pounds per day. In order to set work standards, planters developed contests and offered prizes to workers.

At times the contests became more than just intramural as planters pitted their best pickers against those of other plantations. On occasion the results of these trials would appear in the press. In 1826, for example, the *American Farmer* reported the results of a competition pitting slaves from various plantations near Edenton, North Carolina. The account resembled a modern box score.[20]

1st day—lbs	2nd day—lbs
Derry, 154½	Derry, 178¾
Olla, 117	Olla, 185
Harry, 101	Harry, 167
Jeff, 100	Delilah, 103
Delilah, 99½	Prov, 107
	Primus, 90
	Boy Ned (12 years old), 91

The purpose of these "quota" competitions was to develop a standard of work for a slave. Play was woven into work to enhance productivity. Most planters realized that once slaves decided how much work they were going to perform, they weren't going to work any harder. Wiggins reminds us that numerous planters made it relatively easy for slaves to perform their daily tasks by setting the standard of labor very low. This way the slaveholders could maintain a semblance of discipline and at the same time improve morale.[21] Frederick Law Olmstead noted that many of the slaves on a Virginia plantation he visited would simply go through the motions during the day.[22]

However debasing the institution of slavery, plantation life rarely became so harsh that it destroyed the imaginative nature or prevented slaves from establishing their own singular culture. In spite of the degraded conditions, games orchestrated by plantation owners—making sport of work—provided a competitive outlet for slaves and some enjoyment. Many of the competitive opportunities for slaves were closely linked to the type of work done on the plantation. "Slaveholders were ingenious enough to make these occurrences great social gatherings where work was dissembled in the form of fun and gaiety."[23]

Plantation or slave work-sports had much in common with their non-slave counterparts: measured performances, prizes, regularity of contests, and even some record keeping. And even though they were not spontaneously fashioned by the participants themselves, slaves competed with much more intensity and regularity than most people realize. Cotton picking competitions, for example, may have resembled other work-sports in a traditional sense. Yet the difference was that the impulse and raison d'être came from the slaveholders and the slaves themselves did not have the freedom *not to compete.*

In the years after the abolition of slavery, cotton picking contests, for either nostalgic or entertainment value, became popular, especially in the deep Southern states. By the time of the Great Depression, cotton picking had a national championship with all the accompanying standardization. For example, in 1941 Blytheville, Arkansas, hosted a "World Championship Cotton Picking" competition which drew thousands of spectators.[24] Today there are any number of local or regional cotton picking contests, mostly associated with community efforts to attract tourism.

4

Setting Type, the Story of the Swifts

Joseph W. McCann of the *New York Herald* and William C. Barnes of the *New York World* had been at it for nearly four hours. Setting type as quickly as possible in front of a large number of printing journeymen, neither showed signs of slackening. McCann and Barnes were swifts, 19th century newspaper compositors, and in 1885, they were two of the nation's fastest typesetters. Their backers had put up $500 apiece in October, winner take all, and arranged a challenge match for mid–December for Tousey's Printing Office.[1] And boy, did they fly. The New York City composing room was virtually silent as a crowd of peers watched in fascination. The only sounds were the steady "click" when the compositor completed a line of type, the emptying of the composing sticks, and the low appreciative reaction of the crowd which would occasionally murmur "oh boys, oh you boys."

From a betting standpoint it was difficult to get a fix on who led whom. Both used twenty line composing sticks (trays of set type). McCann filled his to capacity before emptying it. Barnes, on the other hand, emptied his composing stick, perhaps to unnerve his opponent, after only nineteen lines. To spectators, Barnes appeared to be faster but veteran journeymen weren't duped. The match ended after the agreed four hours.

Compositors of the 19th century set type by picking out tiny metal letters from cases and manually aligning them into rows of words. This initial stage in the printing process had not changed much in several hundred years. Typesetting was the final part of the process to be mechanized in conventional printing. Technological leaps in other printing stages had already occurred. Yet even after presses that could produce 15,000 newspapers an hour were introduced after the Civil War, newspapers still needed a plethora of compositors to set type.

Ottmar Mergenthaler's "blower" linotype slugcasting machine first appeared in 1886 and was the earliest viable Linotype. This lithograph appeared on the pages of the industry's trade journal, the *Inland Printer Magazine* in the same year. The appearance of the new machine made all of the old hand-typesetting records obsolete (*Inland Printer*).

Type was prepared letter by letter. A compositor stood on the shop floor facing a case with many compartments containing discrete metal characters: letters, numbers, and punctuation marks. Each of these characters had its own pigeonhole, some larger than others. The cubicles, for instance, for the letters *e* or *a* would be larger and contain hundreds of the metal characters. Other cubicles would be small, holding perhaps a dozen quotation marks or semicolons. There were cubicles with blanks used to fill out lines. The character on each sliver of type was backward, so that when it was swabbed with ink and pressed on a sheet of paper, the final copy would read normally. The compositor would reach into the case for each and every letter, then place them upside down and backward, starting from the bottom left, on a small tray called a "typestick." The letters formed words, sentences and paragraphs,

4. Setting Type, the Story of the Swifts 57

all creating a block of text. The trick was to be able to simultaneously spell upside down and backward. When the typestick (or pan) was filled, he delicately pushed the block of type onto a metal tray called a "galley." The compositor then went back to his case and started again with the next passage.

Once the story (and block of text) was completed, the printer would transfer the type to a completely level table, correct any mistakes, and add other stories, headlines and illustrations to compose a whole page. The printer cast a plate of hot metal from the impression of type and used it to print the newspaper.

Typesetters measured their volume of work in ems, a unit of measurement based on the letter *m*, the widest letter in the alphabet. Printing historian Walter Rumble tells us that a typical compositor would set about 700 ems an hour (including the time spent spacing the lines correctly and correcting typos. At this speed the compositor had to reach into the typecase nearly 2000 times. Racing pace, approximately 2000 ems per hour, required over 5000 reaches; 85 to 100 letters picked up each minute; 7 or 8 letters every five seconds.[2]

Typesetters who had the requisite speed to race one another or accept timed challenges were referred to as "swifts." They were well known in the trade for their dexterity, stamina and ability to quickly and accurately spell the wrong way up and regressively. The task took total concentration. In the mid–19th century the compositor was an elite worker and always a member of the International Typographical Union (ITU), one of the oldest and most respected labor unions in the nation. Union membership was confined to men although women were able to demonstrate that they had the requisite skills of swifts. Women typesetters usually worked for book publishers or in small print shops. But the newspaper composing room was a male domain and every newspaper claimed to employ a swift or two.

Swifts habitually moved from job to job, a trend known as "tramping," and replicated by college athletes a generation later. The International Typographical Union approved this kind of mobility as a way to keep wages high, by increasing the demand for their services. Typesetters with union cards were virtually guaranteed employment anywhere, and so they moved frequently, seeking the highest paycheck. The legendary George Arensberg had worked in most major cities in the eastern United States. The New England typesetting champion George Graham worked in nine different states between 1873 and 1884.[3]

McCann and Barnes, too, had tramped. McCann, for example, was born near Dublin, Ireland, in 1856 and began a printing apprenticeship at age twelve. In the spring of 1881, after working at four different newspapers, McCann applied to his union for a traveling card and immigrated to the

United States. He eventually found a job in the composing room of the *New York Herald,* moved to the *Boston Globe,* and by 1883 was back in New York at the *Herald* where he earned a reputation as a very fast worker. Barnes, a native of Toronto, had held composing jobs at Quebec, Connecticut and New York newspapers. For newspaper journeymen, tramping was a respectable way of life.

By 1885 Barnes was a prominent swift, but McCann was still rather unknown. Barnes had sprinted to a pair of 2000 ems-per-hour performances in 1885 and had won challenge contests in both the U.S. and Canada. That summer a composing room foreman at the *New York Herald* volunteered McCann for a challenge match, and before Barnes could respond, Ira Somers of the *New York World* had arranged a $500, 3-hour match with the 29-year-old Irishman. Barnes was in the audience of 300 when McCann disposed of Somers and felt that McCann, with his inconsistent and rough technique, could be beaten and quickly offered McCann a challenge.

When the McCann-Barnes matched ended it was not clear who had won. Judges and proofreaders pulled and scanned the galleys, counting ems and checking for typos. Barnes had hoped to win using a deliberate style that would minimize typos. But McCann was declared the winner. Not only had he set more type, but he provided a cleaner proof. The swifts shook hands and McCann made a short acceptance speech, then, as was traditional, bought a round of drinks for his supporters. The purse of $500 was substantial since even the top printing journeymen in their trade made between $20 and $30 weekly.

Although no medals or trophies were struck for this race, both were common prizes. And for typesetter races the financial rewards were remarkably lopsided. For example, in 1877, a Montreal challenge match offered $1,000 to the winner, $4 and an inkstand to the runner-up, and $3 and a composing stick for third place.

As for McCann and Barnes, they were about to become famous. Within days of their celebrated match, promoter J.R. Davis contacted both men outlining an opportunity to take their skills on tour. Davis, as a talent scout for P.T. Barnum had been responsible for bringing the renowned Jumbo the elephant, the largest animal in captivity, to New York from the London Zoo in 1882. Davis had traveled extensively in Asia and Africa in search of exhibition animals and knew something about promotion. His orchestrated parade to move the veiled Jumbo from the Battery to his new home in Madison Square Garden took most of a day. The procession engaged 16 circus horses pulling and several normal size elephants pushing and was classic promotion.

Davis, who would die a year later at age 34, now worked for Kohl and Middleton, a chain of dime museums based in Cincinnati. He knew what the public would buy. People would pay to see swifts. Davis proposed a national tour featuring McCann, Barnes and local Swifts. He billed the tour as a "world" or "national" championship, the appellations being commonly used for just about any type of sporting event of the era.

In the 1880s and 1890s virtually every American city had a dime museum. Originally designed to be an uplifting and intellectual showplace, much like the British Museum, the Americanized dimes had become places of amusement. For a dime, one could find displays, a theatre, some wax figures, a comic, even a giant and a dwarf or two. They were entertainment centers that particularly appealed to bachelors, falling somewhere between ballparks and theatres in the taxonomy of entertainment.

Joseph William McCann ("JoeMac" to friends) was born in Williamstown, Ireland, began a printing apprenticeship at age twelve and emigrated to the U.S. in 1881 at age 25. He worked at the *New York Herald* and *Boston Globe* and was the nation's fastest typesetter in 1885. A year later he established a one hour typesetting record at 2,150 ems (*A Collation of Facts Relative to Fast Typesetting*, New York, Concord Cooperative Printing Co., 1887).

Davis intended to take typeracing off shop floors and turn a straightforward, tedious task into public entertainment. He envisioned a national tour and booked McCann and Barnes because he knew they would draw crowds. The South Side Dime Museum in Chicago was first up for the week of January 11, 1886, and the famous swifts were scheduled to compete all week against one another and against the best of the local typesetters, one each from Chicago's five dailies: the *Inter-Ocean*, the *Tribune*, the *Evening Journal*, the *Daily News* and the *Daily Herald*.

The daily race format called for afternoon and evening sessions. Each of the seven compositors participated in an afternoon heat lasting 90 minutes and another in the evening. They were all given identical text and competed against one another in various combinations so that the entire marathon was divided into a string of sprints, easy and entertaining for spectators. Barnes worked deliberately. McCann set more type, but he also made many errors, which allowed Barnes to pull ahead in the proofreading. It was similar on each of the seven days of racing. The museum's proofreader, Fred Rae, insisted on well-composed lines. After a few days the smooth-working Barnes began to attract more spectators than McCann. He was winning consistently and as he worked, hundreds of patrons milled around, fascinated with his work. Barnes was not above showing off some and he entertained the crowds during breaks by reversing his typecases. Capital letters were traditionally placed in the upper cases, small letters in the lower cases. Barnes worked almost as quickly with the cases reversed. He also impressed the crowd by setting type blindfolded, with the copy read to him.

By Wednesday the swifts were a runaway promotional success. At times the crowds were so large that the contestants took to plugging their ears with cotton to block out the racket. On one occasion a drunk and boisterous woman attacked a police officer, her shrill voice elevated above the din. "For God's sake, gag her," one of the contestants pleaded.[4]

By Saturday Barnes had won so frequently that he was declared the new "world champion," with McCann second. The Chicago boys never were in the same class. With first and second place wrapped up, Barnes and McCann by arrangement each made an attempt on George Arensberg's one hour record. Ruthian in stature, the legendary Arensburg, known as the Velocipede, had set 2064 ems in a single hour in 1870, and the record had been around so long that some felt that it might never be surpassed. Both agreed to not to attempt the record until the final heat of the tournament on Sunday evening.

McCann gained a modicum of redemption setting a new shop-floor standard of 2150 ems, fifty more than Barnes. McCann lost the "world championship" but achieved a world record. Happiest of all were Davis and the Kohl and Middleton Dime Museum, which made a pile of money on the worker competitions. McCann and Barnes received endorsement offers. Davis began to plan more tournaments, the next national championship scheduled for Philadelphia in the middle of March.

In 1886 thousands of ordinary people in Chicago were able to view worker-sport. And they paid to do so. Typeracing was now a public amusement. Productive labor became sporting theater. Before Davis's second championship tournament got off the ground in Philadelphia the Austin and Stone's Dime Museum of Boston conducted its own New England championship typesetting race. Not only did it turn the museum's lecture hall into a facsimile of a large daily newspaper's composing room, it also provided a typesetting contest for women. The winner of the men's tournament, over a trio of Boston swifts and amid large and enthusiastic crowds, was George Graham of the *Boston Globe*, and his employer crowed.[5] But it was the result of the women's race, among four unknown compositors (three competed using assumed names), that opened eyes.

4. Setting Type, the Story of the Swifts

While the vase was offered as an afterthought, the "daisies" exceeded all the composing records the men had established the previous week. Not only were they just as nimble in grabbing the type, they made fewer errors and, when the dust cleared, the winner was a part-time and unemployed (at the time) typesetter named Miss Kenney (it was standard for newspapers to substitute "Miss" for first names) who topped Graham's winning weekly total by 950 ems. So too did the second and third place female typesetters (using the names Davis and Hammond instead of White and Hartford) exceed Graham's winning total. During the week and hearing the rumors of fast work, doubters within the trade rushed to Austin and Stone's on Tremont Street to see for themselves and came away shaking their heads but persuaded.[6]

William C. Barnes, a native of Toronto and "Swift" at the *New York World,* was national typesetting champion in 1886 winning the crown in a match against Joseph W. McCann. He occasionally showed off by reversing the upper and lower cases and set type blindfolded (*A Collation of Facts Relative to Fast Typesetting,* New York, Concord Cooperative Printing Co., 1887).

This was an entirely unintended result. In fact, this contest provided one of the few outright intragender work-competitions of the century. A year later when Barnes, McCann and a Cincinnati swift named Alexander Duguid collaborated on a manual called *Fast Typsetting,* which, among other things, offered a history of typesetting races in America, they dismissed the Boston ladies' performances, claiming that too much latitude was given in timing and proofing to the women so that their records were not authentic. In hindsight, although the female marks did not challenge the records of the fastest of the male swifts of the day (McCann, Barnes, and Duguid), their response appears unashamedly chauvinistic.

The Boston tournament had labor overtones. The 1870s had brought hard times for the American economy, and the printing industry in particular felt the blow. ITU membership and the number of locals fell dramatically in the decade. When the economy returned to normalcy in the 1880s, the ITU had encouraged typeracing as it was a way to enhance the reputation of the craft locals. In effect the ITU organized the sport by sponsoring races and standardizing rules. Indeed it is doubtful that any work-sport of the 19th century had more stringent and circulated rules.

In Boston the male swifts were all members in good standing with the ITU. The female compositors, who normally worked for book publishers or in print shops but rarely in newspaper composing rooms, were members of the Knights of Labor, a new and aggressive organization.[7] The results, to be tactful, discomfited the ITU.

As the industry mulled over the Boston results, Davis's second national championship tournament was getting underway at C.A. Bradenburgh's Dime Museum at Ninth and Arch Streets in Philadelphia. To guarantee heavy attendance the proprietor also scheduled a variety of vaudeville acts that included the "Elastic Skin Man"; a minstrel show and a snake charmer; and Nala Damjanta, the "Beautiful Hindoo princess." Typesetting compositors not only competed among themselves but with the other acts for attention.

Bradenburgh, as was now common, turned his main hall into the workroom of a large daily newspaper. The public had an opportunity to see just how a newspaper was prepared. The tournament began on Monday, March 15, 1886, with Barnes of the *New York World* and McCann of the *New York Herald* as the banner performers. They were joined by Alexander Duguid of the *Cincinnati Enquirer*, three local typesetters and Thomas C. Levy of the *Chicago Evening Journal*, who had finished third at the Chicago tournament but who arrived a day late in Philadelphia.

Thousands flocked to the Philadelphia races. Many came to bet and Barnes, just off his Chicago victory, was the early favorite. McCann, however, sprinted to an early lead, lost it on day two, then regained and held it until the sixth and final day of the tournament. The unexpected winner, however, was Duguid, who rallied on the final day to overtake the two favorites. And what a rally. His afternoon tally of 2,259 ems an hour was the fastest on record. Just to make sure no one doubted his effort, Duguid returned that evening and finished with an even faster, 2,277 ems in a single hour.

Alexander Duguid, 29, appeared nervous in the early days of the tournament and was not prepared for the spectators who crowded the compositors while they worked. He was not a complete unknown. He had exceeded 2000 ems an hour in a December race and had been invited to the Kohl and Middleton Museum races but declined because some of the races were scheduled for the Sabbath. He was a teetotaler, and believed that total abstinence from alcohol and tobacco was conducive to both health and fast typesetting.

Surprisingly, the tournament drew thousands of spectators on each day.

4. Setting Type, the Story of the Swifts 63

But even as owner Bradenburgh distributed the diamond-studded medals for first through fifth place, and paychecks based on piece rate wage, and as Levy was leaving with the Hindoo Princess, public typeracing was coming to an abrupt halt. The dime museums had lifted the sport out of the shop floor and into the public eye. Yet just as quickly it ended. Pittsburgh and Indianapolis held local tournaments soon thereafter but museum-sponsored high stakes racing ended at Philadelphia.[8]

Two forces, one economic and the other technological, spelled the demise of the swifts. Not only were union leaders and male typesetters vexed by the gender-dominated Boston results, but the day-to-day work of rank-and-file typesetters paled with the publicized museum racing results. Newspaper journeymen routinely set between 700 and 1000 ems per hour. Knowing that some could work two to three times faster worried union leaders, who had always resisted management efforts to set production quotas.

At Philadelphia's 1886 "national championship" Alexander Duguid of the *Cincinnati Enquirer* set type faster than anyone ever had or would. His 2,277 ems per hour would soon be a victim of rapid technological progress (*A Collation of Facts Relative to Fast Typesetting*, New York, Concord Cooperative Printing Co., 1887).

Union leaders were not interested in demonstrating how much faster their members could work. The dime museum races, especially in Chicago and Philadelphia, had put typesetting skills in the spotlight. Now everyone, including newspaper management, knew. In May 1886, led by New York's Local 6 of the ITU, unions officially condemned such racing exhibitions. In part, the union response represented labor's annoyance at dimes for stealing its thunder. After all, it was the local affiliates which had initially sponsored the races on shop floors and which had codified the rules. They chafed that their best workers had been lured away.

Yet, in the end, the labor union response made little difference. Technological progress was soon to make the swifts irrelevant. Newspaper production had always been top-heavy with labor costs. The printing process was undergoing a substitution of capital for labor, an economic phenomenon

explained by everyone from Karl Marx to Joseph Schumpeter. It had been underway in the printing trades for several hundred years and by 1880 much of the process was mechanized. The invention of a reliable machine enabling type to be set faster than by hand was imminent.

The initial blow came at the *New York Tribune* from its manager and editor-in-chief Whitelow Reid, who had replaced Horace Greeley when the latter died in 1872. Within a year Reid had introduced a new double-cylinder rotary printing press and was on the lookout for a machine that would cut costs by replacing the slow handwork in the composing room. Beginning in 1877, Reid ran his shop floor as an open shop, hiring individuals regardless of union membership and actually preferring those who were not members of the ITU.

The linotype machine altered much of the printing industry. By 1890 print shops and newspapers routinely installed the new Mergenthaler linotype machine,

Kohl and Middleton's South Side Dime Museum built its own newspaper typesetting room and hosted Chicago's 1886 national typesetting championships. The tournament featured Joseph McCann (*New York Herald*), William Barnes (*New York World*), William J. Creevy (*Chicago Inter-Ocean*), and Joseph M. Hudson (*Chicago Evening Mail*) (*Chicago Tribune*, January 7, 1886).

which composed type swifter than the fastest swifts. After a decade of ironing out the deficiencies and dangers of metal slugcasting the linotype damned the male swift and completely eliminated the female counterpart. Even though a few intramural races among handsetting veterans returned by 1888, they were never again conducted in the public arena in the manner of the 1886 dime museum contests. By 1893 linotype operators had demonstrated that an average of 8500 ems per hour was possible. This was a week's worth of work for the old handsetting journeyman.

By the end of the century improvements in the machinery allowed a *Baltimore Sun* operator named William H. Stubbs to set a world record of 12,021 ems per hour over a five-hour period. Compared with hand typesetting, these were outrageous figures. Yet no one called Stubbs a swift. The credit now went to the equipment, not the operator. The swift and one of the most popular work-sports of the century had vanished.

5

Circus Leapers

By the autumn of 1881, the American circus season was winding down but the bad blood that existed between Frank Gardner and William Batcheller was just heating up. Both claimed to be the world's champion circus leaper, an acrobatic occupation that was as entertaining as it was dangerous. That winter both were employed by the same circus outfit, Dockrill & Leon's Circus and Hippodrome, but tensions between the two had reached such a pitch that they didn't speak to one another.

Challenges between leapers, common in circus entertainment and issued via newspapers, flew between the two men, who had been arguing and posturing in the press for over a year. Attempting to settle the issue for good and make a buck, Messers Dockrill and Leon arranged a competition in the last week of December at Leon's Amphitheatre in Havana. Competitions for the right to call oneself the "champion leaper" among acrobats were not uncommon, for the claim paid off handsomely in salary. Eight leaping matches between Gardner and Batcheller were held in a seven-day period. Bob Stickney, another well-known leaper, was also in Havana at the time but did not participate in the contest. The final score of 4 wins, 3 losses, 1 tie was never disputed. But who had the four and who had the three was, and the *New York Clipper* published both versions in early January.[1]

In the years surrounding the Civil War, dozens of traveling circuses crisscrossed America, playing small towns and big. Owners normally offered a "leaping line" which could include as many as 30 male performers, including trapeze artists, tumblers and riders, but which featured the "leapers." Everyone would take has turn pounding the springboard (often referred to as a batoute) at one end and landing on a tick, a soft landing area, at the other. The show would begin with leaps and somersaults of modest distance, before animals would be positioned into pyramids and the leapers would take over, soaring, often with somersaults, over greater distances and heights.

5. Circus Leapers   67

An 1899 poster advertises the Forepaugh and Sells Brothers Circus by highlighting its costumed leaping line of 25 acrobats. They would engage in a contest (a worksport) for prizes by leaping over elevated elephants. The batoute (springboard) is at right (Library of Congress, Prints and Photographs Division, LC-USZ62–24616 for b&w, LC-USZC4–5123 for color).

Often in the early American circus, the leaping act was presented in the format of a tournament, with measured and announced distances and heights.[2] The routine for the leapers was basic. They sprinted down an elevated runway about 18 inches wide, and then bounded off a springy, seven-foot-long hickory board into the air. Each leaper had a preliminary try or two over a pyramid constructed of animals or objects. The landing areas were drawn out to ever longer distances and eventually the pyramid grew to include elephants standing shoulder to shoulder, with the middle animals standing on a platform. Time and again the leapers would take turns until the heights and distances had eliminated all but the featured leaders of the leaping line.

The act thrilled audiences for years. The goal was to see how high, far, or stylishly they could leap. The ringmaster might announce the height or distance beforehand, and with a drum roll, introduce the leaper, who would smile, wave to the excited crowd and begin his approach. The classy leapers threw in somersaults and records were kept for single and double somersaults which could be either backward or forward. Although it appeared that the leapers casually soared through the air, their bodies could take a beating. Hip, knee and ankle joints often buckled upon landing, that is, if the leaper was lucky enough to land on his feet. Since primitive landing ticks were usually made of straw-filled mats, injuries were common. And if a leaper did not land on the mats, the problems were compounded. The danger was a substantial part of the attraction.

By the late 1800s, "the names of the most prestigious leapers were well known throughout the country, and the rivalries which existed between these athletes was a matter of public interest. The art was so well established that every circus of moderate size was compelled to feature a leaping line and such novelties as 'leaping' cats, dogs, monkeys and horses were common."[3]

It seemed that the entire nation was soaring through the air, so much so that it was necessary to make distinctions semantically. In the 1880s a "leaper," as distinct from a "jumper" or "jumpist," was a circus performer who did stunts, usually leaping with the aid of a jump board, over pyramids of people, carriages or animals. He was occasionally referred to as a "vaulter." A "jumper" was an exhibitionist who normally leaped from bridges (the new Brooklyn Bridge, built in 1872, provided wonderful opportunities), while a "jumpist" was a track and field athlete who either long jumped, high jumped, triple jumped or leaped with a vaulting pole. Some individuals competed in multiple camps. For example George Goldie, the younger brother of fireman John Goldie, was a well known circus leaper in the 1860s who went on to become an accomplished track-and-field Caledonian jumpist the following decade.

For circus leapers there were two options to establish a reputation. They could either leap farther or higher than their contemporaries or they could create bigger tricks. In mid-century the most unique and difficult leap was a double somersault over animals. The possibility of turning a triple somersault, "the big trick," was seriously considered by the top leapers. Leaper Ernie Millette, who lived to age 100, described the skill:

> Leaping and somersaulting work requires a very exacting technique. With somersaults the trick is to get hold of your tuck properly, grab your knees and pull them against your chest. This requires a very nice calculation. If you are too anxious to turn over, you tuck up too soon and you *fall heavily*—like a sack of oats. If you're late getting into your revolution, you get stalled or "cast" like a human wheel at dead center. In either case there's only one remedy—send for an ambulance right away.[4]

Double somersaults off the springboard were dangerous enough. Triples were another story altogether. In the decades immediately before and after the Civil War there were more reports of deaths—nearly a dozen, mostly broken necks—than successful finishes during triple attempts. The triple was known as the somersault of death. The most paradoxical part of the triple was that for all but the spectators who had the most discerning and trained eye, it was unnecessary. Most spectators could not distinguish a single from a double somersault, let alone identify three revolutions. For most onlookers the flips were just a flurry in the air, the speed being too fast for the eye to comprehend. To the audience the biggest attraction of the triple was simply the danger.

In the years immediately before the Civil War many significant leaps were well known within the industry but there was no standardization. Novelty reigned. Leapers cleared horses, elephants, camels, and flew through drums and balloons. In 1858, August Siegrist leapt over 24 loaded and bayoneted muskets which were discharged as he made the leap, a trick that became known as the "Spanish Tramplin."[5] The *New York Evening Post,* on July 1, 1859, reported:

> This trick was once spontaneously accomplished by a bored aerialist named Emile Garvelet, professionally known as "Blondin." It seems that Blondin was watching a practice session of the bayonet/musket act with the Ravel and Martinette circus at Niblo's Garden in New York. Unimpressed with the leapers he nonchalantly dashed off the batoute, threw a somersault over the entire group, and alighted on his feet. Blondin was never known as a leaper, but did achieve tremendous fame as the "Hero of Niagara," the first to cross the falls on a tightrope.[6]

Circus historian Steven Goddard tells us that standardization began in mid-century as circuses and menageries began to consolidate and competition among them to offer better and more intricate acts became intense. Leaping performances became a way to provide a quantitative standard of comparison among circuses. So instead of providing only a spectacular or novel leaping act, circus managers became aware of the marketing advantage of claiming that their leaper covered the greatest distance or achieved the highest height. In 1856 when "champion leaper" Thomas King cleared 9 horses it was also notable that the leap was measured as covering 31 feet, 7½ inches, which, at the time, was the longest on record. King, who at one time leaped over a hotel coach in a San Francisco street, was considered the greatest leaper of his time.

In order to indicate superiority, circus managers began to promote quantitative standards of comparison in the post-bellum period. And if managers did not provide the promotion, the leapers did so themselves. King, for example, once offered a challenge to "leap over horses against any man in the world, for a large stake." There were so many leaper challenges floating around that the *New York Clipper* eventually attempted to establish a benchmark for leapers, suggesting criteria for creditable witnesses, procedures for placing animals, the length of the run and use of the springboard, and for landings.[7] No standards were ever adopted and validity remained a problem as leapers claimed sensational accomplishments. It was rarely reported, for example, whether the performer landed on his feet. The permutations for record leaping were boundless.

Champion leapers abounded immediately after the Civil War. In 1865, for instance, George M. Kelly, performing with the Thayer and Noyes Circus, cleared 11 horses in one leap. Within a year he improved his personal record to 16 horses placed side by side with a single somersault. The *Clipper* encouraged competitions between leapers by reporting these performances, while comparing them with previous achievements. When Sam Rheinhart advanced the one somersault leap to 19 horses in Chatsworth, Illinois, and then to 21 in Shelbyville, Tennessee, in 1871, he then issued a challenge for $500 for any man to do better. There were no takers. But that summer Robert Stickney cleared 13 horses with a double and, by October 1874 in South Boston, Virginia, Stickney "executed a double somersault over 20 horses and alighted square upon his feet."[8] A year later William Batcheller, performing with the W.W. Cole Show, upped the mark to 23 horses, prompting Stickney to respond with 24 for a distance of 34 feet. Stickney also performed doubles over elephants and camels and, within a few years, elephants replaced horses as the measuring rod for leapers. The number of announced animals leapt over was always viewed with suspicion. There were alternatives in stacking or positioning animals. It was not until the early 1880s that animals were positioned should-to-shoulder rather than in alternating directions.

In the fall of 1875, in Glens Falls, N.Y., Batcheller claimed that he completed a single somersault over 31 horses and a double over 29, the same year that Fred O'Brien, with Howe's Great London Circus, claimed to have turned a triple somersault and numerous doubles over 5 elephants. With so many claiming to be champions simultaneously, a confrontation was inevitable, and the first major one between Frank Gardner and William Batcheller took place in the late summer of 1878.

Gardner, like his colleagues, began a circus career young. Born in Oswego, N.Y., on March 30, 1855, he moved with his family to Macomb, Illinois, at the conclusion of the Civil War. The James T. Johnson Circus made its winter quarters in a large barn in Macomb, where young Gardner frequently loitered. The circus staff, deciding one afternoon to have some fun, put the twelve-year-old on a horse and sent it flying around the ring with young Frank holding on for dear life. The riding master lashed the horse's flank again and again hoping to dislodge the young rider, but without success. That evening management asked Frank's mother to allow the circus to train her son as a rider. She relented after the circus promised to send her ten dollars per week. The show moved to Galesburg, Illinois, where Gardner would make his permanent home.

5. Circus Leapers

He was billed as "Master Frank, Little Horseman," but within only a few seasons had distinguished himself as a leaper. By 1871, performing for the Van Amburgh Circus of Carthage, Illinois, he was turning double somersaults over 10 and 12 horses. In 1872 he teamed with the legendary Fred O'Brien in nightly contests for the Dan Rice Paris Pavilion Circus. In a Chicago contest between the two, Gardner cleared 14 horses with a double somersault while O'Brien landed on the back of the 13th horse.

In 1877, Gardiner issued a challenge in the *Clipper:*

> FRANK GARDNER,
> *professionally dubbed*
> THE GALESBURG "PUDDIN,"
> TO LEAP ANY MAN IN THE WORLD
> HEIGHT OR DISTANCE
> *for*
> ' FAME OR GAIN.'

He received a nasty but a positive response from William Batcheller, whose original name was Patrick Quirk.

> It is a question but what I adopt an unwise course in deigning to notice the buncombe [a challenge] of one so lacking in every requisite that distinguished an artist, and whose broad back and ample stomach more often finds a leaping bed before his feet; but being in the same company and hourly subjected to his cutcumacious and exasperating blab, I find it impossible to forego the pleasure of squelching his conceit, and, at the same time extracting a few dollars from his not-overfilled purse. The result of the prospective contest, if his nerve does not forsake him, will be sent you from Wheeling.

As a teenager Quirk had been apprenticed in 1865 to George Batcheller, a leaper in a Philadelphia-based circus. As he moved from circus to circus he established a remarkable reputation as a leaper and took his mentor's name. In the fall of 1875, in Glens Falls, N.Y., Batcheller claimed the aforementioned single somersault over 31 horses and double over 29.

Using the *Clipper* as a conduit for the challenge and arrangements, Batcheller and Gardner agreed to meet in Wheeling, W.V., and the contest, for $100, was set for September 6, 1877, as part of the W.W. Cole show. Batcheller's responsive language would surprise us even today. The results were published in the *Clipper* of September 15, 1877. It seems that Batcheller won the single somersault for distance, 33 feet, 8 inches to Gardner's 32 feet, 4 inches. Gardner won the double somersault, covering 32 feet 2 inches of West Virginia real estate to Batcheller's 31 feet, 4 inches. The honors for height were disputed. The contest ended inconclusively and both took public exception to the judge's rulings. Gardner, for example, complained that his opponent never landed on his feet, and that his own performance was hindered because he had agreed to use Batcheller's batoute.

Terms could not be reached for a rematch in 1878 even though Batcheller's language was even more abusive in the press, but their public feud made them drawing cards to whatever circus employed them. Along with Fred O'Brien, they dominated the circus leapers' headlines until the summer of 1881 when O'Brien, after missing the landing pad completing a double, died from the injuries sustained.

Even though they were not on speaking terms, both Gardner and Batcheller were intent on settling the "champion leaper" claim once and for all in Havana. Eight leaping competitions were held between December 24 and December 31. Not surprisingly, the results were disputed. Batcheller claimed to have won four of the contests, with one ending in a draw. He listed, in his report to the *Clipper*, 14 of the circus performers who witnessed the contests. This outcome seemed to have surprised Gardner, who not only claimed the outcome was indeed 4–3, but in his own favor, but he reminded his opponent that he (Gardner) had the right to claim a forfeit victory for a performance where Batcheller was a no-show, but did not because he (Gardner) was a gentlemen. This latter account was confirmed by the owners of the circus, Dockrill and Leon, who also chastised Batcheller for the unauthorized signing of the names of numerous employees. Both antagonists continued to refer to themselves as "Champion Leaper of the World," leaving the question of the highest and longest leaper unresolved.[9]

But by this time the question of who was the champion trick leaper had been definitely settled. That honor went to one John Comish, whose performing moniker was John Worland, a 26-year-old leaper and tumbler with the Adam Forepaugh Circus. Worland had first accomplished a triple somersault in St. Louis in 1874 and repeated it in 1876. He completed it twice more in 1881 in Eau Clair and at La Crosse, Wisconsin. Worland was the only man who ever pulled off the stunt often enough to claim consistency and live to tell about it. His last announced and successful triple was in 1884.

Circus leaping remained a popular sport until the turn of the century and then all but died out, the victim of a large number of serious accidents. A competition for "champion leaper" was hazardous and usually indecisive. Circus performers probably felt that the leaps were not worth the risk, no matter what the reward. In the American circus resurrection of the 1930s there was an attempt to revive leaping, but when attempts at the triple proved fatal, leaping itself disappeared.

Late in the 20th century a form of somersault leaping made a comeback, not in the circus, but in track and field. In 1968 an Oregon State University student named Dick Fosbury parlayed his backward somersault technique into an Olympic high jump gold medal at the Mexico City Olympic Games. The technique, made possible with large and deep polyurethane landing pits, has been since known as the "Fosbury Flop." Six years later a forward somersault was introduced in long jumping technique. After hitting the takeoff board the jumper quickly got into a forward tuck, and came out after one rotation just in time to land, feet first, in the sand. Many who tried it, including 1976 Olympic decathlon champion Bruce Jenner, claimed that it added about a foot to their distance. But after a few broken necks the International Amateur Athletic Federation (IAAF) banned it as too dangerous.

As for circus leaping, the most dangerous of all worker competitions, it had run its course. It made a brief comeback early in the 20th century. Frank Gardner remains among the most enigmatic work-sports figures of the 19th century, right up there with Moses Humphrey, typesetter Richard Arnesberg, cowboy Bill Pickett, and John Henry. He married Cora Mossburg of Wheeling, W.V., who performed many years as a horseback rider in the circus owned and managed by her husband after Gardner retired as a leaper. They resided in Galesburg, Illinois, neighbors of Carl Sandburg. As for William Batcheller, little is known of his life after his leaping days.[10]

Patrick Quirk took the name of William Batchellar when he was apprenticed to accomplished circus leaper George Batchellar. Between 1872 and 1878 William Batchellar engaged in a variety of well publicized contests with the circus industry's top leapers. He claimed credit for completing a single somersault over 31 horses and a double over 29 in Glen Falls, New York, in August, 1875 while with the W.W. Cole show. This woodcut was featured on the front page of the February 11, 1882, *New York Clipper.*

6

Ten Miles of Track in a Day

When, at Promontory Summit, Utah Territory, the cowcatchers of the Union Pacific and Central Pacific engines touched on May 10, 1869, a nation was united–east to west—both symbolically and by rail. As historic as the moment was for the young nation, not yet 100 years old, the bona fide event in the building of the transcontinental railroad occurred two weeks earlier, on April 28, 1869, when a team of Central Pacific workers, to win a bet for their owner, laid ten miles of track in a single work day. At the time the competition was seen as a sporting event and reported as such and the workers went into railroad lore as sporting heroes.

The idea of a transcontinental railroad belonged to an engineer, Theodore Judah, or "Crazy Ted," who failed in a number of antebellum attempts to interest Congress in his scheme. But the discovery of silver at the Comstock Lode interested enough investors—prominent Californians Leland Stanford, Charles Crocker, Collis Huntington and Mark Hopkins—to incorporate the Central Pacific Railroad in 1861. Work began on an eastern march from Sacramento in January 1862 with Judah as chief engineer.[1]

The Union Pacific Railroad, heading west, started work much later, in December 1863. They accomplished little until Grenville Dodge, a former Union general in William Tecumseh Sherman's destructive Savannah Campaign of 1864, took the reins as chief engineer in the spring of 1866. Both groups worked at a steady pace, focusing on completing the transcontinental task by the nation's centennial in 1876, when government subsidies would run out.

But in 1866 Congress abruptly removed the restriction prohibiting the Central Pacific from laying track farther than 150 miles east of the California-Nevada border. Because each mile of track constructed earned the railroad companies a minimum of $16,000 in subsidies and 12,800 acres of right-of-way land and mineral rights that could be sold off, speed became the project's

6. Ten Miles of Track in a Day

Here the completion of the Pacific (transcontinental) Railroad is heralded by a meeting of the locomotives of the Central and Pacific lines at Promontory Summit while the engineers shake hands. The real story occurred a few days earlier when the Central Pacific laid ten miles of track. The entire job of laying 1777 miles of track took six years (Library of Congress, Prints and Photographs Division, LC-USZ62–116354).

principal goal.[2] A race was on. The more track laid, the greater the subsidies. It seemed that everyone wanted to finish the project in a hurry: investors who wanted to claim the financial rewards, unemployed soldiers at the end of the Civil War looking for work, westerners because it would provide transportation for their products to the east; easterners because it would allow colonization of lands beyond the Mississippi River; and the entire population, which felt that the completion of a transcontinental railroad was a matter of national pride.[3] The railroad would be the nation's highway.

And so in 1866 the pace of work accelerated. Yet too much speed presented its own set of problems. Hasty effort without attention to workmanship and detail often required repairs or more ballasting or even the rails to be pulled up and re-spiked. Bridges over water or ravines at times seemed rather flimsy, especially when they swayed in the wind. No matter. Excitement swelled across America as work continued through 1867, 1868 and 1869. The press continually beat the propaganda drums. As the crews approached one another the Union Pacific brought out the whip, requiring longer hours and winter work, while offering extra pay. Thomas C. Durant, the Union Pacific vice president, stressed the need for speed and offered to double wages if workers would stay on the job and work by moonlight. Durant, notorious for squeezing financial gain from his projects, was the designer of the Credit Mobilier of America firm that financed the Union Pacific.[4] It was Durant who hired Dodge and together they moved the Union Pacific efforts westward with alacrity.

Earlier, Durant and Charles Crocker of the Central Pacific engaged in some professional bluster about the competency of their own work crews. Durant was so boastful that Crocker rebutted with a $10,000 bet and challenge: that his own crew could lay more track in a single day than could the Union Pacific, and likely ten miles of it. Ten thousand dollars in 1869 was an enormous sum, worth something in the neighborhood of $170,000 today.[5] And ten miles of track would be an extraordinary feat since one to two miles per day was standard progress. Durant accepted and the race was really on now.

In early 1869, as crews worked incessantly, the two railroad firms agreed on a meeting point, Promontory Summit, just north of the Great Salt Lake in northern Utah Territory. Even though most associate the building of the transcontinental railroad with the Golden Spike ceremony, railroad historians point to the culmination of the Crocker-Durant bet, the "Ten Mile Day," as an event of even greater importance. It represented the final lap of a race between two corporations that had lasted several years.

The Ten Mile Day was a demonstration *and* a competition. It was a staged event, not a typical working day exercise. James Strobridge, the field superintendent for Crocker and the Central Pacific, had the land graded well in advance, and strung railroad ties out along the right of way, two tasks that normally occurred during the work day. It was a choreographed event with press invitations. It had all of the characteristics of a worker competition and "on April 28, 1869, the workers of the Central Pacific entered into their task wholeheartedly, and the eight rail carriers, carefully chosen iron men, became the sporting heroes of the day."[6]

Bruce Rosenberg tells us that, by 1869, both track laying crews had enough experience that they could lay — under normal conditions — four rails each minute, positioning each spike with three strokes. There were ten spikes for each rail and four hundred rails in each mile of track.[7] On April 27, the Union Pacific, moving westward, had its opportunity and put down 7½ miles of track, a new record. It was the Central Pacific's turn the following day.

Edwin Sabin describes what he saw, beginning at 6 A.M. on April 28, 1869:

> With nippers the eight selected rail carriers–four in a squad — seized a pair of rails from the rail truck and running them forward plumped them down. They were

adjusted instantly, the spikes had been dropped, the fishplate fastenings and bolts followed, there was one man told off for each spike, one for the fishplate, and one for each bolt; pursuing them closely marched a solid column of Chinamen, the outside files with picks, the middle file, between the rails, with shovels to ballast the roadbed. Bending their backs another squad of the Chinamen shoved the rail-truck forward onward over the newly-laid rails, keeping pace with the advance.

The moment that the supply [of iron rails] was down to a few lengths, these were thrown off, the emptied truck was tipped to one side, another track, loaded high, galloped forward, up the cleared way, and the work proceeded without a hitch.... Union Pacific watches timed the march at 144 feet a minute — five pairs of rails, or a pair every twelve seconds. End 'o track was moving forward as fast as a horse might walk.

When the panting track-crews slowed through exhaustion, another crew of the pig-trailed host sprang to relieve them. The rail gang was dripping with sweat, but worked with automatic precision.[8]

At one o'clock Crocker called time for lunch. Present-day football and basketball coaches now use his technique for half-time pep talks. Six mile of tracks were already in place. His team was up at the half. Crocker offered to replace any man who wanted to stop, but all eight chose to finish the work. One can imagine his words echoing at the lunch tent: "this, boys, is a great day for railroad history, a great day for the Central Pacific, the Central Pacific is the better outfit, the better team." No one quit. Their motivation was the same as it was for all work-sports athletes. It was the challenge to show what one (or a team) could do. There was pride in their accomplishments, even if it was semi-skilled work and the greatest weight was placed on strength and sheer determination. They would complete the job they started. Laying ten miles of track had never before been accomplished. Nor has it since. It was within their grasp. Those eight men and the accompanying spikers, bolt droppers, and others wanted to demonstrate what could be accomplished. They would win the bet for Crocker.

Work resumed after an hour's break. The progress of the Central Pacific crew was relentless. By 7 P.M. they had surpassed the distance of Charles Crocker's boast. Storbridge claimed they then went another 1800 feet for good measure. Most observers, however, noted that the extra margin was closer to 50 to 60 feet. For the eight Irish iron men, the final measurement did not matter. They had surpassed ten miles, and it went into the record books. My goodness, ten miles! The record has never been broken and no one has tried even though more than 50,000 miles of track would be laid in the succeeding decade.

Wire services dispatched reports but several newspapers had reporters on hand. San Francisco's *Daily Alta California* headlined its front page coverage two days later with "Greatest Tracklaying Feat of the Age — Ten Miles of Rail Laid by the Central Pacific — Their Competitors Give Up."[9]

The paper's coverage was enthusiastic:

> This is the greatest feat in laying track that has ever been accomplished ... it must be understood that all of the paraphernalia of the camp for over five thousand men was transferred over this ten mile stretch over a single day. Two or three miles of track had been hauled out beforehand; but all the massive rail, fishplates, spike, etc., were teamed out today, and a good deal of it had to be brought up from the rear before it was pushed out in front.... The camp equipage, workshops, boarding houses, offices, and in fact, a big settlement, literally took up its bed and walked.... And all this work [the track laying] was done on a heavy up-hill grade, with innumerable curves, some of them so abrupt that rails actually were bent before being spiked down.... And such was the enthusiasm of the men that they were willing to work for hours longer.... The material only exceeded fifty or sixty feet of the promised ten miles.[10]

Crocker had won his bet and western papers were not hesitant to refer to the previous two days as a sectional rivalry. Since the eastern team had laid a mere 7½ miles of track, the western team had won, said the Sacramento *Daily Union*.

The eight Irish iron men became instant sporting heroes. The names of Sullivan, Dailey, Joyce, Kennedy, Killeen, McNamara, Wyatt (some say Elliot) and Shay went into railroad lore. The press, as in any major sporting event, told the tale with statistics. It was reported that 3520 iron rails were drilled to 25,800 ties in a 12-hour stretch. Hourly distances were reported. Nearly 1000 *tons* (two million pounds) of rails were manually handled and spiked with 52,000 pounds of spikes. The numbers themselves, says Rosenberg, were important to a young nation which had little in the way of history. The statistics allowed for some chest-thumping.

If quality might be lacking, then quantity would have to do. The statistics told the world that Americans could place *more* ties, pound *more* spikes, lay more *rails*, in essence, do *more* work than the rest of the world. And the U.S. railroad industry could boast that it could travel *greater* distances and haul *more* passengers or freight over tracks laid in *record time*. America showed what could be done. The numbers, a characteristic of modern sport, were awesome. The *Daily Union* reporter counted everything and peppered his report with data like the number of ties per mile (2,400), the number of ties in all (12,400), the weight of the ties (80 to 90 pounds each), and the total weight of just the ties (622 tons).[11]

There is no record that Durant ever paid up but the bet was less important than what the exercise demonstrated, that is, how much work could be accomplished in a single day. This was no typical work day, as the Central Pacific spent weeks in preparation for the Ten Mile Day. Dodge groused that the Central Pacific had bedded all its ties beforehand. And it seems that two or three miles of iron rails had been laid out beforehand as well. Yet ten miles

6. Ten Miles of Track in a Day

Thomas "Doc" Durant, an engineer and vice president of the Union Pacific Railroad, stands as far as his railroad had reached in 1866, about 245 miles west of Omaha, Nebraska. The roadbeds and ties stretch far to the west and await the track layers. The wooden bar lying on the ties is a "gauger" used to set the space between the rails (Union Pacific Railroad Museum).

had been achieved, with some of the credit going to organization and long-range planning. Dee Brown concluded that, in the guise of competition, both companies "had achieved a high degree of efficiency in planning and organization [of laying rails] ... and had discovered the importance of time-and-motion studies before the technique was given a name."[12]

In the story of the building of the transcontinental railroad, most of the attention went to the Golden Spike ceremony on May 10, a true media event. A telegraph operator was poised to tap out "done" to the world when Leland Stanford (former California governor and later U.S. senator[13]) drove in the final ceremonial spike. Bells would ring out from the nation's capital to San Francisco. The continent would celebrate. At noon Stanford swung, and the key operator typed.[14] It's here that accounts vary. It seems that an inebriated Stanford "missed" and had to be helped in placing the final spike. No matter.

A typical railroad building scene on the Great Plains in 1875 and six years after the "Ten Mile Day." The small covered wagons on the left constitute a supply train, likely from the nearest town or trading post. In the background a construction train has pulled up to within a few yards of where the workmen are laying track. A section of rail is being lowered into place. In right foreground are Union soldiers who accompanied and guarded the work and protected the Union Pacific line from attacks from the Cheyenne and Sioux. The drawing, by A.R. Waud, appeared in the July 17, 1875, issue of *Harper's Weekly* (Library of Congress, Prints and Photographs Division, LC-USZ62–132926).

The job was done. No one denied its importance. A few days later *Frank Leslie's Illustrated Newspaper* summed up the nation's feeling: "This is one of the grand events, not alone of this decade, but of the age itself, and is worthy to be celebrated by pen and pencil, and its anniversary to become a national holiday."[15]

Today a Department of Interior plaque at the site of the ceremony claims that the transcontinental railroad "achieved the great political objective of binding together by iron bonds the extremities of continental United States, a rail link from ocean to ocean."[16]

As for the competitive ten mile feat, it is barely remembered today. Academicians are more likely to debate the impact of the transcontinental (called the Pacific Railroad at the time) railroad on American economic growth. No doubt it significantly lowered transportation costs from coast to coast, offered year-round, relatively safe carriage of goods and passengers, and extended the scope of the market economy. As well the industry became both a sizeable

6. Ten Miles of Track in a Day

employer and an important consumer of basic products like iron, steel, coal, lumber, and machinery. This view has been challenged, by among others, cliometrician Robert Fogel. The traditional view holds that railroads like the transcontinental were prime movers in this country's drive toward extended economic growth. Fogel, who later won the Nobel Prize for economics for his counterfactual arguments, contended that the American railroads were less than indispensable to economic growth.[17] That debate continues. But the Ten Mile Day is mostly forgotten.

PART TWO: WORKER COMPETITIONS IN THE 20TH CENTURY, 1900–1940

7

Rodeo

Bill Pickett, the Dusky Demon

Bill Pickett's (1871–1932) name would find its way on any list of the great American cowboys. Some would place it at the very top. He was world-renowned during his cowboy career but he never quite fit the stereotype of a Western movie hero (tall, square-jawed and white).[1] Pickett single-handedly created a major rodeo event, and though he was black, with a mixture of Cherokee and Caucasian blood, one of his biographers notes that Pickett "was accepted as a performer only because the divided society of his time chose to make him an exception for an exceptional man."[2] One of his employers, Zach Miller, a proprietor of the Miller Brothers 101 Wild West Show, claimed, "Bill Pickett was the greatest sweat-and-dirt cowhand that ever lived — bar none."[3]

Pickett, the first of 13 children of freed slaves, was born in 1870 in Travis County, Texas. According to a widely held account, at about the age of ten young Willie became captivated with ranch bulldogs that could hold cattle by the upper lip until cowhands could rope them. Emulating the bulldogs, Pickett perfected this rather unhygienic "bite-'em-on-the-upper lip" technique on stray calves, then graduated to cows and the longhorn steers which occupied the heavy mesquite brush country of central Texas.

By the 1880s Pickett had hired on with several Texas ranches as a cow puncher and gave demonstrations of bulldogging steers at county fairs across the state. His technique rarely varied. First, a steer would charge into the arena, pursued by a cowhand hazer whose task was to keep the half-ton longhorn on a straight path, usually in front of a long grandstand. In would charge Pickett astride Spradley, his big bay. Urging Spradley forward at a full gallop, Pickett would slide onto the huge steer's back. Pickett, at 5 feet 7 inches, 145 pounds would grab a horn in each hand, dig his boots into dirt to stop the steer's progress, and twist the steer's neck until its head was turned upward.

He would then bite the steer's upper lip or snout, surprising the animal motionless. A quick jerk on the horns or pull of his teeth and the steer would fall over. It was some act.

Even though Pickett's steer wrestling had nothing to do with everyday ranch duties, it was so distinctive and creative that it became a standard exhibition at fairs and Wild West shows throughout cattle country. There is even some evidence that steer wrestling had become a *contest* as early as 1903.[4] Today modern steer wrestling sets a maximum of 750 pounds on the steers, eliminates the biting and concludes when the steer is off its feet and all its legs are straight out. The entire contest lasts no longer than half a minute. Billed as the "Dusky Demon," Pickett once won a 1916 competition in just 8 seconds. Pickett's race made his act even more idiosyncratic to the public.

At the 1904 Cheyenne Frontier Days celebration, Pickett's act brought down the house and accounts appeared in many of the nation's magazines and daily newspapers.[5] By this time he had an

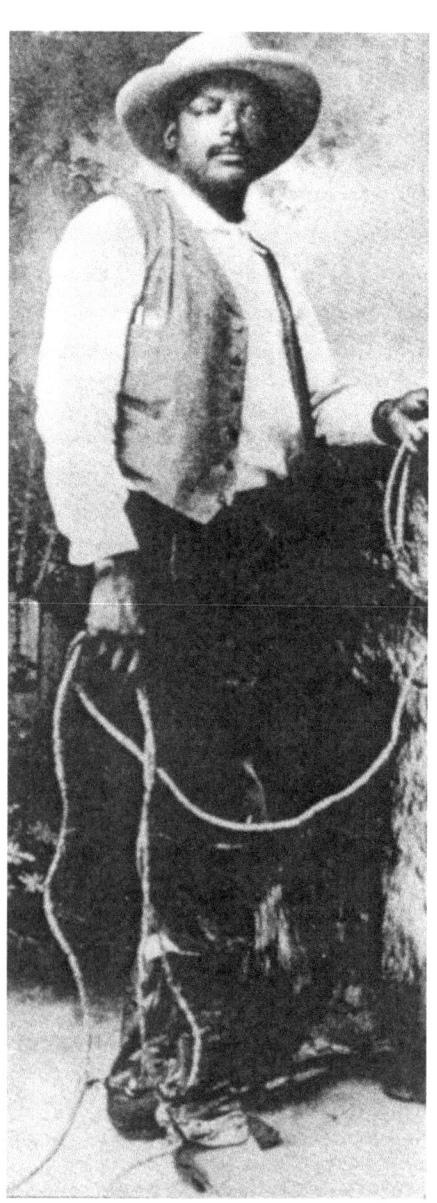

Bulldoggin' Bill Pickett (1871–1932) grew up near Austin, Texas, the son of freed slaves. He was a mixture of African, Cherokee and Caucasian heritages. As one of the earliest rodeo stars, he single-handedly created a major rodeo event and was socially accepted at the time because of his exceptional talents. He was the headliner of the Miller Brothers Wild West Show and over the years worked with every notable western notable, from Geronimo to Will Rogers. In 1994 he was honored with a U.S. postage stamp. 1912 photograph. (*The West That Was,* Knowles and Lansdale, Wing Books, 1993).

Bill Pickett attempting to bring down the bull without using his hands by biting it on the snout or lip, thus scaring the beJesus out of the animal. This performance came from the 1915 Burdick, Kansas, field day. Over the years Pickett lost most of his teeth (James Hoy, *International Folklore Review*, Summer, 1983, plate 57).

agent, Guy Weadick, a trick rope artist from Alberta, Canada, who performed under the moniker "Cheyenne Bill." Weadick, who later established the legendary Calgary Stampede (1912), and Zach Miller signed Pickett to the 101 Ranch in 1905. Pickett would perform as a headliner with the 101 until his death in 1932.

As if his unique style of bulldogging and showmanship were not enough, one particular episode in December 1908 forever assured Pickett's reputation in the world of cowboys. The Miller Brothers 101 Wild West Show was in Mexico City for a two-week engagement when the most electrifying and precarious chapter of Pickett's career was written. One of the Miller brothers, Joe, got into a debate with locals on the relative merits of bull*dogging* and bull*fighting*. In a cantina one evening several bullfighters told Miller that they had seen the 101 show and were unimpressed with Bill Pickett's act. Incensed, Miller challenged any matador to duplicate Pickett's feat if they felt it was so easy. One celebrated Spanish and Mexican matador, Bienvenida, accepted, "to teach the boasting Americans a lesson in courage and grace."[6] When the famous Bienvenida failed to appear at the appointed time on the following day, an emboldened Miller, in front of numerous reporters and unknown to

Pickett, contemptuously berated all matadors in general and bet local organizers that Pickett, barehanded and alone, could handle any fighting bull in Mexico.

The managers of the local Plaza El Toreo bull ring covered the bet, publicized the match, set the date (December 23) and ground rules, and quickly sold 25,000 tickets, as newspapers, handbills and posters stoked the fever over whether Pickett could face down a bull. Local bookmakers gave Pickett four minutes to live upon entering the ring. The Mexican dictator, President Porfirio Diaz, was in the crowd that afternoon as a group of costumed matadors strutted into the ring with a black coffin on which was inscribed *El Pincharino*, "one who has been gored."[7]

The matadors had selected the fearsome Frijoles Chiquitos, a barrel-chested, thick-necked and sharp-horned 1,100 pound fighting bull. Pickett's appearance in the ring atop Spradley drew a chorus of boos, while the crowd roared approval as Frijoles Chitquitos entered. In early posturing, Spradley, unable to avoid the bull's charge, was gored in the flank and went down. Unable to maneuver the bull, Pickett's hazers were of little help. With his horse lying on one side of the ring and a coffin reminding him of his fate on another, the Dusky Demon faced the bull alone on foot.

With some deft dancing, the fearless Pickett managed to get a hold on the bull's horns but was unable to twist the animal's thick neck. He did the next best thing and simply hung on with his arms gripped around the neck. The bull tried everything to unload the cowboy. He bucked and tossed to no avail. Minutes passed while the bull violently shook his shoulders and neck. But Pickett hung on for dear life. It was then that Pickett was injured, not by the bull, but at the hands of an incensed and partisan assembly who felt that his desperation act made a burlesque and mockery of the Mexican national pastime of bullfighting. To Mexicans, bullfighting was a matter of honor and Pickett's rag-doll performance had insulted that honor.

The outraged crowd hurled bottles, cans, bricks and anything else within reach at Pickett. A riot ensued and President Diaz ordered police and troops to restore order. Picket was knocked senseless and sustained two broken ribs from thrown debris. His grip slipped off the bull but hands from the show provided a momentary distraction and the battered and bleeding cowboy was able to stumble to safety.

When the Miller brothers checked the clock they found that Pickett had easily exceeded the criteria of the wager. The Dusky Demon had stayed in the ring for 38½ minutes and on the bull's neck and horns for 7½ minutes. The bet being 15 minutes in the ring and 5 on the bull, the Millers collected their 5000 pesos and another 48,000 pesos in gate receipts. But it took more than two hours for 200 mounted soldiers to restore order and escort the 101 crew to safety. Pickett and Spradley, who eventually recovered, escaped with their lives. It took almost a year for Pickett to recuperate from his bull ring ordeal and he missed most of the Millers' 1909 show season.

This implausible episode would have been unbelievable to an American audience, a literal fantasy story, if it had not been for the Pathé-Frères motion picture company, which happened to be in Mexico City at the time and captured the entire surreal event on film. When it played in American theatres in the following spring Bill Pickett became a household name. In the next decade Pickett and hundreds of other real cowhands found an outlet for their workman skills and turned their display into a spectator sport. Eventually rodeo became the most popular of all worker-competitions.

Early Bulldogging

The rodeo today may be a window into the past, but at times that window is blurred. We can trace the invention of only a single major rodeo event, bulldogging or steer wrestling. In rodeo's evolutionary days, the colorful Bill Pickett, even before he rode for the Miller Brothers 101 Ranch in Oklahoma, had created and perfected his bite-'em style trick of bringing down steers. He was displaying his distinctive knack at Texas county fairs as early as 1886 and by the 1890s was a well-known cowboy performer.

There is evidence that bulldogging had become a competitive event at Wild West shows and country fairs as early as 1903. By 1910 it had become standard rodeo fare, almost exclusively because of Bill Pickett had caught the eye and imagination of the public as well as of other cowboys. Some working hands and Wild West performers for the Miller Ranch copied Pickett's technique. There were even some early-day cowgirl doggers.

Pickett even succeeded in bringing down steers *without* the use of his hands. After leaping onto the steer's neck, he proceeded to stop the steer, twisting the head upward and biting the upper lip. Pickett would raise his hands or have an assistant tie his hands behind his back. He then simply forced his weight onto the steer, toppling the animal while falling with it. When the applause died down he unclamped his teeth and rolled free.

Rodeo History

Pickett's bulldogging career closely matched the formative years of American rodeo (approximately 1880–1920). The sport itself is tied to the *criollo*, a breed of longhorn cattle found in the Western areas of North America. By the early nineteenth century there were an estimated 5 million of these 700-pound, open-range, bad-tempered cattle and they belonged to any enterprising individual persistent and tough enough to corral and brand them.[8] From 1860 to about 1890 teams of cowhands pointed thousands of longhorns north and drove them on trails from the Gulf area of Texas onto railheads in Kansas as well as northward as far as Canada and westward as far as California. They were delivered for commercial use as breeding stock, beef and tallow. It was the requisite trail drive riding and roping skills that formed the basis of competitions that eventually grew into modern rodeo.

Conventional rodeo history begins here, on the trail, with gifted cowhands. Rodeo historian James F. Hoy contends, "Rodeo is borned of brags."[9] It is likely that cow outfits, sponsored by large ranches, frequently got together and, among other things, bragged about the relative merits of their respective hands. Disputes were settled by pitting one rider against another, or through an impromptu roping contest. In the 1880s, competitive riding and roping were just part of the everyday job of working cattle. During roundups and cattle drives, spontaneous riding and roping competitions and demonstrations were staged on the range, at ranches and at line camps, often to relieve boredom. Long cattle drives created pockets of loneliness, an impetus for games. Men from different ranches would gather and bet on these mano-a-mano contests, with the winners being awarded a prize.

The practice became so popular that they were frequently repeated, often annually, in the same location. By the 1890s many western towns were sponsoring cowhand competitions although the Spanish term *rodeo* was not commonly used until much later.[10] The terms "roundups," "stampedes," and "frontier days" were more commonly used.

Yet much of this traditional American rodeo history is myth since it fails to take into consideration the Hispanic influence on these contests. Rodeo historian Mary Lou LeCompte reminds us of that virtually all of the contests, collectively known as *charreria* (with the exception of Pickett's invention, bulldogging) were popular in some form in Mexico, Texas and California *before* the nineteenth century. The first American cowboys were the vaqueros, who worked ranches near San Antonio as early as 1718 and in California by 1786. Their riding and roping skills were legendary, well-documented and incorporated in numerous fiestas. *Charreria* proliferated on the California and Texas cattle ranches in the early days of the nineteenth century when Anglos and Hispanics often worked side by side.

The earliest written accounts of riding and roping contests come from Anglo observers of Spanish fiestas. A Captain Vancouver recorded roping contests at the Santa Clara Mission near San Francisco in 1792.[11] The highly literate fur trader Zenas Leonard recorded riding and roping contests in his diary after traveling overland to California with Joe Walker in 1833. A few years later, after returning to his native Pennsylvania, Leonard was prevailed

7. Rodeo

Buffalo Vernon bulldogging at Cheyenne Frontier days. The rodeo event created by Bill Pickett was popular by the time this 1910 photo was taken in Cheyenne but Vernon did not use Pickett's unique method of bringing down a steer (Library of Congress, Prints and Photographs Division, LC-USZ62–55216).

upon to publish his observations, and the result, *Adventures of Zenas Leonard, Fur Trader,* was a literary sensation.[12] *Zenas* was a bestseller which went through several editions. Western historian Bil Gilbert believes that Zenas Leonard's work is the single best description of the American West before it was settled.

In the days just preceding the Mexican-American War (1844), a Texas ranger, captain Jack Coffee Hays, recorded roping and riding contests, what at the time was known as *charro,* in the Spanish settlement of San Antonio.[13] Another reported rodeo in Santa Fe in 1846 and often referred to as the earliest American rodeo, has turned out to be bogus, a case of mistaken location.[14]

A well-known intercamp bronc-busting competition arranged by a trio of trail bosses was held on July 4, 1869, at Deer Trail, Colorado Territory. Outlaw horses–those difficult to break — were selected for the contest in which an Englishman, Emilnie Gardenshire, from the Mill Iron Ranch, won the title "Champion Bronco Buster of the Plains." For his efforts he was presented with a suit of clothes.[15]

LeCompte reminds us that "it is important to recognize that these competitions, incorporating popular charro sports, took place in the midst of

Anglo society for over sixty years before the Anglo sponsored cowboy contests were introduced."[16] American rodeo was neither a new nor a distinctive sport. Rather it was a continuation of years of tradition, just differently structured, organized and packaged.

Commercial rodeos, where admission was charged and cash prizes were awarded to the winners, began in 1888 in Prescott, Arizona. Such celebrations, commonly called "Frontier Days," proliferated. They became annual affairs, competed directly with Wild West shows, and did much to create the modern sport of rodeo. Among the better known are: the Frontier Days of Cheyenne, Wyoming (1897); the Round-Up at Pendleton, Oregon (1910); and Alberta's Calgary Stampede (1912). These festivals were so popular that they created an informal circuit for professional contestants. No two festivals were alike and there were no standards. Rules differed from place to place.

We have little evidence about cowboy contests, formal or informal, before the 1880s. This is partly because cowboys themselves were not writers. Nor, in the eyes of the public, were they overly popular or respected characters. The Wild West shows would change that.

Wild West Shows

Wild West shows (offered as early as 1883 and as late as 1931) turned the public's attention toward cowboy sports and skills, making the cowboy a fashionable symbol of the West. At the time the public was hardly aware of the American cowboy and what was known was not flattering. Before 1880 cowhands were seen as unsavory characters. Texas historian Mody C. Boatright says a cowboy was seen "at best ... [as] a provincial rustic, and at worst, as a ruffian and a thief and a murderer."[17] For a generation Wild West shows, focusing on cowboy work skills, gave cowboys a public relations makeover, so that in the next century the cowboy became the leading American folk hero.

Initially staged by William F. (Buffalo Bill) Cody, these flamboyant extravaganzas criss-crossed the nation for nearly half a century, and in the process created the modern myths of the old West and the American cowboy. The response by American journalists was enthusiastic. Prominent Americans like Theodore Roosevelt and Mark Twain waxed eloquent about cowboy skills.

By the early days of the 20th century the Miller Brothers 101 Ranch in Oklahoma provided the nation's largest, and often most successful Wild West shows. Their shows included parades, sharpshooting exhibitions, stagecoach holdups, Indian raids with rescuing cavalry, buffalo hunts, Indian dances, trick riders, visits by famous outlaws and Indian chiefs, mock battles, lariat spinners, *and* some cowboy roping and riding contests. One Western historian asserts that "from 1883 to the mid–1930s, more than one hundred Wild West

A group of cowboy (and one cowgirl — second from right) contestants at the 1909 Seattle Yukon Exposition. Second from left is Tom Mix who had been hired in 1904 by the Miller Brothers 101 Ranch. Mix became Hollywood's first cowboy superstar, making 336 films, almost all of them silent (*The American West Magazine,* July, 1971, p. 46).

shows came and went, although some were simply repackaged shows with fresh names, new partners or different owners."[18]

Riding and roping contests at the Wild West shows competed directly with local affairs: county and state fairs, festivals, frontier days, carnivals, stampedes and roundups. Cowhands kept a foot in both camps and it was often difficult to tell the difference between a competitive event and a demonstration. Often Cody or the Millers displayed their wares and conducted Wild West shows in the East, creating an enthusiastic audience for rodeo skills. Although financially draining, Wild West shows staged at New York's Madison Square Garden *made* American rodeo. Riding and roping events were scaled down to fit the confines of the Garden floor, yet they continued to depict cowboy work in wide open spaces. In all respects the Garden performances were sporting events, and not just a show. These extravaganzas faded during World War I and completely disappeared by the Great Depression, but they nonetheless helped put rodeo on the sporting (and work-sport) map.

Rodeo Becomes a Spectator Sport

Few work-sports so clearly represent the transition from folk game to professional sport as rodeo. Only lumberjacking and professional firefighting competitions come close. Despite today's showmanship and commercial promotion of rodeo, the fundamental skills, riding a horse and catching cattle with a rope, are still in place. They were part of the life of real cowboys.

As a sport, rodeo most resembles track and field, with its collection of long-standing contests. Like track and field, rodeo events have been added or deleted over time, but unlike its counterpart, rodeo began as an amateur sport in the West and moved eastward. Track and field, on the other hand, began as a professional sport in the mid 19th century in the eastern U.S. and moved westward.

Today rodeo events fall into two classifications: rough stock events and timed events. In the former, worker athletes attempt to ride a bucking animal for a minimum amount of time, usually eight seconds in standard professional events. Rough stock events include bull riding (for which there was no original working task), saddle bronc riding and bareback bronc riding. In timed events the opponent is the clock. Standard timed events include calf roping, steer roping, team roping, barrel racing (for female competitors) and steer wrestling, also known as bulldogging. Only the last can be pinned down to the creativity of a single individual, Bill Pickett.

For the most part competitive rodeo events are an extension of daily 19th century range work where cowhands had to drive and corral cattle. Rodeo is, in today's parlance, the oldest of the extreme sports. Most of the events are the direct descendants of the cowhand's manual labor, a job that was "dirty, rough, exhausting, lonely and often monotonous."[19] In America, unlike in virtually all other horse cultures, cowboys turned their work into play. James Hoy claims that American cowboys turned roping and bronc riding into sport, while this transformation did not occur in other horse cultures. His analysis is based on an examination of the major horse cultures of Asia (especially among the nomadic tribes like Huns, Mongols, Tartars and Afghans), Europe (notably the Spanish and Portuguese), Africa (Berbers and Moors), North America (Native Americans of the Plains and Mexican vaqueros) and South America (Argentine gauchos). Each of these cultures developed games of skill and speed involving horses, but the major thrust of these games has been preparation for war, not herding. Only in America did horsemen themselves invent games for the fun of it.[20]

Rodeo standardization, rules, sponsorships and advertising came late in the American work-sports era. Many of the riding and roping events were in place early on. Over the years some were eliminated, like fancy and trick roping, and some arrived late, like bull riding, which had little utility on the ranch/range. Yet rodeo's long life reflects continued popularity. A distinguishing feature of rodeo is its showmanship, as much of the event is wrapped up in parades, music and the American flag.

Although it may be difficult to compare the quality of athletes from one sport to the next, no one questions that rodeo performers are terrific athletes. Some famous performers became champions in other sports, including Baseball Hall of Famer Tris Speaker and Olympic pole vault champion Stacy Dragila, both of whom began their sporting careers in rodeo.

Rodeo is a true folk festival and many of the sport's qualities–its relation to everyday ranch work, the animals and equipment, the patriotic ritual and community involvement — have been around since rodeo began to make the transition from games of cowboy life to a professional sport.

Bill Pickett Again

As for the fearless Bill Pickett, he continued to be a headliner with the Miller Brothers Wild West extravaganza. He shared top billing with the likes of Will Rogers, Geronimo, Tom Mix, Buck Jones, Hoot Gibson, Ken Maynard and cowgirl Lucille Mulhall. Pickett had signed on with the 101 ranch/show in 1905 and, as the sport of rodeo emerged, entered more and more rodeos when he was not performing. In the 19th century the evolving sport had drawn contestants directly from the work place, and many cowhands were black, Hispanic, Native American or female. At the time rodeo exhibited more racial diversity than any other sport. But by the second decade of the 20th century, many blacks and other minorities were excluded from rodeo contests. "Pickett would have been a contestant in many more rodeos between 1910 and 1930 had it not been for the color line at many of them, both large and small."[21] Sometimes he was identified as part Indian or Mexican. In fact, he was part everything. Nevertheless he was exploited like many black athletes of his day.

Humane societies bedeviled the "Dusky Demon" for much of his career. For example, in 1914, with the 101 show in England, the London Humane Society convinced local bobbies to arrest Pickett and charge him with cruelty to animals. The Millers, no fools over cost-benefit analysis, promptly paid the fine, and then encouraged Pickett to continue his "bite-'em-on-the-lip" routine, since the fines were smaller than the enhanced gate receipts driven by the legal publicity. The bite-'em style was frequently banned by rodeos and eventually it was prohibited altogether.

In August of 1916, at age 45, Pickett entered a series of championship rodeos beginning with the New York Stampede, a 12-day competition. There he was accused of hoolihaning his steer. Hoolihaning is the fine art of landing on the neck and horns of the steer with such force as to sack the animal without twisting it to the ground. But a week later he won his event at the Chicago Roundup, although he was prevented from using his rather unsanitary biting technique because of humane society protests.[22] No matter. He won in 11 seconds, near the world's best time. Two weeks later he won $75 and the steer wrestling title at the Cattleman's Carnival in Garden City, Kansas, downing his animal in 8 seconds, a tick off the world record.

In 1923 the Norman Film Manufacturing Company produced a film starring Pickett entitled *The Bull-Dogger*. A poster shouts "BILL PICKETT, WORLD'S COLORED CHAMPION, Featuring the Colored Hero of the Mexican Bull Ring in Death Defying Feats of Courage and Skill. THRILLS! LAUGHS TOO!"[23] He was the first black cowboy to be honored with a postage stamp although his brother's image was inadvertently used on the stamp. In a perverse way, the public admired Pickett for his grit and courage in handling animals. On several occasions while in England he successfully bulldogged a wild Scottish Highland steer. Earlier in his career he had subdued a large bull elk with the same technique. In 1930 Pickett estimated that, over his career, he had bulldogged more than 5000 steers using his teeth, many of which he had lost.

Pickett died April 2, 1932, in Ponca City, Oklahoma, after being kicked in the head while taming a gelding on the 101 ranch. In 1971 Pickett became the first black cowboy elected to the National Rodeo Cowboy Hall of Fame.

Rodeo Today

With the passing of the Wild West show, rodeo became its own sport by going through a standardization (events, rules, scheduling, prize money) process. The Cowboys Turtle Association (CTA), founded in 1936, was the sport's initial sanctioning body and cowboy union. The name is a reference to the sluggish organizational process of a sport in which cowboys stuck their collective necks out in an effort to both promote the sport and earn a living. In 1954 the CTA changed its name to the Professional Rodeo Cowboys Association (PRCA).

By 1975 more than 500 amateur and professional rodeos were being held annually in the United States.[24] By 2006 the number had grown to over 3000, in which more than 60,000 men, women and children compete.[25] The most profitable contests are the more than 700 rodeos sanctioned by the PRCA, which is largely responsible for the sport's popularity, standardization and increases in prize money at the professional level. Since 1984 the PRCA has organized the National Finals Rodeo, a 10-day national championship event in Las Vegas, Nevada, and today has a national sponsor (Wrangler), a $4 million dollar purse and an extensive TV contract (ESPN).

In 1992, recognizing their growing popularity, professional bull riders broke from rodeo and formed the Professional Bull Riders, which now has television contracts and revenue from advertising and sponsorship of $25 million per year.

Today American rodeos thrive in cattle country, although they can be found in 46 states. They cater to professionals, amateurs, intercollegiate

Cowboy life — riding a yearling. Steer riding was a diversion of cowboy life during roundup time. From this pastime modern rodeo developed. This illustration is based on a photograph by C.D. Kirkland of Cheyenne, Wyoming, a pioneer photographer of American cowboy life. It was converted to a lithograph and appeared in *Frank Leslie's Illustrated Newspaper*, May 5, 1888 (Library of Congress, Prints and Photographs Division, LCUSZ62-102085).

participants, women, prisoners, Native Americans, gays, high schools students, senior citizens, and children. Rodeo is one of the nation's most fashionable sports and certainly its most popular work-sport. In 2006 more than 20 million Americans either watched or attended a rodeo event, making it one of the nation's most popular spectator sports.[26]

8
Lumberjacks

Frank Cookson thought little of the claim. Some of his men in a Michigan logging camp near the west branch of the Fox River, about 16 miles north of present day Seney, had been reading about John Ross, a Maine lumberman whose feats on lumber drives had made it to the periodicals. One newspaper claimed that Ross could cut down a tree, hand carry it to a river, then have the log carry him to the other side in a given amount of time. The trick, besides the balancing act on the water, was to select a tree that was light enough so that it could be carried on land, yet heavy enough that it could carry the lumberman on water. The diverse skills of judgment, strength, speed, balance and agility made the protagonist a virtual lumber decathlete.

The Michigan lumberjacks thought the feat quite impossible. But Cookson, a legendary log driver who lived a dangerous life on the water, thought otherwise. In fact, he claimed that on this spring day in 1892 he could do it himself and would happily demonstrate it if the stakes were high enough. The jacks offered to bet a pound of tobacco, which was currency in 19th century lumber camps. "If you make it seven or eight pounds of tobacco, I'll show you that it can be done," said Cookson.[1]

The jacks eagerly took up the bet, whereupon Cookson gathered his axe and cut himself a cedar tree about 25 feet long. After swamping it, he clean and jerked it to his shoulder and carried it several hundred yards to the dam on the Fox. He slid the cedar log into the water, leaped on it (it was buoyant enough to support him) and used a pike pole to push himself out onto the pond. Deciding to show off (and earn a lifetime supply of tobacco) he lay down on his back with the pike pole across his chest, then rose and, without ever getting his feet wet, pushed his way back to shore.

For Cookson, the feat seemed simple enough since he spent his days separating jammed logs in sluiceways, leaping to safety when the released logs rushed through the dam. Yet his hazardous tumbles and narrow escapes were

8. Lumberjacks

Among the lumberjacks of Northern Michigan. This 1910 photograph demonstrates the skill necessary to break up log jams on the river, skills that eventually turned into the sport of birling. Originally published by the Detroit Publishing Company (Library of Congress, prints and Photographs Division, LC-D4–71045).

indicative of a few of the many physical skills which were required daily in 19th century logging camps. Many of the lumberjacking skills (Cookson's is called birling) soon became part of lumberjack competitions. And even though trees are harvested much differently today, lumberjack contests featuring 19th century skills are one of the nation's most popular modern worker sports.

The Lumber Industry

One of America's great treasures was its lumber belt, a vast forest which supplied a new nation with permanent, sturdy building materials for homes, factories, barns, railroad ties, fences, implements and more. The region began in New Brunswick and Maine and continued through the Great Lakes before tapering off in western Canada and the Pacific Northwest. The timber wealth of this area was virtually immeasurable. Historian Robert Fries says it amounted to hundreds of billions of feet of commercial timber—"a wealth far surpassing all the fabled treasure troves of the world."[2]

Nineteenth century lumberjacks could be found from Maine to Washington. In the East (including Canada) they were known as shanty men or woodsmen and the lumber regions were known as the bush. In the old northwest (Michigan-Wisconsin-Minnesota) they became known as lumber-jacks or lumberjacks. They were, in their time, a hard crew, hardy, self-reliant and resourceful. Nothing was too hazardous or difficult for them to attempt. They possessed great courage and strength as they toiled on the edges of civilization.

The labor supply for the lumber industry did not come from any one source. Before 1860 they were mostly of native American stock (mostly from the New England states). But in the 1870s a strong influx of Europeans ... Irish, Scandinavians, Germans and French-Canadians—filled the camp rolls. By 1880s there were so many Scotsmen entering the Michigan, Wisconsin and Minnesota camps from Canada "that the camp clerks faced real problems in identification. The many MacDonalds with the same given name in one camp were entered on the payroll as Big Dan, Black Dan, Curly Dan, Dirty Dan, and Dan with the gold watch."³ In the latter one-third of the 19th century approximately 20 percent of the total employment in the lumber industry nationwide was Canadian.

It was common in the Wisconsin winter to pile the logs high on sleds for transport to either a waterway or railhead. This was a rather common size load for a two horse sled and lumberjacks kept records on the size of lumber loads hauled. The job became a demonstration event at the 1893 Chicago World's Fair (Library of Congress, Prints and Photographs Division, LCUSZ62-104898).

"Many of the men who were hired by the Lake States lumber operators were employed for only part of the year. Large numbers of axmen, raftsmen, mill hands and teamsters were pioneer farmers who worked in the woods or mills when farm work was slack."[4] W.T. Orcutt claims that they "as a rule, were illiterate and of mediocre intelligence. Yet they were quite proficient in their line of work, canny, and generally trustworthy and industrious, generous and dependable.[5]

During the winter logging season, "jacks" would be thrifty. After the Civil War, wages ranged from fifteen to thirty dollars per month and by the time the logs were safely in the boom, the loggers usually had fat bank rolls. Instead of banking their earnings (in part because in some Great Lake states banking itself was looked upon suspiciously), many would spend it freely on liquor and women after the logging season. Once their bankroll was gone they would hire on to another logging camp and repeat the same routine the next year.

Lumber Camps

U.S. lumber camps moved west after the completion of the Erie Canal (1825), which provided water transportation of lumber to the Atlantic Coast states and after the Black Hawk War (1832), which helped advertise places like Wisconsin to Easterners. "But it was really the advertisements placed in New England newspapers and large amount of promotional literature sent from Wisconsin. For e.g., the following appeared in the Bangor (ME) *Daily Whig and Courier* (Oct 9, 1938) 'Wanted to Go West, one first rate head Sawyer, two of the second class, one who understands circular Saws, and one Teamster ... the above to start immediately. Also, in 3 to 4 weeks, and gang of 10-to 12 Wood Choppers ... the best references will be required.'"[6]

Lumbermen from eastern states flocked to new sources of pine lumber on the Great Lakes, transplanting their methods and habits in logging. "White pine was called cork pine on account of its light weight. A younger growth of white pine was called sap pine and was more or less mixed with another species called Norway pine."[7] Yet lumbering was a passing phase in the history of many states, coming to an end when trees ran out. In Wisconsin, where the lordly pine was king, lumbering began in 1842, but by 1890 the crop was exhausted. Yet in that half a century, the industry provided work, merchantable timber and picturesque heroes.

In the 1870s lumber camps contained from 50 to 200 men who produced difficult work under difficult conditions. Trees were initially felled by axes. Many of the larger pines were 120 feet in height and 3 to 4 feet in diameter. After the Civil War it was customary to begin the task with an axe and then do most of it with a cross-cut saw. Once on the ground the swampers smoothed the logs by taking off the branches.

Sawyers cut the trees into various sizes, usually 12, 14, or 16 feet in length. The logs had to be taken to the bank of a stream where they were temporarily piled or "decked" to await the spring floods, as much of the logging occurred during the winter. Oxen were used for hauling in in the early days almost entirely, but the beasts gave way to horses, tractors and the railroad. Heavy hauling gave way to numerous demonstrations and competitions within the camps. Some went into the record books. At the 1893 Chicago World's Fair, some Michigan loggers decided to show off. At the time a load of 60,000 pounds (a load of 6,000 feet of logs) on a horse-drawn sleigh was significant hauling on a well-iced road. The loggers at the Nestor Estate Logging Company in northern Michigan, using 18 foot logs, loaded a sleigh 33 feet, 3 inches high (three stories) and the logs, if laid end to end, stretched more than one-half mile and weighed more than 180 tons! It required nine railroad flatcars to move the sleigh and logs to Chicago, where a two-horse team hauled it easily.[8] There were so many physical tasks in logging camps that it is no wonder that many of them were turned into challenges, exhibitions or competitions.

In the 1880s, spring in the Great Lakes region found thousands upon thousands of logs stacked along the riverside awaiting the day when the ice would break and the river would swell to begin the drive. River drivers, armed with spiked boots and poles, drove the logs downstream, herding the cranky mass through the river's twists and turns.

The lumber drives were similar to cattle drives of the Plains but had their own peculiar problems and dangers. A river driver's life centered on his ability to keep his footing as he stepped or leaped from one slippery log to the next. Many of the jacks had to ride the logs to avoid jams and thwart other lumber companies by getting their logs through dams and sluiceways first, the way pre–Civil War fire companies raced to be the first at a fire. River space was precious and many lumber companies derived keen pleasure from thwarting other companies. Drives were competitive and treacherous and the slightest misstep or miscalculation sent many to their deaths. Jams had to be avoided and many exacted a heavy toll in both men and money.[9]

The logs had to be sluiced, that is, directed through the gates of a dam. Often jacks had to help the logs down a sluiceway with pike poles. It was dangerous work. If a man happened to be washed into the sluice there was not much hope for him, as swiftly moving following logs would knock him senseless. John Nelligan recounts an incident in which "a tall Frenchman made a misstep and fell into the water with a strong, swift current. Doyle was closer to him than I was so I raised my voice above the roar of the water and yelled: 'Hey Doyle, save that man.' 'To hell with him,' replied Doyle, with charac-

8. Lumberjacks

The 1888 photograph illustrates the end of a log drive in Saginaw, Michigan where the logs will be hauled in off the water and to large steam powered sawmills. The skills necessary in driving the logs downriver (stamina, balance and courage) resulted in the sport of birling (Library of Congress, Prints and Photographs Division).

teristic abandon. 'He's no good anyway.' So I had to go in after the Frenchman myself. I managed to pull him to safety, but almost got sluiced myself in the bargain."[10]

When jams formed on the rivers the logs would pile up on top of one another so tight and so high that they would almost dam the stream. Nothing moved. As a last resort dynamite was used to break up the jams. But in most cases the job was left to agile rivermen who pried the logs away with pikes and peavies. Jams of two to four miles in length were not uncommon on Wisconsin and Michigan rivers. One jam, located Little Falls, Minn., was almost seven miles long and a half-mile wide. A celebrated jam on the Mississippi River in 1894 took 150 lumberjacks, five teams of horses, and one steam engine six months to break up.

Some of the drivers were very dexterous in riding logs. Orcutt tells us:

> They could get on top of a log that little more than carried their weight, start it revolving, and cuff it with their feet until it made many revolutions per minute, then stop it from revolving almost instantly and hold it stationary in the water, keeping their equilibrium during the whole performance. Another favorite stunt was to ride a log through the sluiceway, where, as it descends, it stands, part of the time at an angle from 30 to 45 degrees. Some drivers were about as dexterous in performing their tricks on logs, as the western cowboys are in riding broncos.[11]

The Birth of a Sport

Jacks were so playful on moving logs that they initiated a sport which showcased their water/logging skills, birling. John Nelligan reports that when a drive came to an end, "rivermen would indulge in a bit of sport on the logs. Two or sometimes more would jump on a log together and roll and snub it furiously to see who could stay on the longest. Sometimes they all took a ducking, sometimes one proved himself better than his comrades by staying atop the spinning timber and forcing it into subjection."[12]

Birling appears simple. Two men leap on a floating log and spin it with their feet to see who can ride it longer. Different species of wood rode differently in the water and every river bragged of its champion birler. By the turn of the 20th century birling contests had become standard at the end of drives. They were announced well in advance and developed well understood although unpublished guidelines.

A 1901 Labor Day birling contest in Ashland, Wisconsin, watched by 3000 spectators, made a marathon seem effortless by comparison.

> "I witnessed the best log birling I have seen in fifty years of following the timber," recalls Jack Mahoney of Bend, Oregon. "It was claimed to be for the championship of the Lake States and was held in Ashland. Ten or twelve men, I forget which, got past the preliminaries. Then they rolled until only Tom Oliver, Michigan's best and Jim Stewart, of Eau Claire, Wisconsin were left. It was up to Oliver or Stewart.
>
> "They started in right after noon. Stewart was the taller and heavier man. Stronger too. With his superior weight he had control of the log at all times. But roll it as he would, he never had the lighter man in danger, while a number of times Oliver nearly got Stewart trapped — making him do a back roll. About seven o'clock that evening, the judges ordered the men from the log. It would have to go until the next day."
>
> "Next morning at ten Stewart and Oliver went back to the log ... they birled until noon when time was called for dinner. When the contest was resumed it was easy to see that Stewart's greater strength was going to win. He was wearing Oliver down with terrific bursts of speed that seemed to turn the log as fast as the headrig of a circular mill. At about half-past four Oliver fell exhausted from the log. He wasn't rolled into the water; he simply collapsed and fell in.
>
> "Tom Stewart received 100 dollars prize money and a gold medal that said he was the best man on logs in three states."[13]

Twelve-hour birling contests were far from the norm but the sport was soon firmly established. And competitions of all kinds — using crosscut saws, throwing or chopping with axes and pole climbing — relieved the monotony of camp life. At logging's peak, around 1906, it is estimated that in-camp lumberjacks numbered 500,000. Most logging was done in the winter months and evenings were taken up with shop talk, rough banter, tall tales, feats of physical prowess, and games. After a few hours of this, the smoky oil lamps were blown out and the tired men would roll into their bunks. It was slow on Sundays when there was little to do except repair axes, saws and clothing.

Most lumberjacks wore "wool caps, heavy flannel shirts, mackinaw cloth jackets and pants, heavy German socks and low rubbers. This was the warmest, most comfortable and most efficient costume for woods work."[14] Underclothes had to be washed every so often, usually to keep free of body lice, which were called "graybacks." Carl Leech reminds us that jacks mostly quarreled over their boots, the most important part of their outfit.[15] Daily boots had to withstand ax cuts, snags, wetness, burns or theft. Frequently jacks gambled for boots.

On spring drives, outfits needed to be much lighter. Drivers wore their overalls staged, that is they were cut off at a point just above the boot tops. This cutting was usually done with a knife or ax, and as a result was very uneven. They carried peavies or pike poles with which they wrestled logs and directed their course along the wandering rivers.

Ultimately, the routine and monotonous life in logging camps led to logging competitions. Jacks also loved to fight and "putting on the gloves" was always considered great sport. Loggers had a peculiar set of skills that turned into recreation. Cutting, sawing and climbing trees were transformed into contests. Initially these were informal contests to settle bragging rights, crown camp champions or just kill time. By the 1880s, when the lumber industry was booming, they became more formal. Contests like the underhand chop, standing block chop, two person crosscut saw, pole climbing, axe throwing, single bucking (one person using a crosscut saw), tree falling, and log rolling on water (birling) became standards at such affairs.

Modern Timber Sports

With the exception of rodeo, timber sports competitions are the most successful of modern worker competitions. Both sports were relatively slow starters in formalizing competition schedules, equipment and rules. Both could brag of competitions in the last half of the 19th century, though it was not until the first quarter of the 20th century that they became major spectator happenings. There is some discussion as to whether timber sports, in the second decade of the twenty-first century, are in decline.[16] In fact, just the opposite may be the case. In spite of losing national TV coverage, the timber sports competitions, especially in the east and south, are on the rise.

The competitions evolved from the actual tasks required of lumberjacks just prior to the appearance of the chain saw. The first acknowledged world lumberjack champion was Howard Paul Criss Jr. of Webster County, W. Va., who dominated competitions in the 1930s. Criss was so handy with an axe that he gave chopping demonstrations nationwide, shaved bearded men with his five pound axe, and could split an apple, held by his wife between her thumb and forefinger, and a block of wood simultaneously. He was known as Paul Bunyan Criss.

The nation's current top lumberjack is Arden "Jamie" Cogar, of Charleston, W. Va. He is 6–3, 270 lbs., and, in a major competition in 2001, chopped through a 13-inch horizontal white pine log in 14.02 seconds, and, in 1996, axed through a 13-inch vertical white pine log in 15.01 seconds.[17]

These workday skills that were perfected in the forests in the 19th century have become 21st century popular pastimes, with at least 80 state, regional and national competitions held annually by a myriad of logging federations and organizations.[18] A Lumberjack World Championships, begun in 1960, draws upwards of 12,000 spectators to a permanent site in Hayward, Wisc., on the site of a huge holding pond formerly owned by the Weyerhaeuser North Wisconsin Lumber Company. About 100 professional lumberjacks from around the world (the figure has never been large and New Zealand and Australian jacks have come to dominate) compete in 21 events ranging from men's and women's logrolling to chopping and sawing, to pole climbing. Prize money exceeds $50,000.

ESPN's *Great Outdoor Games* series has been discontinued, yet over the years it increased the sport's popularity, bolstered the fan base and provided prize money for this roving band of pro-jacks. And lumberjack competitions continue at hundreds of woodsmen's field days, Paul Bunyan Days, state and county fairs, craft shows, maple festivals, and museum openings, even at rodeo and firemen's events. Many colleges have woodsmen teams or forestry clubs which compete regionally and nationally. Stihl (the manufacturer of chainsaws) introduced the Timber Sports Collegiate Series Events, which are now emphasized by ESPN.

The most famous 19th century lumberjack in folklore is Paul Bunyan. He is the industry's recognizable icon and, although there were Paul Bunyan tales bantered about in logging camps in the 1890s, he and his faithful blue ox Babe do not make a formal appearance in literature until 1906.[19] So important to the lumberjack history is Paul Bunyan that today there are at least 16 giant statues of him in former lumber communities, eight of which claim to be his home.

American lumberjacks, as were cowboys and frontiersmen, are seen today as picturesque and heroic figures. In truth they were hard-living, hard-working, hard-fighting, individuals who have gone the way of our other typically American pioneers. Their memory is now relived in traditional worker competitions.

9

Rock Drilling and Steel Drivin' Men

Nothing in the history of rock-drilling contests can match a collegiate competition on the University of Arizona campus in early 2011. Mining students were competing in a rock-drilling contest (with modern drills) outside of Old Main when they hit something that was not granite. The huge rock had been transported from a mine near Tucson for the students to practice on. Geological engineers immediately stopped the contest and discovered the foreign material to be a unique dinosaur fossil. Experts from the Academy of Natural Sciences and the Smithsonian Institute hastened to Tucson to identify and date the new dinosaur species, which was named Wilbursaurus and determined to be 76 million years old.[1] Needless to say the competition was discontinued until university officials could obtain another rock. Surely it was the first and only time in history that a sporting event was interrupted by a dinosaur.

Dinosaurs notwithstanding, rock drilling has had a lengthy and colorful history as a worker competition and can claim as practitioners both a literary genius and a cultural icon. Ironically, although separated by 2,500 miles, Mark Twain and John Henry were contemporary rock drillers during the American Civil War era. Twain (Samuel Longhorne Clemens), at age 26, was prospecting in search of a livelihood and found himself drilling rock in a Nevada silver mine in the fall of 1861.[2] His was one of the first descriptions of how mining was accomplished at this time:

> That was the weariest work! One of us held the iron drill in its place and another would strike with an eight-pound sledge — it was like driving nails on a large scale. In the course of an hour or two the drill would reach a depth of two or three feet, making a hole a couple inches in diameter. We would put in a charge of powder, insert half a yard of fuse, pour in sand and gravel and ram it down, then light the fuse and run.[3]

The procedure would be repeated indefinitely in the process of producing ore or a tunnel. Twain's accounts may have been lighthearted but he found this extremely difficult work. He soon resigned, his drilling and blasting career lasting all of two weeks. He quickly turned to literary pursuits.

John Henry's tale is grimmer. As a prisoner/convict assigned to work digging tunnels on the Chesapeake and Ohio Railroad in Virginia in the immediate post–Civil War era, he became a cultural icon while racing a steam drill in 1871. Scott Reynolds Nelson's recent Henry biography details the life of the true John Henry and the dangers and consequences of the rock drilling occupation.[4]

19th Century Mining as an Occupation

By the mid–19th century, the increasingly important railroad and mining industries, hand-in-hand, created a demand for skilled rock drillers. The railroads needed tunnels built. The mines needed mineral deposits retrieved.

In mining especially, whether it was in the Appalachian coal regions, the lead mines of the Ozarks, the Michigan copper range, or the vast silver deposits in the Sierra Nevada and Rocky Mountain range, experienced rock drillers were required. The initial wave of miners came from the played-out (and sometimes flooded-out) mines of Cornwall and Wales in the 1840s. Another wave of immigrants, this time Irish, swarmed to the United States seeking work after Ireland's mid-century potato blight. After mid-century, the work in American mines was likely to be ethnically divided, with the Cornish (dubbed "Cousin Jacks") in administrative, surveyor and drilling positions, and the Irish ("Paddies") taking orders from a Cornish shift boss, while manning the heavy-lifting jobs of hauling and mucking.

Mining was big business. No matter what was being retrieved from the ground (gold, silver, lead, coal, copper, or zinc), mining was a labor-intensive, low productivity industry. The California rush for gold beginning in mid-century is well documented. Before 1900, U.S. coal production had doubled every ten years, increasing from 8¼ million short tons in 1850 to over 270 million short tons by the end of the century. In the 19th century the major coal producing states were Pennsylvania, Ohio, Illinois and West Virginia. In 1910, the coal mining industry employed three quarters of a million men (as opposed to around 80,000 today).[5] In the same year approximately 2 percent of the entire U.S. labor force worked *inside* coal mines, as opposed to less than a tenth of 1 percent currently.

In 1858 a large silver deposit, the Comstock Lode, was discovered in Nevada, stimulating prospecting all across the Great Basin. This resulted in the United States becoming the world's largest silver producer of the century.

9. Rock Drilling and Steel Drivin' Men

In addition, U.S. copper ranges stretched from Michigan's Upper Peninsula to Arizona to Butte, Montana, whose copper vein deposits were called the "richest hill on earth." Silver and copper wires were vital in production of electricity, communications and coinage. With the discovery of lead and zinc deposits, American mining, along with the railroad industry, carried the western half of America from an agrarian economy to one more industrialized and diversified.

Gold, silver and copper mining were especially dynamic forces in the settlement of western North America. Butte, Montana, for instance, was a major gold supplier until the placers were exhausted in 1867. Soon thereafter prospectors discovered silver veins, and, in 1882, large copper veins. In 1909 approximately 1 out of every 35 non-farm male workers in America was a miner. Today there are but 220,000 miners or approximately one out of every 300.[6]

Mining Camps

The mining camp, Twain tells us, was a strange place. It was a beggar's revel, distinguished by a lack of money and boundless optimism. There was no productive effort in the camp. Yes, alcoholic, food and amatory services abounded. But the focus was on the work and the chance of success. "Prospecting parties swarmed out of town with the first flush of dawn, and swarmed in again at nightfall with spoil — rocks. Nothing but rocks. Every man's pockets were full of them; the floor of his cabin was littered with them; they were disposed in labeled rows on his shelves."[7] The rocks were the product of relentless drilling and blasting. Single-jack drilling was done by a lone miner. Double-jack drilling

> was done by two man teams, one man striking with an eight pound sledge at the drill steel held, rotated, cleaned and changed by the other member of the team. The stroke was a steady 50 beats a minutes, and as a drill dulled the man turning extended a finger as the signal to stop. The steel was pulled and changed and the members of the team exchanged positions. The holder had to have great confidence in his mate, for a broken arm or ruined hand was the price paid for an instant's inattention in the candle-lit gloom of the drift, where the target was only a bright spot the size of a quarter dollar.[8]

After the holder declared that the hole was deep enough, it was filled and tamped with sticks of black powder, the tighter and harder the better. A blasting cap and fuse was carefully installed and lit and the miners high-tailed it out of danger. The resulting explosion left a muck pile of rock and gravel which had to be carried away by muckers. The drilling for the next blast began straight away. And so it went, two shifts a day, seven days a week until the mine played out.

Many miners migrated from camp to camp. "Tramp miners began to fade from the western mining scene after the turn of the twentieth century. Unionization and technical change conspired to render his caste obsolete."[9] Yet life in the western mining towns was not completely dreary. The inhabitants of isolated camps or towns were clever in providing their own amusement and diversions. And everyone looked forward to celebratory days like Labor Day, Railroad Day (the day the railroad arrived in communities) and most importantly, the Fourth of July. In some towns July 4th festivals lasted as long as three days.

The chief business of many a July 4th was the drilling and mucking contests. Contestants competed for purses, usually supplied by local merchants. It is easy to imagine how such contests originated. They were initially informal, the result of watering hole or on-the-job challenges. Boasting, pride, gambling and alcohol all likely played a role. Since these contests made a fine spectacle, they quickly became popular and institutionalized, with rules, schedules and a troupe of roaming professionals. We date the heyday of the rock-drilling era from 1880 to approximately 1910. Historian Otis Young estimates that national championships were held as early as 1885 in big camps such as Butte, Montana; Tonopah, Nevada; Bisbee, Arizona; and Kellogg, Idaho, the latter the center of the Coeur d'Alene mining district. "The national winners received as much adulation as toreros in Spain. Champion drillers were kings, known and feted throughout the mining world."[10]

On the day of celebration the mucking contests came first. They were the simplest, timing contestants who transferred one ton of assorted rocks and waste from one ore car into another. Micromucking contests, which prevail to this day, were common in gold mining camps. Sixteen tiny gold nuggets would be placed in a standard 18-inch pan mixed with pebbles, gravel and silt. The object was to eliminate all but the tiny gold bits using a spraying cistern.

Rock Drilling Contests

The feature of most celebrations was the 15-minute "double jack" drilling contest. Two men working as a team — one holding a steel drill while the other pounded with a sledge hammer — would change places every 30 seconds, and change drills every 60. Normally one team drilled at a time. Few sports required the same combination of skill and strength as this concocted worker team-game which duplicated the necessary skills of the mining or tunnel driller: a strong arm, a quick stroke, good eye-hand coordination and lots of trust and courage.

There were also "single jack" contests in which one individual held the drill with one hand and hammered with the other. Here being ambidextrous helped. In some mining camps ladies' nail driving contests were conducted in which women of all ages pounded nails into boards or flat timber.

The men's drilling contests, which drew large crowds, were normally conducted on a raised platform set flush with a wide, six-foot-thick block of granite. These uniform granite blocks, preferred for their hardness and absence of flaws, were quarried and shipped to the celebrating town at considerable expense.[11]

The contestants provided their personal drills and hammers. They forged, sharpened and tempered their own steel drills. Drills may have been iron in Twain's day, but the more durable steel was in vogue by the 1880s. Usually 15 were needed as drills were changed each minute. They came in an array of sizes, short ones for the first minute of pounding, and then progressively longer (to fit in the hole), eventually reaching up to 5 feet in length, optimistically for use in the last minute of drilling. In the early 20th century it became standard to make single jack drills ¾ inch and double jack drills ⅞ inch in diameter. Single drilling hammers weighed 4 pounds, double jack sledges 8. No doubt the experimentation with suitable tools helped productivity of the industry.

In some camps competitors were separated into weight classes, heavy and light. A number of contestants possessed legendary size and strength. Forty years after the fact, well-known driller Atha Richie touted Big Jim Pickens (6'3", 240 pounds) as the best of the bunch, a driller rarely beaten. Richie also recalled half a dozen top drillers in his day who weighed in at over 210 pounds.[12]

The contestants, normally in shirtsleeves or stripped to the waist, carried their hammers and a heavy roll of canvas containing their drills to the platform and, in a precise manner, laid out the drills in the order they would be used. They also positioned a slow-running hose attached to a barrel of water. The running water was used to clean the hole of granite after each stroke. With each blow the grimy water would squirt out making the men look as if they had been spewed with cement. During a 1903 contest in El Paso, Texas, the winning double jack team of Chamberlain and Make added beer to the water on the theory that the foam would bring the cuttings to the surface faster.[13] In this case they didn't drink beer so much as they wore it.

In cases where no hose was available the contestants aligned a number of tin cans filled with water for the same purpose. It was important that the hole get cleaned frequently of stone cuttings and muck, and that the drills did not stick. If a drill stuck it had be tapped and dislodged, losing precious seconds. If it did not come loose the contestants had to start a new hole, resulting in an almost certain loss.

When the contestants were in position, one kneeling and clasping the shortest drill pointed at the exact position, and his partner standing over him ready for the first blow, the contest began with either a gunshot, a shout or a simple tap on the shoulder. The initial rap was just hard enough to give the drill a straight direction. Each successive blow was a bit harder, and, as the hole deepened, the strokes grew ever more powerful. The holding partner turned the drill 90 degrees after each strike. The drills were expected to last one minute.

Every 30 seconds the partners changed places. As the moment of changeover approached, the man holding the drill gave it a final turn and simultaneously grabbed his own hammer. A timer, with stopwatch in hand, tapped the standing partner on the shoulder, who immediately crouched, grabbing the drill with both hands. His partner leapt to his feet and delivered the next blow, continuing the rhythm without any loss of time. Rock drilling changeovers had all of the precision of today's NASCAR pit stops.

As the hole deepened and longer steel was necessary, the former drill had to be yanked out and a new one inserted without slowing the drillers' rhythm. This precision was especially difficult late in the contest when 3-, 4- and 5-foot drills were being used. A loss of a stroke could mean the difference between winning or losing.

Stroke counts were announced by one of the judges each minute. Fifty was a pedestrian pace. Frank Crampton recalled that he and Irish Jack Commeford, early in the 20th century, beat a couple of Cousin Jacks in Grass Valley, California, with a steady beat of 61.[14] As in rowing, where a coxswain calls the stroke, the pace was critical. Young's description claims that "drift" pace was 50 blows per minute, but contest pace "was forced as high as eighty, and, everything else being equal, the team that could press the pace was likely to be a winner."[15] Suffice it to say that sixty blows per minute, *or one blow per second,* was astonishing work.

There was plenty of danger involved, which may help explain the event's popularity. A missed stroke could crush the hand, wrist or arm of a partner and accidents were not unheard of. Mrs. Hugh Brown, in her memoir of railroad days, recalled:

> Once during my life in Tonopah I saw a man's hand struck. Suddenly the hammer poised in midair. The crowd groaned, knowing what had happened. After an instant flinch, the man crouched over the drill, looked up at his towering partner, and yelled, "Come down, you!" Down came the hammer. The men cheered and the women cried. The hand on the drill began to turn red, but still it held on to the drill. When the injured man's turn came to rise and hold the hammer, the blood crept down his arm until it looked as if it had been thrust into a pot of red paint. The blood ran into the hole and mixed water from the hose. Every time the hammer descended, the red fluid sloshed up and spattered nearby onlookers. The man

9. Rock Drilling and Steel Drivin' Men

sagged lower after every blow, but he never gave up until the timer's hand signaled fifteen minutes. Then he fell over in a dead faint. The platform looked like a slaughtering block.[16]

At the end of a contest, oftentimes marked by a gunshot, the last drill was yanked and the depth of the hole was carefully ascertained with the help of a steel measuring rod. The result was chalked on a scoreboard. Oftentimes the crowd had a fair idea of the winning depth of team since they had kept track of the announced minute-by-minute count. Top teams could get in over 900 blows in a fifteen-minute time span.

Drilling a granite hole 42–43 inches deep (they were measured in 32nds of an inch) was considered very good and would win most side bets. It is believed that the 15-minute record is 45–7/16 inches, put down by Pickens and Page in Tonopah in 1912. According to Atha Richie, an alleged 46⅝ record into Gunnison granite in Bisbee in 1903 was incorrect. The team had actually drilled 42¼ inches but, just before the 14-minute mark, Chamberlain and his partner, even though on record pace, laid down their hammers, believing they would never be able to place another side bet if they had set such a prodigious record. Had they continued they probably would have drilled between 45 and 46 inches.

A double-jack drilling contest held on July 4, 1908, in Telluride, Colorado. The holder on right has just changed drills and the previous drill is flying out of his left hand (Ross Thomas in Young, O. E., *Black powder and hand steel: Miners and machines on the old Western frontier*, Norman, University of Oklahoma Press, 1976).

The champion single jack driller of the first decade of the 20th century was Fred F. Yockey, a 150-pound dynamo who used personally crafted hammers and who would have been a perfect subject for Frederick W. Taylor's time and motions studies then in vogue. Yockey, who died in 1919, was literally unbeatable for a few years, setting records at every stop on the circuit of Western mining camps. Using ¾ inch steels, he drilled 23¼ inches at Bisbee in 1903, 28⅞ inches at Tonopah in 1905 and 30 inches at Goldfield, Nevada, a few days later.

Prize money for champion drillers was significant. The 1905 Labor Day celebration at Tonopah offered $1000 as a double-jack purse. Yockey won the single jack prize money of $587.50 at the same affair. However Richie reminds us how important gambling was to the sport, especially side bets placed by the contestants themselves.[17] Successful drillers could earn half a year's wages with the right odds. Some competed under assumed names and moved frequently. Hand drilling contests suffered from the same 19th century problem that afflicted track and field. Often successful drillers, realizing they were well ahead of the competition, would loaf through the last few minutes of a contest to guarantee better odds on future bets.

John Henry — Steel Drivin' Man

While Yockey, Chamberlain, Page, Big Jim Pickens and others toiled away for prize money and fame in the early days of the 20th century, their occupation began to acquire a patron saint. Recent research now verifies that John Henry, once believed to have been a fictitious figure, was indeed a "steel drivin'" man. Scott R. Nelson researched the legendary figure, and recently uncovered the actual person who rose from a convict to an occupational, musical and cultural icon. And John Henry did, indeed, engage in an 1871 contest with a steam drill.[18]

Using company files, penitentiary reports and census data, Nelson tracked John William Henry through the Virginia penal system to his death while working on one of the day's most dangerous enterprises, the first rail route though the Appalachian Mountains. Nelson found the following information in the formerly sealed records of Virginia penitentiary:

John William. Henry c[olored] (#497)
When received: 1866 Nov. 16
Where sentenced: Prince George
Crime: Housebreak and larceny
Term: 10 years
Nativity: U.S.
State or Province: New Jersey
County Dist or city: Elizabeth City
Height: 5 ft 1¼

9. Rock Drilling and Steel Drivin' Men 113

Age: 19
Complexion: Black
Col of Hair: Black
Col of Eyes: Black
Marks or other peculiar descriptions: a small scar on left arm above elbow. A small one on right arm above wrist.
When pensioned, discharged, or died: Transferred [in pencil].[19]

In May 1866, a nineteen-year-old John William Henry was found guilty of burglary of a small dry goods store near Petersburg, Va., in the Tidewater. He was harshly sentenced to ten years, the victim of Virginia's notorious Black Codes, and was shipped to the infamous Richmond Penitentiary. As prisoner number 497, John Henry was soon leased, like so many other young inmates, to the Chesapeake & Ohio Railroad by the Virginia governor and the prison superintendant. The C&O was then engaged in digging tunnels and laying track in the western part of the state and had arranged for cheap, pliable labor through the state's prison system. Further investigation of engineering reports of the Chesapeake and Ohio Railroad revealed that convicts and steam drills worked side by side to cut through the Lewis Tunnel, a mile-long stretch on the Virginia-West Virginia border just east of White Sulphur Springs, W. Va., located deep in the Appalachians and approximately halfway between Charleston, W. Va., and Charlottesville, Va.[20]

Henry was shipped to the mountains as unskilled labor and likely began his C&O tenure as a mucker. His strength made him a natural to handle the 12-pound sledge hammer. The side-by-side working of man and machine provided the gist of John Henry's legend. At the time, steam drills were seen as potentially economical, but they were often unreliable. Newer versions were continually being introduced. By the summer of 1871, John Henry, despite his size, had developed into a highly regarded and powerful rock driller.

Legend has no answer as to who arranged a contest between John Henry and a new steam drill. There is no mention of it in the C&O engineering reports. Yet it is easy for us to see how a competition came about, just the way it did in many other nineteenth and early 20th century work situations. Here a new and highly regarded machine was next to a powerful driller. A contest would be natural and would give the railroad a way to gauge the machine's efficiency. It is fair to say that many worker competitions began in the same manner.

It seems that both were given a limited amount of time to drill through rock. Given what we know about hand drilling, this contest must have taken several hours. We do not know the type of rock drilled or if John Henry double or single jacked. But legend does tell us that he drilled like a man possessed. The results of this drilling contest, as captured in a ballad, read like a modern football score:

> The man that invented the steam drill
> Thought he was mighty fine
> John Henry sunk her 14 feet
> And the steam drill only made nine
> Steam drill only made nine.[21]

The legend has it that, in his desire to out-drill a steam engine, John Henry died at the end of the contest. In fact, many of the convict drillers died in the Virginia Alleghenies, hammer in hand, normally victims of a lung disease and John Henry may have become their metaphor.

> John Henry went down that railroad track
> With his 12 pound hammer by his side
> Went down the track but he never looked back.
> Because he laid down his hammer and he died.
> Yes he laid down his hammer and he died.[22]

John Henry may have been a particularly popular driller with co-miners and co-prisoners. An immediate ballad of John Henry's challenge and death was initially sung by other black railroad workers and was spread beyond the world of tunnels, mines and prison cells. By imposing their own experiences on the lyrics, workers kept John Henry's story from disappearing. Over time the legend grew. John Henry eventually morphed into a giant wielding 30-pound hammers. It was, of course, pure hyperbole. There are no 30-pound hammers.

The legend grew and John Henry eventually entered the world of tall tales and occupational folklore, on a par with Paul Bunyan and Pecos Bill. As the years passed, he grew taller, more heroic and amazingly powerful. We are told in the legend that, as he drilled, he drove steel down 2 inches with every strike. Contrast this with the double jacking records from the Western mining towns where it took 900 blows to cut 45 inches of rock.

Ironically, another hammer wielding hero was pounding his way through the Caledonian and Highland games at the very same time John Henry drilled in the Virginia mountains. The sports' first superstar, Scotsman Donald Dinnie, carrying his personal collections of sledge hammers,[23] toured North America in 1870 and again in 1872. Dinnie did not pound steel with *his* hammers, he *threw* them, and at such distances that thousands came to watch.[24]

Americans flocked to Highland/Caledonian gatherings not only to watch Dinnie compete but simply to *see* Dinnie, an incredible physical specimen. Thin-waisted, Dinnie stood 6–1 and possessed a 48-inch chest. At 218 pounds he had 26½-inch thighs and sported no fat. It was said that when Dinnie shed his robe before competing he made men's hearts and women's knees weak. Dinnie was in fact what John Henry later became in legend, a giant strongman and athletic hero.[25]

The ballad of John Henry was finally copyrighted in 1922. His legend grew in popularity over the 20th century as he morphed into a working-class hero. By the late 20th century he became a shorthand symbol for size and strength. Numerous black athletes in sports where size and strength were required, were referred to as John Henrys. These included Rutgers' All American football star (and later entertainer) Paul Robson; world heavyweight boxing champion Joe Louis; and world champion decathlon performers Big Bill Watson, Milt Campbell and Rafer Johnson.

At least four states claimed that John Henry had died battling a steam drill within their borders. His image appeared on a line of clothing and on historical markers throughout the southeast. Shaquille O'Neal appeared as John Henry in a lamentable 1997 movie adaptation of his life. In April 2010, John Henry's life was recalled in a Washington, D.C., stage production.[26] But mostly John Henry is remembered in song. By the end of the 20th century more songs had been written about John Henry than about any other American figure. Pete Seeger, Woody Guthrie, Johnny Cash and numerous others all have recorded John Henry ballads.

Demise and Return of Drilling Contests

By 1910 compressed air and electric drills were common in mining establishments and hand drilling contests faded away. Like other worker competitions, rock drilling became a victim of technological innovation. Many of the new drills were manufactured by Holman Brothers in Cornwall. They made hand drilling obsolete. Soon enough (1910) South Africa was conducting World Rock Drilling contests with compressed air drills.

Hand drilling competitions made a brief comeback in 1934 in both Idaho Springs and Boulder, Colorado.[27] Today there are dozens of rock drilling contests in the old mining states. Leadville Colorado's Boom Days and Carson's Nevada Days are extremely popular, drawing dozens of competitors annually and thousands of spectators. Annual hand drilling contests dot the western map: Salt Lake City; Tombstone, Arizona; Allegheny, California; Silverton, Colorado; Bisbee, Arizona, and the list goes on. Several claim to be national or world championships.[28] These contests are typically 10 minutes long and, for single jacks, a 14-inch hole is considered top drilling. Emmit Hoyl of Rollinsville, Colo., is a frequent world champion. A blacksmith by trade, he comes from five generations of miners. Today there is a rock drilling competition circuit, as there is for lumberjacks and rodeo cowboys. Rock drilling is even a collegiate sport. The annual Intercollegiate Rock Drilling Championships are usually held in Bisbee, Arizona. There ought to be a national organization, sort of like the NCAA, for intercollegiate work sports. The program could include rodeo, timber sports and mining competitions, all of which are tendered at American colleges.

Rock drilling as a work-sport and John Henry existed in a world left behind — a time before the machine age, scientific management and the assembly line. The legend of John Henry serves to remind us that there was a time when men swung their shovels, axes, rakes or hammers from sunup to sundown, and occasionally made time to play. Every now and again, to make their occupational lives more palatable, a challenge and a worker competition resulted. Johnny Gunn, a popular hand-drilling announcer throughout the West, reminds everyone that his sport is a throwback, an old-time game, and should be remembered as such. In 2007 Gunn was requested by the University of Nevada-Reno to introduce its collegiate competitors as representing the "Mackay School of Earth Sciences." Reluctant to use the modern educational terminology, the old-timer told the university to go to hell, and said, "It's the Mackay School of Mines."

10

Office Games

Speed Writing

A 1918 office scene found two practitioners engaged in an ad hoc shorthand contest, the likes of which had occurred repeatedly in American offices since Sir Isaac Pitman first published his phonetic shorthand system eight decades earlier. On one side of a large and decorated mahogany desk sat a 61-year-old executive offering dictation to an 18-year-old high school graduate seated on the desk's opposite side. They then reversed roles. For 30 minutes they listened and scribbled, then noted errors and scored, in words per minute, each other's aural tests.

Although the impromptu stenographic contest itself was not out of the ordinary, the contestants and the setting were. For this was the Oval Office. One contestant was the nation's twenty-eighth president, Woodrow T. Wilson. His opponent was one William Rosenberg, a New York City stenographic dervish who had captured the city's high school shorthand contest a year earlier. Rosenberg had left Commerce High in Brooklyn in May of 1917 and taken a position with the government's War Production Board, then managed by tycoon Bernard Baruch. Rosenberg soon came to Baruch's attention and before long was employed as his private secretary, offering Baruch a transcript, each evening, of *everything* Baruch had said during the day. After Baruch had boasted about his speedy stenographer to Wilson, the president sent for the 5–4, skinny lad to have a look for himself.[1]

Wilson fancied himself a stenographic connoisseur. Rosenberg's stenographic skills were well known. Shortly after pleasantries they got down to the business of fashioning a contest. Although there is no record of the results, a later biography hints that the recent high school student had the better of the former Princeton professor.

In the last part of the 19th century shorthand was the sport of intellectuals and a time saving measure of lawyers, authors, preachers and politicians, most of whom were males. It would later become the property of court reporters and those preparing for secretarial positions. By the turn of the 20th century the Pitman system faced competition from a newer stenographic technique invented and promoted by Irish educator John Robert Gregg (1878–1948). In 1909 the professional association of court reporters, (National Shorthand Reporters Association or NSRA) began to conduct national speed contests at their annual convention. The national contests were initially designed as a platform for reporters using both the Pitman and Gregg systems to demonstrate their ability and to expose fraudulent claims that stenographers could record dictation in the 400 to 600 word-per-minute range.

In the early days of the 20th century shorthand contests were frequently reported in the local press. For example, when the 1912 national speed writing championships were held in New York City, the *New York Times* published 7 stories about the event and the work-sport in general.[2]

The Remington company purchased a typewriter patent in 1873, then designed and marketed a convenient typewriter; 40,000 machines were in use by 1888. The female typist working on a Remington machine in this 1910 postcard was typical of the day, for, according to the 1910 census, 81 per cent of all typists were female, a vast jump from just 20 years earlier as increased office work pulled women into the workforce (http://www.websters-online-diction ary.org/definitions/typewriter).

Shorthand contests required the reading and transcribing of passages at various speeds. By 1910 three readings at national contests became standard: a literary passage read at 200 words per minute (wpm); a jury charge at 240 wpm; and question-and-answer testimony at 280 wpm. Over the years the reading speeds have become more rapid. Winners were judged on the fewest errors.

10. Office Games

Nationwide boards of education carefully watched the results of the national speed contests, as both the Pitman and Gregg methods attempted to win acceptance for their system with high school shorthand departments. The 1909 nationals at Lake George, N.Y., marked the beginning of the first of two great eras of championship steno writing that didn't end until 1927. A second and current era, begun in 1952, has been dominated by machine shorthand writers (stenotypists).

Early national competitions were won by professional court reporters, but by 1914 groups of specifically trained high school students began to win some of the individual contests. The aforementioned William Rosenberg, for instance, possessing a good ear, nimble fingers and excellent recall, was such a contestant.[3] He was tutored and groomed by Gregg himself, and Rosenberg's reputation was so widespread that he went to the 1919 national speed writing competition in Detroit as a favorite. Unfortunately (or perhaps fortunately?) the teenager spent too much time in a Windsor, Ontario, speakeasy the night before the contest, suffered from a hangover the next morning, lost his favorite pen, and passed out during the contest. Humiliated, he gave up reporting as a career and turned his attention to songwriting. He soon shortened his name from William Rosenberg to Billy Rose and headed for Broadway. Within a dozen years he had become, although often and deservedly vilified as a despicable rascal, a renowned songwriter and producer.

The early speed writing contests were not without controversy. Many court reporters complained that the competitions were dominated by high school kids who had been explicitly trained for the contests and who had no intention of making reporting a profession. At the same time, their employers—judges and attorneys—took note of the speed of the youngsters and wondered aloud why they had to pay such great salaries to their own reporters. The situation was similar to the one 40 years earlier when competitive swifts demonstrated astounding work speed and newsroom managers wondered why the rank and file compositors weren't as speedy. And everyone complained about the Gregg and Pitman publishing companies, who were overt in their commercial misuse of contest results, each claiming the majority of champions. And so, in spite of the astonishing records for accuracy in the pen and shorthand era, the national contests were dropped after the 1927 NSRA convention.

National speed contests for stenographers were resumed in 1952 and have been popular ever since. World championships (run by INTERSTENO) have been conducted bi-annually since the mid 1990s. Today all contestants are machine shorthand writers. In the mid 1970s the premier national class competitor was J. Edward Varallo (known in a Newmanesque fashion as "Fast Eddie"), who turned in a perfect transcript in the 280 wpm testimony reading section. Varallo won the 1974, 1975 and 1976 nationals, and then retired from competition. After a ten-year absence he returned to win the 1986 nationals, and then re-retired, only to re-emerge in 1996 to win yet again. He retired once again, then, just to remind the profession who was top dog, he re-appeared in 2006 to win a sixth national speed writing title, with 32 years between his first and most recent national victory. Incidentally, Varallo will be 70 years old in 2016.

As for the impresario Billy Rose, he died in 1966 after having amassed an enormous fortune. Among his seven wives were starlet Fannie Brice, swimming beauty Eleanor Holm and socialite Joyce Matthews, whom he married twice. One early Rose biography claimed that he had been the national shorthand champion. Not so. But Rose could claim a 1–0 won-loss record against U.S. presidents.

Typing Contests

Shorthand contests may be older, yet the most popular office competition was the speed typing contest. Although there were numerous early patents for "writing machines" the age of the typewriter really began after the Civil War. The first typing machine that enabled operators to prepare a page appreciably faster than a person could write by hand was perfected by Christopher Latham Sholes (with a patent awarded in 1868) after numerous keyboard design experiments. Sholes solved the problem of jamming keys by spacing commonly used letters. His effort was the QWERTY keyboard, named for the letters in the upper left hand row. Sholes's patent rights were purchased by E. Remington and Sons in 1873, which, a year later, marketed a machine for $125. Other firms, with their own keyboard designs, competed in this youthful market at a time when many businessmen considered typing a letter to a customer to be rude because it lacked the "personal touch" of a handwritten letter.

Expense and mechanical problems prevented the typewriter from becoming an immediate success. Early machines were heavy, cumbersome and finicky. Remington ads claimed that 40,000 of its machines were in use by 1888.[4] The typewriter's advantage over handwriting was enhanced as the speed of the operators improved and because multiple copies could be made with the use of either carbon paper or stencils.

In the late 19th century, the operator of such an apparatus was frequently known as a *typewriter,* and later known as a *typist.* Competitions to assess the speeds of typists were soon common. A great deal of economic and historical importance has been attached to a typing contest in 1888 in which the contestants chose different typewriter models. In what has become known as

10. Office Games

the QWERTY story, a pair of speedy typists met in Cincinnati in July of 1888 to settle a challenge, both claiming to be the world's fastest typist.

Frank E. McGurrin, a court stenographer from Salt Lake City, had challenged "any one or more typewriter operators to a speed contest in typewriting, for a purse of not less than $500" in the occupational trade journals *The Typewriter Operator* and the *Cosmopolitan Shorthander*.[5] The challenge was accepted by Louis Traub, a proprietor at Longley's Shorthand and Typewriting Institute in Cincinnati, Ohio.

The trade journals and popular press enthusiastically covered the contest. McGurrin chose a Remington No. 2 (with its QWERTY keyboard), while Traub selected a Caligraph No. 2. McGurrin had memorized the QWERTY keyboard and was an early practitioner of ten-finger touch typing. The myth still circulates that Traub was a two-finger, hunt-and-peck typist. In fact he used an eight-finger method common to the Caligraph machines, which offered a double keyboard, one for upper and the other for lower case letters. Traub was no slouch. He had exhibited his skills on a *blank* Caligraph keyboard at the Indiana State Fair a year earlier.[6]

The contestants typed for 90 minutes, half dictation and half text copying. McGurrin won in a convincing fashion, crushing his opponent, 8709 to 6938 words. So dominant was McGurrin (at a rate of 96.7 words per minute or wpm) that he could have taken a 15-minute coffee break and still won. He laid claim to the title "the world's fastest typist" and to the $500.

The results and significance of this contest have attracted the attention of economists, who wondered if this was a victory for the man or the machine, and why the QWERTY keyboard has become the industry standard? The conventional wisdom is that McGurrin's choice of a QWERTY keyboard for the contest was simply fortuitous and his victory and resultant success by Remington illustrate that the first product that attracts consumers will have an insurmountable advantage in the market place over subsequent superior products. This is the doctrine of "path dependence," which claims that the past so strongly influences the future that consumers get locked into choices that are inefficient. Specifically, due to the 1888 speed typing case, Remington fictitiously claimed that its QWERTY *keyboard* was victorious. As a result we put up with inefficient typewriters for the next century in spite of evidence of more workable layouts. Nobel Laureate Paul Krugman tells us that "in QWERTY worlds, markets can't be trusted."[7] This traditional interpretation of the famous typing contest is all poppycock.

The notion that later superior keyboard designs have been unable to unseat the QWERTY design because of path dependence has been dispelled by Stanley Liebowitz and Stephen Margolis in their now famous "The Fable of the Keys" article published in the *Journal of Law and Economics* in 1990.[8]

World War I recruiting poster advertising the need for office workers in 1917. Not only were soldiers needed for the fight overseas, but clerks and typists were needed to staff the new government offices. Stenographer's skills were in particular demand (Library of Congress: Prints and Photographs Division).

It proves conclusively that the claims that August Dvorak, a professor at the University of Washington, to have produced a superior keyboard design are nothing but hokum. Dvorak manipulated data to make his claim. Yet the story of the Dvorak keyboard has been repeated so frequently that modern scholars, without consulting original documents, now simply accept it as fact. It can be found in newspaper and magazine stories, documentaries, and even successful economics texts.[9] Nothing is further from the truth.[10] The moral: repeating false conclusions is common and not the exclusive property of sporting and labor historians or even Nobel laureates.

McGurrin won the 1888 speed typing contest because he had mastered a ten-finger touch typing system, while Traub, although highly nimble, just was not as fast. The 1888 contest was not one between machines or competing keyboards—it was one of typists. The results simply proved that McGurrin was a faster typist. Nothing more. Afterwards McGurrin became somewhat of a celebrity, participating in contests and demonstrations across the country.

McGurrin and Traub squared off one additional time, in January 1889, again in Cincinnati. Traub insisted on a 10 percent handicap and *won* the competition, typing 434 words in 5 minutes, while McGurrin typed only 447 words, a margin of only 3 percent.[11]

But the concept of typing contests caught fire after 1888 and became a staple of professional meetings, trade shows, fairs, the YWCA, and educational institutions. Liebowitz and Margolis claim that "typing competitions are somewhat underplayed in the conventional history. In fact, typing contests and demonstrations were fairly common during the late 19th-early 20th century. They involved many different machines, with various manufacturers claiming to hold the speed record."[12]

The *New York Times* began to publish accounts of speed typing contests in 1888. McGurrin continued to win contests, The *New York Times* reported on August 2, 1888, that he typed 95.8 words per minute to win a five-minute New York contest. His opponents, Miss May Orr and M.C. Grant, seemed to be pressing him, recording speeds of 95.2 and 93.8 words per minute.[13] Other manufacturers held their own "championship for fast typing." Just months after the Cincinnati affair, Thomas Osborne of Rochester, N.Y., in a Brooklyn demonstration, reached 142 wpm in a five-minute test, 179 wpm for one minute and 198 wpm for 30 seconds, using a Caligraph machine with a non-QWERTY keyboard. The Underwood Company also claimed its machines were on the winning side of many contests. So did other manufacturers. Unfortunately there was no standardization of the competitions so comparison of speeds across typewriters and typists is hazardous.

As the population of typists grew, so did the popularity and frequency of their contests. The number of stenographers and typists in America grew from approximately 200 in 1870 to 811,000 in 1930. Even more arrestingly, in the earlier period only 5 percent of stenographers were female. By 1930 the figure grew to 96 percent.[14] Work-sports in the office became the prerogative of women. For example, in the early 20th century the world's fastest typist was Rose L. Fritz of New York City. She first entered speed typing contest in Chicago, at the International Business Show of 1907. She won that competition at age 19 and held the title for six years. She was soon hired by the Remington Company, a major typewriter manufacturer, as a promotional agent, and she was allowed abundant time to practice and enter competitions.[15]

Because typing speed is an important secretarial qualification, there have been more typing contests than any other form of work-sport. Business shows, high schools, public and proprietary business schools and typewriter companies all promoted these easy-to-conduct competitions. Standardization took hold and there are now well-accepted typing records. According to the *Guinness Book of World Records*, today Barbara Blackburn is the world's fastest English typist: 150 wpm for 50 minutes, 170 wpm for shorter periods and a peak speed of 212 wpm. Ironically, she failed her high school typing class.[16]

Morse Code Competitions

A third example of office competitions in the 1830–1930 period also came about because of a technical improvement, some would say revolution, in communication. In 1843, Samuel F.B. Morse made a successful attempt to interest the American government in financing the telegraph, a project he had experimented with over the previous eleven years. He built the first successful telegraph line from Washington, D.C., to Baltimore, Md., and transmitted its first message ("what hath God wrought") on May 24, 1844. Quickly the telegraph and Morse's code found practical commercial, news-gathering, military, maritime, and railroad applications.

Morse code has always been popular with amateur radio operators. When Morse code was sent via the traditional telegraph key (straight key) and later adapted to radio, the dots and dashes, short or long pulses to signify letters, numbers and punctuation marks, were either sent by nimble fingers or heard and transcribed by attentive listeners. For the second half of the nineteenth and the first half of the twentieth centuries, the majority of high speed national and international communication was conducted in Morse code, using telegraph lines, undersea cables and radio circuits. It should not be surprising that those who became proficient in sending or receiving the signals engaged in demonstrations and contests to display their skills. The transmission speed of Morse code is typically specified in words-per-minute (WPM).

In his autobiography, Alan Greenspan, longtime chairman of the Federal Reserve Board of Governors (1987–2005), recalls his fascination with and participation in telegraph contests while growing up in Brooklyn in the 1920s, an era when competitions proliferated.[17] Unfortunately Greenspan makes no mention of his personal records. But in a contest in Asheville, N.C., in July 1939, Ted R. McElroy set a still unbroken record for *copying* radio-sent Morse code, 75.2 WPM. And *senders* have exceeded 100 WPM. Harry Turner demonstrated at a U.S. Army base in 1942 that Morse code could be *sent* at 35 WPM using a straight telegraphic key.[18]

Although satellite and high frequency communications systems have essentially rendered Morse code obsolete, nonetheless high speed telegraphy competitions in which individuals correctly send, receive and copy Morse code transmissions abound today. It is most popular in Eastern Europe and the competitions (there have been seven world championships since 1995) are organized by the International Amateur Radio Union (IARU).

Technological Transformations

The growth and interest in shorthand, typing and telegraphic competitions in the late nineteenth and early twentieth centuries reflects technological change in the nature of work in America. Until 1860 American businesses employed very few clerical workers, mostly bookkeepers, document copyists, filers and message boys. The share of U.S. non-agricultural labor force that was clerical workers was under 2 percent at the time of the Civil War, 5 percent in 1900 and 11 percent in 1920.[19]

The growth of large corporations and railroads which served more than local markets contributed to the expansion of offices and office workers. So too did technology: telephones, elevators, safes, the telegraph, writing inks, typewriters, calculating machines, mechanical pencils, and rubber stamps were innovations and inventions that created a need for individuals with specific office skills. And the shift to services made intensive use of clerical workers. Specifically, telegraph firms, commercial and investment banking companies, insurance firms, mail order companies and all levels of government employed a growing number of clerks. In 1870 there were less than 75,000 clerks nationwide. In six decades the numbers were 500 times as large (3.74 million).[20] As a share of the clerk population, the number of females ballooned from approximately 2.5 percent in 1870 to virtual parity with males by 1920.

Thus, by the end of the American work-sports era (approximately 1840–1940) a significant number of contestants of worker competitions were likely to have been women. The finest female athlete of the 20th century, Mildred Didrikson-Zaharias, claims to have been a work-sports champion. The "Babe" was a top professional golfer, outstanding basketball player and the owner of three world records and three Olympic gold medals from the 1932 Los Angeles games. She was voted by the Associated Press as the top American female athlete of the first half of the 20th century. In 1930 she was employed as a typist at the Employers Casualty Insurance Company of Dallas, Texas. Often, during her athletic career, she reminded the press that she had won a gold medal for typing 86 words per minute (a world class pace) in a high school typing contest.[21] Although the story is apocryphal, it does illustrate that the nation and the nation's best female athlete of conventional sports had a high regard for worker competitions.

As the nature of work changed in America, so did the nature of work-sports. It should not be surprising that there were thousands (perhaps hundreds of thousands) of ad hoc and formal typing, shorthand and telegraphic contests. Interestingly, the transformation in the character of work, from outdoor hard labor to indoor and non-physical, made worker athletes out of the likes of Woodrow Wilson, Billy Rose and Alan Greenspan, three of the least athletic-looking individuals in U.S. history. Few would lump them with the stereotypical Paul Bunyans and John Henrys. But they all competed, often successfully, in contests of worker skills.

11

Corn Husking and Other Agricultural Contests

Cornhusking

Fred Stanek, a 25-year-old Bohemian farmer from Webster County, Iowa, drove his black Model T through the morning of November 23, 1924. After four hours he managed to locate a field of sod corn adjacent to the town of Alleman, midway between Des Moines and Ames, and one-half mile from any paved road. There he found frenetic preparations for the Iowa State Cornhusking contest, the leading contest of a relatively new farm sport. Professor L.C. Burnett of the Iowa experiment station[1] was waiting for the ten invited contestants and preparing for a large crowd

Stanek, a confidant young man who stood 6-0 and weighed 180 pounds, worked on his father's farm in Fort Dodge. He had no invitation to the well-advertised, ten-man contest that offered a $100 first prize, but hoped that, somehow, he'd be allowed to take part. When one of the ten invitees, all winners of regional contests, failed to show, Stanek and three others with the same intent drew straws for the final spot. Stanek was the lucky one, and was immediately offered $10 by one of the others for his spot.

He declined, preferring to take his chances in the field and, lo and behold, put 24 bushels in the bin, more than any of the other nine competitors. But because he used a palm hook, his ears were dirty and penalties relegated him to second place and the $50 prize. Twenty-one-year-old Ben Grimmius, a 6-0, 170 pound farmer from Grundy County, won the $100 prize in front of several thousand spectators. The ten huskers, all of whom competed simultaneously, were pitted against a new mechanical corn picker supplied by a local farm implement company, which put up three times as much corn as Stanek.[2] Unlike in the mythical John Henry rock drilling contest, no one died

WALLACES' FARMER

Good Farming   Clear Thinking   Right Living
A Weekly Journal for Thinking Farmers

Published Weekly, on Friday, at Des Moines, Iowa
BY THE
Wallace Publishing Company
Under the Business and Editorial
Management of
JOHN P. WALLACE and **HENRY A. WALLACE**

Wallace's Farmer newspaper did not invent cornhusking but was responsible for turning it into a major spectator sport. The weekly paper, published in Des Moines, IA, was a family project. Henry A. Wallace was the general editor in the early 1920s, and later U.S. Secretary of Agriculture and Vice President in the Franklin D. Roosevelt Administration (Wallace's Farmer).

at Alleman, Iowa. His second place finish earned Stanek an invitation to the first Midwest cornhusking contest against the top two finishers from Illinois and Nebraska, to be held a week later in the same field. Stanek started slowly and trailed badly after the first 30 minutes.

> About this time Stanek began to speed up. He had been throwing about 36 ears to the minute, but now he was (thoroly) warmed up, he increased to 42, and finally, during the last ten minutes of the contest, he passed 50. He knew that excess husks were the only thing that had beaten him for the Iowa championship, and he was therefore husking cleaner. He figured that he could afford to let the gleaners pick the nubbins behind him, but he didn't pass up any big ears. The thing about Stanek's husking which impressed every one was his rhythm. The swing of his arm was almost as even as (tho) he were keeping time to music.[3]

The above was part of a 1,500-word article in the widely read *Wallaces' Farmer*, which, like other midwestern farming papers like the *Prairie Farmer* and *Nebraska Farmer,* tendered elaborate coverage of cornhusking contests. In fact the story's author was Henry A. Wallace, editor of the family farming weekly, who is traditionally given credit for transforming the back-breaking farm chore into a formal sporting event. Many farmers kept track of their cornhusking work, and frequently engaged in informal timed contests.

A Monoma County, Iowa, farmer boasted to *Wallaces' Farmer* in late 1924 that

> I have picked corn for 23 years and belive that I have husked more corn than any other man in that time. I am thirty-seven years old and I don't consider it has ever hurt me.

11. Corn Husking and Other Agricultural Contests

Spectators enter a field in Ontario, Oregon, for a firsthand look at a cornhusking contest. Crowd control was always a managerial concern as such affairs, especially at the state and national levels where crowds could overwhelm the event. Championship events drew as many as 100,000 enthusiasts (Library of Congress, Prints and Photographs Division, LC-USF33–013209-M1).

> In the nine year I have husked in Monoma County, Iowa, I have picked 43,901 bushels, or an average of 153 bushels for 287 days. Last year I picked 2,073 bushels in ten consecutive days. One week, 2,239.7 bushels. For nineteen days I had an average of 193 bushels. The thirty-six days I picked last fall, I had 6,657 bushels. And I wasn't in a contest, either.

As early as 1916 the *Prairie Farmer* had encouraged its readers to send the results of their informal husking contests to the paper. But it was Wallace who conceived the idea of proving some of the tall husking tales by actually staging an official competition. Tired of all the unproven claims, Wallace, whose father, Henry C. Wallace, was secretary of agriculture in the Warren G. Harding administration, suggested it was time to either put up or shut up. In October 1922 he printed an editorial asking huskers to submit their records, and inviting the best to a competition held on his family farm in Polk County, Iowa.[4]

Three showed up and the initial winner was Louis Curley, of Lee County, Iowa. In 1923 Wallace encouraged counties to conduct contests and send their champions. Eleven huskers turned up at the Wallace farm to husk and he gave the event extensive newspaper coverage. Wallace was like another newspaper editor and sporting promoter, Henry Chadwick, who gave far-reaching

A contestant in a 1941 cornhusking contest, Ontario, Oregon. Cornhusking contestants were typically given 80 minutes to husk (remove from stalk and toss into a bin/cart) as much corn as possible. The resulting take was weighed rather than counted. This was one of the last major corn husking contests before World War II put a stop to the sport and ended a century of customary and popular worker competitions in America (Library of Congress, Prints and Photographs Division, LC-USF34-070796-0).

coverage in the New York metropolitan area to another new game called "baseball" 80 years earlier.

Approval of the new sport was not universal. To his credit Wallace ran editorials pro *and* con. Typical of the objections was this diatribe: "It is rather puzzling why *Wallaces' Farmer* persists in holding its so-called husking contests. As an actual cornhusker I can not but regard them as a somewhat revised edition of the late marathon dance. To exalt the dreariest and most grueling of farm tasks to the position of sport rather strains the imagination."[5] Another groused, "It does make a fellow who can't husk more than sixty or seventy bushels a day feel like 30 cents."[6] Others lobbied to make the contests longer. Alva Gay, a Minnesota farmer, suggested "that a whole season's corn husking contest would be a better test for real merit than the hour or day plan. Lots of short time experts do not make enviable records when it comes to a whole season's work ... let's hear from the season huskers."[7]

But Wallace's idea and influence prevailed. In 1924 he pressed his case.

"Local corn husking contests are a fine affair for the local farm organization to put on as a feature of the fall program. Often local business men and bankers will be glad to help. So, of course, will we."[8] He envisioned a bunch of boys husking corn for fun in front of a cheering crowd. Although he professed to be settling arguments while having fun — "actual husking would come nearer to deciding the champ than talking"[9] — Wallace had an ulterior motive — productivity. He imposed penalties for both the corn left in the field, and husks left on the corn ("husking dirty"). He concluded that contests with ground rules would foster equipment advances and faster husking methods and spectators could not help but become better huskers themselves.[10] He was right. Husking information was shared and soon "county farm advisers, elevator operators, farm bureau groups, implement dealers and other local businessmen took part, while groups of women set up food stands."[11] The result were local cooperative efforts which created tradition, spirited rivalries among counties and states, and a fan base.

At this time Nebraska was known as the Cornhusker State. In 1900, a Lincoln, Neb., sports editor, Charles S. (Cy) Sherman, tired of referring to the University of Nebraska football team with then-current nicknames: Bugeaters, Old Gold Knights and Rattlesnake Boys or Antelopes. He called them the "Cornhuskers" and it stuck. Quickly Nebraska rushed into cornhusking competitions. By 1924 Nebraska and Illinois were also conducting statewide competitions. The Illinois contest was noteworthy because it was sponsored by another newspaper, *The Prairie Farmer*, and attracted 3,500 spectators. Wallace arranged a contest among the top two huskers from each state and it was this competition, originally called "The Mid-West Championship," that Fred Stanek won.

This contest became the National Corn Husking Championships. Minnesota and Indiana sent entries in 1925, South Dakota and Missouri joined in 1926 and Kansas joined in 1927. By the 1930s Ohio, Wisconsin and Pennsylvania were sending their champions. And Fred Stanek was the sport's initial superstar, winning four national titles.

The National Corn Husking Contest Association, created by the Chicago based *Prairie Farmer*, most of whose readership came from Illinois and Indiana, and *Wallaces' Farmer* hosted the national contests, which rotated from state to state.

John Strohm, a staff writer at the *Prairie Farmer*, articulated the pressure and thrill of America's new sport:

> The corn field on contest day is a gridiron, a bull ring, a cinder track, basketball court, and boxing ring rolled into one. The husker must have the strength of a football player, the grace of a bull fighter, the speed of a sprinter, the accuracy of a basketballer, and the stamina of a boxer if he wants to go places in the corn husk-

ing contest field. There are no time outs in corn husking. No rests between rounds. No trainers to work over aching muscles at the ends of the field. No coaches offering advice. The husker must go on his own for one hour and twenty minutes throwing corn every second. For eighty minutes huskers beat a steady tattoo on the bangboards, like a machine gun spitting bullets. Fast huskers can throw 50 to 60 ears a minute. Irv Bauman, national champ last year, threw an average of 50 ears a minute for the entire contest. That means that that every six seconds he threw five ears. In the space of one second he spotted an ear, grabbed it, peeled it, broke it, threw it and reached for the next ear while the other was on the way to the wagon.[12]

The indispensable piece of equipment was the husker's hook or peg, a leather aid fitted or strapped onto the hand. These hooks or pegs slashed the ear of corn while the other hand pulled back the remaining enveloping husks. The hooked hand grabbed the ear near its bottom, broke it from the shank and flipped it into a following wagon. The whole process required astonishing eye-hand coordination, strong wrists and arms and the stamina to continue for 80 minutes. Top-end huskers could and did throw upwards of 4000 ears of corn in the allotted time. This could work out to *three quarters of a ton* of corn, given the standard conversion to 70 pounds per bushel. It was what the farming community came to see ... an amazing amount of human work accomplished efficiently in a short period of time. Top huskers trained assiduously, running wind sprints and longer distances and husking whenever they could. During contests many wore short sleeves or even went shirtless, so relentless was the action.

Cornhusking contests began to draw crowds, big crowds. *The Prairie Farmer* kept meticulous attendance records for the Illinois state contests, which peaked at 95,000 in 1939. The national contest drew even more— 125,000 both in 1935 and 1936. In both years the national cornhusking contest was the best-attended sporting event in America and the *All Sports Record Book* of 1935 recognized it as a national sport.[13] In May 1936, *Prairie Farmer* introduced a fixed sports page.

Farm equipment dealers saw these events as an opportunity to display or introduce their products. Site selection for the nationals became a problem since the event required not only acres upon acres of evenly rowed corn, but additional acres for parking and exhibits. Crowd control was an issue, for spectators liked to traipse through the fields with the contestants. At major competitions "between 20 and 40 volunteers followed the wagon of each contestant to see that the crowd did not interfere with the husking or give help and ensure that everything went according to the rules."[14] In early years coaches accompanied the contestants into the field, pointing out ears and dispensing advice and encouragement. Imagine a basketball coach stationed at mid-court calling plays. After 1929 no coaching was allowed and only offi-

11. Corn Husking and Other Agricultural Contests

cials, gleaners (picking up the overlooked corn) and security accompanied the worker-athletes into the field.

At times the noise could be deafening. Crowds were huge and the competitive field was frequently a half mile long, or longer. A shotgun was often used to start the competition. Occasionally a contest began with a stick of dynamite. To get everyone's attention for the 1929 nationals in Missouri, a detail of soldiers from Fort Leavenworth, Kansas, brought an artillery piece to start the contest.[15]

The numbers of spectators attracted pickpockets and the radio networks. To contain the former, police used livestock transport trailers as makeshift jails. By 1928 radio networks were covering husking contests live. WLS of Chicago broadcast the Illinois state contest live that year. In 1929 cornhusking became only the second American sport with national live radio coverage (on NBC). Elaborate systems allowed announcers to cover the action. Towers were erected high above the center of the field where an announcer would relay records, background of the athletes and progress of the 80 minutes-contests. One announcer confided that "his most trying ordeal was during a state contest in which the starter's gun jammed [and he had to] adlib for 13 minutes until a state policeman ended the suspense by pulling out his revolver and starting the contest."[16] Field reporters, using portable shortwave sets to follow the huskers on the field and in the wagons, provided the sounds of ears thumping the bangboards. It was all state of the art.

Over the 18 year span of cornhusking nationals, thirteen different farmers won, but only Fred Stanek of Fort Dodge, Iowa, won more than twice. He won in 1924, 1926, 1927 and 1930. Although national contests grew in geographical reach and status, the prize money was never large. After winning a third national husking competition in 1927, Stanek, who by this time was one of the nation's best known farmers, complained that if the prize money (still $100) was not increased appreciably he would no longer compete. He became the first husker holdout and refused to enter the 1928 or 1929 contests. In late 1929 it was rumored that L.E. Phillips, an Iowa native and founder of the Phillips Petroleum Co., would award the 1930 national corn husking champion a check for $1,000. The offer was widely reported in the press and when Stanek read of the proposition he returned to competition and subsequently won a fourth national title in Kansas. When the money had not arrived within a month Stanek looked into the matter. He enlisted the help of Arthur M. Hyde, U.S. secretary of agriculture in the Herbert Hoover administration. Hyde informed Stanek that the contest-sponsoring newspaper bristled at Phillips's interference and told him to butt out. "A disappointed Stanek never received the grand prize and pointedly never again entered farm magazine-sponsored contests."[17]

The two nationals boycotted by Stanek (1928–29) were won by Walter Olson, a grain former from Rio, Illinois. After his second victory Olson was offered a breakfast cereal endorsement contract by the Quaker Oats Company, four years before General Mills and Wheaties got into the business of sporting endorsements. The farming papers guarded their own turf. Olson was immediately informed by *Prairie Farmer* that he would be considered a "professional husker" if he accepted the fee, and as such, would be barred from the newspaper's sponsored contests. Olson was confused and chagrined. Corn farming (and husking) *was* his profession. Forty years later, in recalling the incident, he surmised that he was not husking for the Cubs or the White Sox.[18]

An understanding and connection to the task, colorful champions and vigorous, non-stop action made cornhusking contests appealing and popular among farm people. Recall that in the corn husking heyday, 1924–41, 45 percent of the U.S. population was rural, and most people lived and worked on farms. On average that amounted to 50 million people, a big potential audience for a single sport.[19] The sport grew dramatically in the 1930s and the events took on all the characteristics of county or state fairs with displays, commercial exhibits and musical entertainment.

The number of competitions proliferated. In Illinois for instance, in 1938, 48 county competitions were conducted before the state meet. Iowa held competitions in every one of its 99 counties with winners advancing to four regional sites before finalists were selected for the state championships. A conservative estimate for 1938 puts the number of husking contests nationwide at over 600, with attendance in excess of one million.[20] In 1936 *Time Magazine* declared cornhusking the fastest growing sporting spectacle in the world.

The end came quickly for corn husking as a national spectator sport. Innovation did its part, as corn harvesting was machanized. By 1940 mechanical pickers were harvesting half of all the corn grown in Illinois. Five years later the figure was up to 75 percent. Hand husking quickly died. *Prairie Farmer* hosted the 18th and final national contest in LaSalle County, Il., just one month before Pearl Harbor. Cornhusking contests suffered the fate of many sports during World War II. Contests were cancelled for the duration of the war and were never revived on a national scale. Ultimately and ironically, *Prairie Farmer* called for more agricultural contests, including trapshooting, horse pulling, milking and plowing.[21]

One cannot overestimate the significance of husking competition in buoying the spirits of the farm community during the Great Depression. This aspect alone makes it a unique sporting event. And the sport, via the Heritage Foundation, now has its own documentary, *When Farmers Were Heroes: The Era of National Corn Husking Contests*, made in 2010. Today virtually all corn harvesting is mechanized. Yet the tradition of corn husking continues with a small but stable constituency within the Midwest farm belt. No longer are huge crowds the norm, but nine states offer a championship contest. And the National Corn Husking Association, since 1975, has conducted an October national for ten classes of pickers.

Plowing

Although the most popular and widely attended, cornhusking was hardly the only work-sports which developed from the American farm. From the very beginning of the republic, work-sports were common. In 1800 America was a rural nation, as 93 percent of the population lived and worked on farms.[22]

The first farming work-sport to achieve formality and recognition was plowing. These contests were held in Britain in the late 18th century, and, even today, many still refer to the exercise using the British spelling, *ploughing*. The first real county fair in America, held in Pittsfield, Mass., in 1811, had a plowing contest.[23] Plowing contests were also the very first American work-sport to be reported in the national press. In 1828 the weekly *American Farmer*, founded in 1819 by John F. Skinner, included a sports column, "Sporting Olio," which reported on a plowing contest at a Maryland agricultural fair in Baltimore in 1828.[24] Because competitions among workers which emphasized useful skills, like plowing, reaping, rock drilling and tree cutting were common in the antebellum and post Civil War periods, they often drew large crowds and the attention of sporting journals. For the next 40 years, plowing competitions were a staple of Skinner's *American Turf Register and Sporting Magazine* (founded in 1829), in various versions of *Spirit of the Times* (1831) and in the *New York Clipper* (1853).

Herbert Applebaum reminds us that plowing and grass and grain cutting contests were not new. In fact they date to the time of Homer.[25] Plowing competitions quickly spread westward. For instance, a plowing match was the feature of the Milwaukee County agricultural fair of 1842.[26] The idea was to completely plow an allotment of land, within time limitations, in tidy and straight furrows (today at least 6 inches deep). In the 19th century teams of horses, oxen or mules were used, often driven by a separate companion than the contestant behind the plow. Today tractor plowing competitions abound but animal-team competitions are still common.

Nineteenth century contests gave farmers an opportunity to display their skill in the handling of a walking plow, but also the opportunity to show off a fine team of horses or oxen. Family teams were not uncommon, frequently with the husband behind the plow and the wife or child handling the team of animals. Contests usually lasted several hours with teams competing simultaneously.

Of interest to many of the onlookers was the plow itself, which became the first major implement in America to be significantly improved. The contests were an opportunity for farmers to demonstrate and try new plow innovations, and the 1820s was an era of abundant plow patents. The earliest plows were modest-sized, homemade wooden mouldboard types. Cast iron plows, usually fashioned by the local blacksmith, were introduced in the early 1800s and were first used in contests in Worcester, Mass., in 1820. They gradually replaced the wooden plows. Plow makers sought to increase the depth and ease of plowing. The result was improved rotation, turning the sod over more frequently, which, in turn, resulted in increased crop yields. Cast iron plows were labor saving on man and beast, and required less maintenance from the village blacksmith.

Cast iron plows dominated the East but proved troublesome in the West, where prairie soil did not have the grit of New England soils. Blacksmiths and plow makers experimented with steel mouldboards in western states. Western soil stuck to iron mouldboards, causing greater resistance. An Illinois blacksmith from Grand Detour, John Deere, turned out his first steel plow in 1837. Within ten years the Vermont native was manufacturing 700 steel plows annually.

The popularity of metal plows and plowing contests grew noticeably in the ante-bellum period. In the 1830s, plowing contests in Worcester, Mass., attracted as many as 150 teams of oxen. Canada offered its first agricultural fair with a plowing contest in 1826. New York State founded a State Agricultural Society in 1832 and plowing contests became a feature of its annual state fair in the 1840s. Pennsylvania held its first statewide farming trade fair (with a plowing contest) in 1851. It is possible the state followed the lead of western Pennsylvania, where plowing matches were common.[27] In 1857, under the auspices of the State Agricultural Society, the Iowa State Fair conducted its first plowing contest. There "each of the seven contestants plowed a one-fourth acre of land in 'old, loose and sandy' soil turning a furrow at least six inches deep ... the shortest time required was 48 minutes and the longest 61 minutes. In the 1858 plowing match the prize was actually awarded to the slowest plower on the principle that it is 'vastly more important that the plowing be well done, than that it be speedily done.'"[28]

By the 1850s, because of their proliferation of plowing contests, America's sporting weeklies, in particular the *New York Clipper*, *National Police Gazette*, *New York Sportsman* and *Spirit of the Times*, all reported details. In 1856, the *New York Clipper* tendered this report of a plowing contest in Harlem:

11. Corn Husking and Other Agricultural Contests

Plowing and Spading Match— Premiums being offered by the American Institute for plowing and spading, a match came off on the 24th (October) at Harlem. The ground selected was a piece of light, dry, sandy soil, not far from the house of Mr. Leslie, River House, where the Committee assembled, and on land belonging to the late Mr. C.H. Hall.

The stipulations as to plowing were: that the quantity of ground for each team should be one-eighth of an acre of green sward. The time occupied to be an hour. The furrow not less than seven inches deep. Each plowman to do his work without a driver.

The first premium, a silver cup, value $15, was awarded to Ira Peck, of Orange, New Jersey. The second, a cup, worth $10, to Asa B. Munn, of Orange, New Jersey. The third, a silver medal, to Andrew Fitzpatrick of Harlem.[29]

Plowing matches could be formal, scheduled and rule-laden affairs conducted by an agricultural society, but just as frequently were ad hoc challenge events, farmers having as much self confidence and pride in their occupational capabilities as anyone else. Charles Ogden of Clinton, Mass., issued this *New York Clipper* taunt in 1856:

Challenge to Plough—I hereby challenge to plough with two horses, against any man in the state of Massachusetts, one quarter of an acre, or more, for $100 or $200. The furrows to be 8 inches deep and 9 inches wide—$25 or $50 to be deposited in the hands of two parties, as shall be agreed upon, who will also decide as to the best ploughed piece, and, in the event of their not agreeing, they do appoint a third part, whose decision must be final. Address me for one month from this date at Mr. Jas. Smith, 15 Greet Street, Clinton, Mass.

Charles Ogden.[30]

In the 20th century plowing matches became both mechanized and politicized. Henry Ford produced his first experimental gasoline powered tractor in 1907, under the direction of chief engineer Joseph Galamb. It was referred to as an "automobile plow" and the name tractor was not used.[31] After 1910, gasoline powered tractors were used extensively in farming and began to appear at plowing contests.

Various county and local contests proliferated with both animal-driven teams and tractors. By 1940 the U.S. had 6 million farms and 18 percent of the labor force in farming. Several of the local matches were elevated to state level contests. At the end of the war Herb Plambeck, farm director of radio station WHO, Des Moines, took the next logical step and organized a national plowing contest.[32] The 1948 nationals were scheduled for Dexter, Iowa, at the height of the national presidential campaign. In September, President Harry S. Truman "used the national plowing contest to issue a major statement about U.S. farm policy reminding listeners that 'How well you must remember the Depression of the Nineteen Thirties. The Republicans gave you that greatest of all depressions.'" The "Give 'em Hell" performance before assembled farmers has been reported as a major turning point in the 1948 presidential election.[33] Republican candidate Thomas Dewey had passed up the affair.

Each September, for the next three presidential campaigns, no major candidate skipped the national plowing contests. Republican candidate Dwight D. Eisenhower and Democratic counterpart Adlai Stevenson gave major speeches in Kasson, Minn., in 1952 and again in Newton, Iowa, four years later. Democratic candidate John F. Kennedy and Vice President Richard M. Nixon did so in 1960 when the contest was conducted in Sioux Falls, S.D.[34]

Plowing matches are now more popular in Canada. The International Plowing Match and Rural Exhibition is an event organized yearly by Ontario's Plowmen Association. More than 500 acres of land are reserved for plowing competitions and 600 plowmen compete annually for prize money before enormous crowds.

Today, with farmers making up less than 3 percent of the American labor force, plowing contests continue to be popular for a small group of loyal contestants and spectators. A conservative estimate put the number of American plowers at between two and three thousand.

The 2013 U.S. nationals were held under the auspices of the USA Ploughing Organization in Greenville, Ohio.

Sheepshearing

A major influence on farmer work-sports has been the agricultural fair. Begun in the earliest days of the 19th century, these fairs exhibited products, mechanical innovations, labor saving devices, tools and gadgets.[35] Many of the fairs offered competitive premiums, monetary prizes, for work contests. One work-sport which developed through the agricultural fair was sheepshearing. These early contests were especially important for a young nation for their commercial implications. "The raising of fine wool for cloth implied domestic self-sufficiency and the beginnings of a competitive trade base for agriculturalists."[36]

As a work-sport, American sheapshearing contests have a 200-year history. Sheepshearing is a simple, timed contest in which sheep are relieved of their thick coats with either mechanical or electric shears. Following are some of the sports' highlights.

In 1805, a sheepshearing contest designed to encourage the development of the native wool industry was conducted in Arlington, Va., by George Washington Parke Custis, the grandson of Martha Washington and her first husband, Daniel Custis.[37] Custis's contest became an annual event.

At a New York State Fair in Buffalo, an Erie County farmer named James Bicknell brought his never-shorn ewe to the sheep shearing contest to make a political statement. His eye-opening animal sported fleece 17 inches thick. Bicknell announced that he would not sheer his sheep until the U.S. president,

11. Corn Husking and Other Agricultural Contests

who had engaged America in an unpopular and unnecessary war, left office. Although the description could fit many presidents, the year was 1848 and the president, James K. Polk, had conducted the Mexican-American War. Presumably Bicknell sheared his sheep after Polk left office in March of the following year.

Sheepshearing contests made their appearance in Wisconsin in 1854 at the state fair in Whitewater. A year later the winner took 78 minutes to shear six sheep.[38] By 1894 sheepshearing was appearing annually at Madison Square Garden in New York City as part of a livestock/farm show. For a number of years the contests drew substantial crowds.[39]

Organized by the International Sheep Shearing Festival Association, an extensive set of contests were offered at the St. Louis World's Fair in 1904. Professionals and amateurs competed in both speed and quality events. E.S. Bartlett, a freshman at Michigan Agricultural College (now Michigan State University), won the $125 trophy offered in the college class on October 13, 1904. Bartlett immediately became one of the original sporting heroes at the college, an institution which would later produce the likes of Robin Roberts, Earvin "Magic" Johnson, "Bubba" Smith and Duffy Daugherty. It took him just 4 minutes and 18 seconds to complete the contest. He then entered the free-for-all (professional and amateurs combined) and finished fourth, shearing his sheep in 3 minutes and 2 seconds.[40]

Con Pickett of Illinois took home the first place prize in the professional speed contest, shearing three sheep in a world record one minute and 30 seconds.[41]

Sheep shearers were so proficient at their trade that some contests were completed in a matter of seconds. This led to declining spectatorship and new types of shearing contests: *endurance* sheep shearing and sheep-to-shawl contests. Records vary depending on the tools used and breed of sheep. In endurance competitions, shearing continues for an extended period of time. For example, Wade Kopren of Bison, S.D., claims the world record for shearing 787 sheep in eight hours.[42]

Sheep-to-shawl contests use five-member teams. They became popular in the 1980s. One shearer, three spinners and one weaver shear a sheep, spin the wool into yarn and use it to make a 22-by-78-inch shawl. The entire process takes between two to three hours.

So ingrained were sheep shearing competitions at Pennsylvania's Farm Show Arena in Harrisburg that, in 2008, a prankster got away with the following facetious news release about sheep-to-shawl contests:

Jan. 6, 2008 Sheep-To-Shawl Replaced By Horse-To-Glue at PA Farm Show
  (Harrisburg)- In a move state agriculture officials said is designed to "throw a

new twist" into the Pennsylvania Farm Show, the Sheep-To-Shawl Contest is being replaced this year by a Horse-to-Glue Contest.

"Much like the name would suggest, teams will be on the clock to turn a horse into a quart of glue as quickly as possible," said Agriculture Secretary Dennis Wolff. Each team's first task will be to slaughter their horse on the spot. "The key will really be to get to that bone and connective tissue, which are the main components of glue, as quickly as possible," Wolff said.

While the event promises to be considerably more messy than its predecessor, Wolff said he remained convinced "that it will be even better family fun, both for participants and for spectators." He said bystanders will be provided with parkas to protect them from flying horse guts.

"Horse-To-Glue will be a chance for us to better incorporate Pennsylvanians' love for killing animals into this exhibition for all ages," Wolff said.

Previous attempts to replace Sheep-To-Shawl proved unpopular. They included the Kitten-To-Mitten and Bull Penis-To-Keychain contests.[43]

All of the New England states are home to a thriving cottage industry of spinners, weavers and crafters of handmade fiber products and today there is a plethora of sheepshearing contests. Most are conducted by wool growers' associations at local festivals. For example, the New Hampshire Sheep and Wool Festival is celebrated each May, usually at the State Fairgrounds in Contoocook.[44]

Cow Milking

Examples of farming work-sports abound. Allow me to add one, the first work-sport I witnessed, although I didn't realize it at the time. As a youngster I would attend minor league baseball games in my hometown of York, Penn., a farming community which surrounded an industrial base. I was a White Roses fan and can recall more than once that games were preceded by cow-milking contests. As a city kid I usually visited the concession stand when they began. Yet I did notice that infielders usually won these affairs. Perhaps they had better hands. Hall-of-Famer Brooks Robinson spent part of his minor league career at York.

Cow milking contests were part of New York State Fairs as early as the 1840s, and made an appearance at World Fairs in Chicago (1893) and St. Louis (1904). Contests varied by objective — speed or quantity. Often the cow was the contestant. For instance, at the 1908 Whitman County Grange and Livestock Show, the cow giving the highest number of pounds of butterfat in two days was declared the winner of the $125 first prize. Forty-five cows were entered in the two-day contest and a Cloverdale farms cow owned by George Nelson took first prize for "her record for two milkings [of] 47½ pounds of milk and 2.471 pounds of butter fat."[45]

The Grand National Live Stock Exposition, which began in 1941, takes place in the San Francisco Cow Palace. "The sobriquet 'Cow Palace' was bestowed on the exhibition hall during the depression-plagued 1930s when a local newspaper editorial writer criticized the city administration for failing to provide adequate low-cost housing for people although it spent thousands of dollars on building a palace for cows."[46] Milking contests are a principal Cow Palace event.

Although many kinds of animals are milked competitively, including goats, reindeer and even polar bears, cow milking contests remain popular today. Thousands are conducted annually, but are local in scope.

Farm Work-Sports' Influence

Agricultural fairs, agricultural colleges and localized civic festivals endorsed and advanced formal worker competitions. Following the American Revolution, farmers in the United States independently developed methods and technologies for food production. They formed agricultural societies and associations whose purpose was to disseminate new farming practices and display livestock and produce. The *New York Herald* championed the concept in 1858.[47]

> They acquire an immense fund of information from this commingling and competition, and are stimulated more and more to study the arts of husbandry and cattle raising.... But though the plan of holding agricultural fairs is not a very ancient adaption here, it is by no means backward in its development. On the contrary, it has entered largely into our social policy and forms quite a feature in rural life. We have extended it up to national fairs, and down to county fairs.

The fairs fostered competitions and awarded prizes, initially for plowing and sheepshearing contests. Other contests followed such as blacksmithing, shoeing, baling, butchering, mowing, scything, threshing, hay stacking, spading, reaping, cradling and more. Many of these worker-competitions never moved past their local origins. But occasionally accounts found their way into the national press.[48] The agricultural fairs became, in a sense, farming colleges and their competitions, besides providing fun and rewards for the contestants, became trial and error lab research for improved techniques.

Agricultural fairs started in New England and soon took on regional characteristics. The initial county fair was held in Pittsfield, Mass., in 1811, and offered a plowing competition. Other New England farming expositions followed. Agricultural societies spread from New England to the South and to Western states by the 1820s.

The Topsfield (Mass.) Fair, initially a cattle show formed by the Essex Agricultural Society, was started in 1820, and with the exception of a three-year break for the Civil War and another three-year hiatus for World War II, has run continually since, for 192 years.

Often held at harvest time for the dominant local crop, agricultural fairs developed into countywide events and later gatherings for the entire state. A group of farmers and lawmakers in Albany, wanting to promote agricultural improvement and local fairs, founded the New York State Agricultural Society in 1832. By 1841 the society planned and held in Syracuse the nation's first state fair. Ten thousand visitors assembled for speeches, livestock and produce exhibits and a plowing competition.

By 1959 the *New York Clipper* listed 22 state fairs. Eight years later the *Clipper* cataloged 292 state and county fairs.[49] In 1967, Meyer claimed that "every year some 2000 farm fairs are staged in the United States."[50] A recent Web check for 2013 puts the current number at over 2300.[51]

Agg schools, too, were part of the farming work-sports equation. At the urging of farm journals and the aforementioned agricultural societies, Senator Justin S. Morrill of Stafford, Vt., introduced into Congress a bill for the establishment of agricultural and mechanical colleges in every state. The measure was signed by Abraham Lincoln in 1862 and offered states large plots of land. Some states elected to give the land to existing institutions whole others established new agricultural and technical colleges.[52]

One overlooked group which promoted farming competitions was the New England Federation of Agricultural Students at the University of Massachusetts in Amherst. The group organized in 1907 for the purpose of bringing together agricultural students at New England colleges for the study and advancement of agriculture and to set up and manage annual contests in field crops, packing, and livestock.[53]

Ted Ownby tells us that "the harvest and work sharing celebrations once so meaningful in rural culture, fell before the commercialization of agriculture and technological innovations that accompanied it. With the decline of sufficient family farming came a new desire to mechanize most agricultural processes."[54] Thus work sharings and harvest games are part of an almost forgotten past. Well, not quite. Today civic groups, chambers of commerce, and regional and state agricultural societies provide an opportunity to display farming skills, mostly in the form of harvesting contests. Many are conducted at local fairs or celebratory festivals. These are not on-the-job contests per se, but competitions which developed from local harvesting work. It seems that every farm community in America is famous (or claims to be) for growing something and many offer festivals celebrating the community history, often with a harvesting competition. Examples would include potato peeling (Barnesville, Minn.); cotton picking (Gosnell, Ark.); coffee bean harvesting (Kona, Hawaii); blueberry picking (Six Mile, S.C.), orange picking (Orlando, Fla.), strawberry picking (Bluemont, Va.), watermelon tossing (Hope, Ark.), asparagus eating (Stockton, Calif.), rhubarb stalk throwing (Lanesboro,

11. Corn Husking and Other Agricultural Contests 143

Minn.), huckleberry homesteader pentathlon (Trout Creek, Mont.), chili pepper toss (Hatch Valley, N.M.), grape stomping (Silver Creek, N.Y.), cabbage bowling (Canfield, Ohio), and generic harvest games (Marlinton, W.V.). Some even refer to themselves as a "national championship."

Often overlooked, or simply ignored as a sporting venue for 200 years, the American farm has provided more worker competitions, contestants and spectators than any other industry category in this volume.

PART THREE: WHAT HAPPENED TO WORKER COMPETITIONS, 1940 TO THE PRESENT

12

Obsolete Work-Sports

Worker-competitions surface as ad hoc affairs, or responses to a challenge or wager. "Hey, I think I can finish this job faster than you can," or "5 bucks says I do more of that than you can in the next half hour," or, "slow down, will ya,' you're making the rest of us look bad." These might be typical ignitions to a challenge, a demonstration or a contest. Virtually all worker competitions start this way, that is, informally. Some games become popular locally, regionally or beyond, and eventually end up as established sports. Others, like a match stick, burn out quickly, never to be attempted again. A few attain some modest notoriety before being relegated to the footnotes of history.

We can identify some of these competitions because they either conducted a national championship or their reports turned up in the national sporting press. Recall that between 1850 and 1880, at least four sporting weeklies circulated across the nation: *The Spirit of the Times*, the *New York Clipper*, the *National Police Gazette* and the *New York Sportsman*. Of course many more worker competitions would have been reported in the local press. By 1870 there were over 5000 daily and weekly newspapers in America.[1] But the work-sports examined in this chapter, some of which lasted for years, were important enough to attract wider than local attention and thus achieved a modicum of notoriety before eventually fading away.

In these samples it is easy to see how work situations, with laborers working side-by-side, would have matured into competitions. Listed alphabetically, here are a few nineteenth and early 20th century worker competitions that, at least for a short period, caught the public's fancy.

Blacksmithing

Every town had a blacksmith shop which manufactured plows, nails and other tools and which fashioned horseshoes and also shoed hooved animals.

Blacksmiths were indispensable to the progress and prosperity of American towns and cities and many earned reputations for strength and quality workmanship. Blacksmiths played a secondary role in the development of a number of American sports including track and field (the hammer toss) and horse-racing. But they could also fabricate their own games and it was quite natural that blacksmith challenges abounded in both the nineteenth and 20th centuries.

Early American sporting papers were filled with reports of blacksmith contests and work demonstrations. A favorite activity was to make as many horseshoes as possible in a single day. The January 30, 1858, *Clipper* announced that Thomas Rambo "made in one day, one hundred and twenty horseshoes." A record. The following week the paper's editor, Frank Queen, was corrected. It seems that the previous year one Jim Nolan, a Brooklyn blacksmith, made at his shop on Nevins Street and Flatbush Avenue fourteen dozen (168) shoes as one day's work.[2]

Many blacksmiths kept track of their work and often mailed their work results to the sporting journals. For example, it was reported that Robert Walsworth, employed at the Norwich, N.Y., blacksmith shop of Messrs. Vosburgh and Reed, with the assistance of George Foster as striker, made 260 complete horseshoes, with 8 double punched holes in each shoe, in seven hours and fifty-seven minutes' working time. He had taken a 39-minute dinner break. Four weeks later, in the same shop, R.J. Leaden made 2,400 horse nails in seven hours and fifty-four minutes. The report chronicled his progress hour-by-hour:

First hour:	321 nails
Second hour:	300
Third hour:	321
Fourth hour:	300
Last ½ hr before dinner:	160
Forenoon subtotal:	[1402] one hour break for dinner
Afternoon 1st hour:	300
Second hour:	292
Third hour:	280
Last 24 minutes:	*128*
Total:	2400

The report noted that Leaden, who averaged 5 nails per minute (or one nail every 12 seconds for approximately eight hours), was so buoyed by his work that he issued a challenge to any blacksmith to beat his total for $1,000.[3]

A horseshoe was as close to a standard product as there was in a blacksmith's world. Thus, matching a pair of blacksmiths to determine who could hammer out the most horseshoes became a typical timed event. Likely, no fictional story has ever grasped the concept of a worker competition with more insight than Edward W. O'Brien's 1940 *Saturday Evening Post* story "Blacksmith's Boy—Heel and Toe." The tale, set in 1907, pitted a small town blacksmith against a "floater," a blacksmith who drifted from town to town engaging in shop contests.

> ... and both forges driving like fury, for all the song. Pop has a Stillson-wrench grip on his tongs, as though he'd just begun, instead of whaling away at the anvil since seven a-morning, and his arm, from the strong fulcrum of his elbow, rose and fell the same as it did ten hours ago, and like black magic, the iron, the black metal from which comes the name of the trade, shaped itself hurriedly at his will. Striking or not, his hammer never idled. Often, squinting a moment at his shoe, he'd keep his hammer dancing on the face, and he'd break the tempo; clatter the heel and ball. Then, swiftly, "Wallop! Wallop! Wallop!—wallop!" he'd strike in miniature thunder, and McCann'd dance a challenging answer from the back forge, as though they were two fiddles, one dropping the melody, the other taking up the tune, and, as old Jimmy said about McCann, the big devil having himself a fine time of it, still confident as all hell.[4]

Even more engaging was the *Post's* accompanying illustration by Norman Rockwell, which has become an American classic.

The passage of time and innovation have rendered blacksmithing much less significant and the contests have faded away. There are occasional demonstration challenges here or there, but nothing like the pre–horseless carriage days when competitions, both ad hoc and arranged, were widespread. For instance, in 1869 a pair of New York City smiths, Harry Clinton and Bill Weaver, got to bragging about their abilities. The fans of these "Knights of the Anvil" arranged, organized and publicized a competition in making "crow's feet" for boilers. The first to five would forfeit $100 and a champagne supper. The match was arranged for New Year's Day 1869 at the Fox Brothers Shop on West 34th Street, and the superintendent of the Wharton Iron Works of Philadelphia was engaged to referee. The affair attracted a large crowd and considerable betting. The contest was 34 minutes old, with each contestant striking 1,068 blows with a 14-pound hammer (a whack every two seconds), when Weaver gave out and conceded the match.[5]

Butchering

By 1885 American butchering records, set in competitions, challenge matches or demonstrations, were well established. For example, the *New York Clipper Annual*, the nation's sporting record book, listed records for categories like 10 sheep dressed; 25 sheep dressed; 200 chickens dressed; and more. Walter Dennison, a Chicago butcher, held the record for "bullock dressed market style" in 4 minutes, 29 seconds, set on August 18, 1883. Another Chicago butcher, John Malone, dressed a bullock in the "go-as-you-please" style in 3 minutes, 40 seconds in the same competition.[6] Animal butchering is one of civilization's oldest and most skilled professions. In the middle of the 19th century, butchers were employed at meat packing houses or in proprietary butcher shops.

Traditional butchery includes slaying and skinning the animal, removal of viscera and splitting the carcass in half longitudinally, all referred to as primary work. Secondary butchering consists of boning and trimming cuts in preparation for sale. For much of the 19th century, primary and secondary butchering were performed in the same establishment. There were so many types of animals to be butchered — hogs, steers, deer, poultry and fish — and so many steps in the work that "butchering" became an umbrella term.

As worker-competitions, indeed, sports of all types, developed in the mid–19th century, the butchers went along. Yet no two butchering competitions were alike. There did not seem to be a consensus on what a butchering contest should look like. Some began as public challenges. For example, this 1858 Iowa challenge of speed and skill which appeared in the *New York Clipper,* was typical:

> Mr. George Ellison, of Keokuk, having boasted that he could dress a bullock quicker than I can, I now challenge him on a wager of fifty or one hundred dollars, to a test of our skill in dressing, say a six hundred pound steer. If he accepts, the time, place and other preliminaries can very readily be arranged.
> J. F. Kelly
> Davenport, March 11, 1858.
> Mr. Kelly hails from Newburgh, New York. A reply to the above challenge will meet with prompt attention.[7]

Match contests varied by number and type of animal, timing and purpose. For instance, a pair of 1861 New York City competitions were very different. At Kerrigan's Hall in February, Roger Gorman and George 'Darby' Macomb squared off to dress five sheep apiece in a well publicized match. Gorman won by over 10 minutes in 22:03.[8] One month later Lalors Slaughterhouse on 4th Street conducted a $10 match of "neatness" between two fast "killers of critters," Patrick O'Brien and Edward Lawrence. The judges ruled the outcome a draw to the displeasure of O'Brien, who then suggested another challenge, one of killing and dressing 20 steers for $200, where speed would be considered decisive.[9]

Some events were actually endurance demonstrations. In 1859 four Milwaukee butchers, in front of an audience, killed and dressed one hundred and twenty five cattle in 3½ hours, averaging one kill-to-completed dressing every 100 seconds. The same butchers returned two days later for a 7½-hour exhibition. Other contests featured butchering whole herds. In 1868 in Chicago, William Colz and Patrick Sullivan "challenged any two men in the west to slaughter 100 sheep the quickest and best for one hundred dollars or upwards. The money to be held at Martin O'Neil's saloon near Reid and Sherman or, if necessary, to be sent to the editor of the *Clipper*."[10]

Chicago provided a good deal of appeal in the butcher's profession because of its stockyards and slaughterhouses. In 1869 interest ran so high that the city's Butcher's Society, boasting that the nation's finest practitioners worked locally, instituted a Butcher's Championship of America competition, with the winner to receive an elegant silver- and gold-plated belt with the figure of an ox engraved upon it. The first "butcher's nationals" took place on May 15, 1869, in Bridgeport, a short distance from Chicago, at Reid and Sherwin's Packing House. A large crowd of sporting men, cattle dealers and butchers gathered to watch, and betting was brisk.

Specific rules were enforced as each butcher, in turn, worked on a single bullock and prepared it "for market use, the work to commence after the animal had been pretched up, with the two fore feet; each butcher to be allowed a helper, the latter to open the beast and neck, but not chop or saw them, with the privilege of washing the carcass on the floor — also to adjust the 'beef tree' and hoist up the bullock, clear of the entrails and split the kidney." Five butchers had qualified for the competition, one each from St. Louis, Toronto and Buffalo and a pair from Chicago.

The times for the first four butchers had ranged from 7 minutes and 41 seconds to 5 minutes and 11 seconds. The final *athlete* (as they were called by the *Clipper*) was Charles Leyden of Chicago, a 19-year-old Irish-American. Slight in appearance, he contrasted physically with his older and brawnier adversaries.

> On the call "go," his knife flew over the carcass with electric swiftness. In an incredibly short space the beef was hanging on the "tree," the hide was stripped to the neck, the keen axe cleft the backbone with amazing dexterity, and having dressed the bullock, the time-keeper, amid the wildest excitement, declared the young man's work performed in the space of four minutes and forty five seconds. Leyden was immediately hoisted on the shoulders of the crowd and borne off in triumph."[11]

The conditions of Leyden's victory were not unusual for the times. He was required to accept challenges every three months and would retain the belt as personal property if he was still champion within one year. He did have the privilege of compelling any challenger to put up anywhere from $500 to $1,000 as a wager and insisted on four weeks' notice prior to any match.

Yet butcher's competitions never became big stuff. The events suffered from a lack of standardization, rules and purpose. And they had logistical problems. Some spectators liked to be close to the action when the cutting began and were fascinated by the dipping meal. But many others were repelled by the unpleasant flying slop that was part and parcel of any contest. As well, the meat-packing industry suffered from what today might may be called bad publicity. In 1906, Upton Sinclair published *The Jungle*, a powerful and popular novel about the meat packing plants of Chicago. A Baltimorean, Sinclair exposed poor conditions and precipitated a public uproar, prompting Congress to pass the Pure Food and Drug Act and Meat Inspection Act in 1906.

Refrigeration eventually separated primary and secondary butchering and turned a local industry into a national one. And marketing of food products changed the butcher's landscape. The corner butcher shop has disappeared and many secondary butchers are now employed by supermarket chains. Much primary butchering continues in slaughterhouses and meat processing plants.

Today we occasionally hear of butchering contests. They are usually sponsored by supermarket chains and involve secondary butchering. For example, *Whole Foods* offers an annual "Top Butcher Competition" where local winners advance to regional events and regional winners advance to a *Whole Foods* national title contest.[12] The emphasis is on meat cutting, merchandising, food display, customer service and, of course, on speed without severing fingers.

Coopering (Barrel Making) Contests

Today barrel competitions are an integral part of the wine industry. But they are different than their 19th century counterparts. Today wine barrels are judged on how they impact the flavor of the wine. Barrel makers supply barrels from the same oak species to a vineyard. The wine going into the barrels is identical while the finished wine in each barrel is different. A panel of wine experts judge the impact of the individual barrels on the wine. This subjective game, usually played in California, showcases the tradition and history of the barrel making trade but is nothing like barrel making contests of the 19th century.[13]

Today barrels can be made of stainless steel, aluminum or various types of plastic. But in the 19th century, barrel makers, or coopers, traditionally fashioned their product from vertical wooden staves and bound them by metal hoops. Coopers were skilled artisans who made similar products like casks, buckets, tubs, kegs (a small barrel), butter churns, hogsheads, firkins (a standard antique wooden bucket), rundlets (a wine cask), and more. Traditionally a barrel was a standard size of measure holding a specific capacity (originally 36 gallons), and this customary size allowed coopers to compare one another's speed in finishing a job. Thus a work-sport was born.

An astounding coopering feat was reported initially by the *Vermont Patriot* of Montpelier in August 1857. It seems that John Londergas, a local cooper, accomplished the most extraordinary feat ever achieved in a cooper shop until then, and perhaps since. Coopers had their own techniques in bending wood into shape through heating, a technique likely borrowed from boat building, and constructing a barrel was time consuming. Londergas, working steadily for 12 hours, made *fifty-four* timber barrels. As word spread of his intentions, many of townspeople hustled over to his cooper shop to watch him work. He had methodically readied his timbers and barrels came out of his shop as if on a modern assembly line. At a time when 4 to 5 barrels was a good day's work, Londergas *averaged* 9 barrels every two hours, or roughly one barrel every 13½ minutes. A few weeks later he demonstrated his speed by making two barrels in 15 minutes. One Vermont resident was so proud he reported the achievement to the *New York Clipper*, who treated Londergas as a work-sports hero.[14]

Today there are frequent barrel-making demonstrations, but no one attempts to construct a wooden barrel in 7½ minutes.[15] Modern barrel contests, instead, involve filling the newly made casks with water and rolling them downhill to ascertain which rolls the straightest.

Hat Making Contests

Hat making in colonial America was one of the earliest industries to take prominence over its European counterpart. Felted fur was the primary material for making hats and the European beaver population was almost extinct by colonial times, but beavers thrived in the northern part of North America. Hat making, which began as a cottage industry, shifted there. Small village shops and, eventually, hat factories dominated. The first American hat factory was in Danbury, Connecticut, which, became, for a time, the world's hat making capital, with 56 factories making more than five million hats per year.[16]

An 1867 hatter's challenge appears to have been an aberration.

> Challenge to Hatters: Chas L. Henriele, writes us from Cincinnati, O, to say that he is ready to make a match at hat finishing with any (old?) shop man in the country for any reasonable amount. The work to be done on ladies hats and the match to come off at Cincinnati, Cleveland or Buffalo, within sixty days. An answer through the *Clipper* will be attended to promptly.[17]

Although some local challenge matches may have materialized there is no evidence that this worker-competition gained any traction. A trade union of hatters had been organized in 1819 and it is possible, as occurred in other unionized work-sports situations (e.g., typesetters) that the union discouraged its members from displaying their hat-making skill or speed for fear of bringing about increased production quotas. There is no evidence of hat-making competitions in the 20th century. It should be noted that members of the hatters union engaged in a much more important competition against a Danbury hat manufacturer (they boycotted), and the U.S. Supreme Court, in one of its most in famous cases, applied the new Sherman Anti-Trust Act against the union and its individual members.

Newspaper Folding

The American newspaper industry took off in the 1830s with the creation of the so-called penny press: inexpensive papers that were sold for one cent by street hawkers, instead of the previous up-front subscription model. The industry grew in importance, profitability, and influence, including the rise of sensationalist "yellow journalism" in the late 1800s.[18] Some U.S. cities had as many as eight newspapers and many ran multiple daily editions.

Hat making required manual skill (*Scientific Hat Finishing and Renovation*, Henry L. Ermatinger, New York, Roberts and Cushman, 1919).

In 1830 there were approximately 700 U.S. newspapers. Forty years later the number had risen to over 5000. The two-cylinder press was first used in the U.S. in 1835 by the *New York Sun*, which, by 1851, could print 18,000 copies per hour. But the presses cold not *fold* the papers and hundreds were employed just to fold newspapers, a monotonous and mind-numbing occupation. Of such stuff worker competitions were born and soon enough there were reported newspaper folding feats. The *New York Clipper Annual* kept track of these reports and claimed that the record was 13 minutes and 26 seconds for folding 500 papers with 3 folds. Charles Flynn of the *San Francisco Examiner* set the record in April 1883. This was six years before William Randolph Hearst purchased the paper and made it a platform of yellow journalism. A separate record was maintained for 500 papers that had to be piled, evened and ready for delivery. In this case Joseph P. Willis of a Boston daily held the record of 19 minutes, 21 seconds, set in August of the same year.[19]

Although it was hard, physically demanding work, newspaper folding never excited the public and the occupation disappeared when newer presses folded the papers as they came off an assembly line.

Picking Up Potatoes

In the antebellum period both track and field and work-sports escalated. The former (literally running/walking and/or jumping contests) were professional in nature. The nation's sporting papers, *Spirit of the Times, National Police Gazette, New York Clipper* not only gave great play to these sports but also sponsored, promoted and organized many of the events.

The 1850s were a chaotic era of competition and the variety of walking and running contests knew no limits. Someone whose name is now lost to us in a spark of creativity combined pedestrianism and a farmer's harvesting chore and a new event, picking up potatoes, was born. The rules were simple. Contestants had to pick up, one at a time, 100 potatoes, which were placed one yard apart, and return each separately to a basket at the starting point. Imagine a potato placed on every yard marker of a football field. (In 1850 American football had yet to be invented). Usually matches were timed, but there were also match races with 2, 3 or more rows of potatoes stretching 100 yards. What this amounted to was a 10,000-yard (about @ 5⅔ miles) race with lots of bending and 200 stops and changes of direction.

The sport appealed to those with stamina. The potato was a durable if indifferent piece of sports paraphenalia. It had to be placed in the basket, not tossed. Organizers who sought strict compliance to this rule used eggs instead of potatoes but eggs were much more expensive. It is difficult to describe how popular this work-sports became. The *Clipper* handled the arrangements for many of the competitions and kept records.

The following, sent in by an interested observer, is representative coverage of the sport.

Picking Up Potatoes-Amsterdam, NY, March 10. Friend Clipper: Our town was the scene of no less excitement on Tuesday and Wednesday of last week grew out of the fact that the feat of picking up 100 potatoes, one yard apart, to be taken separately and deposited one at a time in a basket placed 3 feet from the first potato, was to be accomplished within an hour for a wager of $10; for the first day to be performed by Phillips, and the succeeding day by the well known pedestrian, George Ireland, against the time made on the first day; for a purse of $50 a side. The weather on both days being remarkably fine, quite a large concourse of people were present to witness the sport. H. Phillips started and accomplished the feat in 57 minutes, giving him 3 minutes to spare.

On the succeeding day the trial against time came. The time being fixed at 10 o'clock, A.M. and long before that time the race ground was crowded with one deep mass of beings, including ministers and deacons. All seemed to take a deep interest. Thus the potatos were gathered, sometimes at the centre and others at the ends, until the great array were dwindled down. As the last potato was deposited within its place and time being known, there rose up one universal cheer for the Champion Potato Picker which made the ground quake. The time for the same being 47½ minutes, beating the time made on the proceeding day by nine and one half minutes. We are to have another trial to come on the 3rd. The stakes being $50 and between the same parties. Due notice will be given of the same.

Yours, A Lover of Good Fun.[20]

In 1858 the record was established at:

- 51½ minutes in Chesterton, Md., then in April lowered to
- 47½ minutes in Amsterdam, N.Y., then lowered later in the month to
- 44½ minutes in Newburgh, N.Y., and later in April to
- 44 minutes in Newburgh, N.Y., and then in July to
- 43 minutes in Dover, N.H.

By today's standards, 43 minutes for 5 miles plus does not raise any eyebrows, but it should if the runner had to stop and turn around 200 times. As track and field formalized after the Civil War, potato picking races disappeared.

Road Bowling

One sport which never caught the public's fancy was road bowling. The *New York Clipper* endorsed the sport in the summer of 1859, claiming "this is a very fine exercise and tends to develop the various muscles of the physical system."[21] The only facility necessary was a flat (and presumably un-crowded) road and the only equipment, a cannonball. The author is uncertain if this is a work-sport for a road crew or artillery men. On August 18, 1858, a match came off between a Mr. Dillon of New York City and a Mr. Kenney of Staten Island. The rules were quite simple. Each would roll a 2-pound cannon shot along a road, starting from a specified point, and terminating at any other previously agreed upon point. The match could be a sprint (say 100 yards), a middle distance event (perhaps a mile), or even longer with repeated tosses (say ten miles away). The one whose ball reached the terminus first won the match. There is no report on who won the Dillon-Kenney match or that that this game was ever attempted again. Thirty-two months later cannonballs were used for their original purpose as the American Civil War began.

Spading

In the 1850s the American Institute of the City of New York, a group founded in 1828 to promote agriculture and industrial arts, sponsored spading matches in the metropolitan area offering both premiums and prizes. The rules were simple enough: plots of ground 20 feet by 10 feet had to be spaded (turned over by a shovel) at least 10 inches deep. In other words contestants had to move about 200 cubic feet of earth usually within an hour.

Accounts of the competitions are found in the *AI Annual* reports and in some newspapers. For example, the 1852 contest (and $8 and a silver cup) was won by D. McVane. Joseph P. Lodge of Harlem won the silver medal and Alexander McCullum was given a diploma for 3rd place.

Four years later the first place premium was increased to $10 and William Beatty of Mott Haven in Westchester County won the silver cup. James Vance of Harlem was 2nd and Roger O'Connor was 3rd. O'Connor's 80-year-old father, Edward, was one of the contestants.[22] The American Institute, which offered annual premiums for produce, plants and livestock, survived for another *century*. Yet, by the outset of the Civil War, the AI spading competitions had vanished, probably from apathy.

Telegraph Pole Climbing

The advent of the telegraph and the resulting erection of telegraph poles throughout the nation led to linesmen who needed to be able to climb telegraph poles quickly and safely. Thirty poles per mile is an industry standard. In the 1850s, pole climbing challenges began to appear in print. The following 1857 taunt is typical.

> Pole Climbing—House Telegraph Office, Philadelphia, Oct. 24, 1857—Frank Queen—*Dear Sir:*
> I see in the last number of your worthy sheet a challenge from Mr. Chas. Simmons [his actual name was Timmons] to climb a pole for $100 or $500, with or without spurs. As this is the first challenge of the kind I have seen since I have been in this country I will accept it, and will climb him both *with* and *without* spurs-—a pole not less than 100 feet high, clear of bark, $100 a side, with spurs, and $200 a side without spurs. As we are both telegraph men, and personally acquainted, I wish no blowing in the matter, but if Mr. Simmons is serious and disposed to back his challenge he can find man and money ready as above.
> Andrew Wynn[23]

A few years later, after having won a number of contests, Timmons was referring to himself in print as "champion" and "champion climber," which another pole climber, John Green, thought to be more than a little presumptuous. Using the "champion" appellation was not uncommon among athletes of the day, including worker athletes, but this time it got under Green's skin. Green prepared a detailed contract with specific rules on height of the pole (43 feet was a standard for telegraph poles), the selection of judges, acceptable descent tactics (no free falling) and more. He included two curious insertions:

First, "no excuse for accident will be accepted by the judges;" second: "Mr. Timmons to climb himself, Mr. Green reserving the right to climb himself, or name his man on the day of climbing." The right to name (and compensate) a stand-in may have been acceptable for the U.S. military, but was virtually unheard of in the history of American worker competitions.

Green published his contract in the *Clipper* with the following message:

> "I will match Timmons to climb 43 feet up and down, best two in three, for $100, or as much more as he desires. He agrees to meet me halfway between Philadelphia and New Brunswick; and I therefore name Trenton, N.J., as the climbing ground ... play or pay. To convince you, Mr. Queen, as well as your readers, that I mean climbing, and not blowing, I forward with this a deposit which I wish you to please hold. Should this deposit not meet the demands of the "champion" ...I will cover any amount he may see proper to deposit in your hands."[24]

It appears that the match never happened. But lots of others did and, for a few years, pole climbing competitions, with a lot less formality than the Timmons-Green affair, were quite common.

Tinkering/Sewing/Stitching

Amid patent wars and infringement lawsuits between Isaac Singer and Elias Howe, sewing machines became commercially feasible and went into mass production in the 1850s. Needles were powered by a foot treadle and the machines provided an opportunity for "stitchers" to race one another or the clock. Called "Knights of the Wax and Thread," sewing machine operators frequently offered challenges. For example, E.M. Schofield of Chicago made a $25 bet with O.P. Sellers of Savannah, Ga., that he, Schofield, could perform 12 *dozen* double seams on 2-quart fabric buckets in 12 minutes. The competition was set up at Wheeler and Blakes in New Orleans on November 14, 1859. Using a Burton's Patent machine, Schofield "went in lemons" and accomplished the feat handsomely in 10 minutes and 45 seconds and was immediately handed the $50 stakes.[25]

Some sewing establishments conducted intramural competitions for their employees. Lentill and H.W. Baxter, harness makers in San Francisco, matched two of their employees, Charles Miller and Charles Winter. The conditions were to sew two rows of stitches, ten to an inch, on traces six feet in length. The prize was $40. Miller never trailed and won handsomely by 27 stitches.[26]

Competitions where the contestants were the machines themselves were not uncommon in the last part of the 19th century, but stitching competitions became infrequent. Today the American Sewing Guild offers contests of fashion and creativity.

Mowing

The scene of contestants headed to the competitive fields bearing sheathed scythes in hand or slung over shoulders is long past. Mowing contests were commonplace before mechanical mowing machines and reapers appeared in the 1850s, as farmers were able to display their endurance and skill in handling a scythe while cutting down grass or grain.

The *True Californian* offers an example from Vallejo, which was twice the state capital before 1853. The contest came off in the Vallejo Valley, located in the San Francisco Bay Area on the northeastern shore of San Pablo Bay. Two eastern farmers, Addison M. Ripley from Maine and a Mr. Ball from Vermont were matched in a timed mowing contest in the autumn of 1856. Each put up $500.

With scythes in hand, they were each given 5 acres of grass to mow, the grass at the time being estimated as weighing two and one half tons per acre. Ripley finished his work in just under 8 hours, mowing 12½ tons of grass. This amounted to mowing, for eight hours, 50 pounds per minute. At the finish Ball had a quarter of an acre left to mow. Ripley *earned* his $500 and the contest richly illustrated the need for mechanical mowers and reapers.[27] Hand-mowing contests became increasingly less frequent and were replaced by recurrent trials of mowing machines, with manufacturers anxious to demonstrate the ease by which they accomplished this strenuous task. Even poet Emily Dickinson, in her autobiography, recalled repetitive contests in 1858 for mechanical mowing machines designed to replace scythes.[28]

Mowing, like many other farming labors (and therefore the work-sport), was rendered obsolete by mechanization. But mowing contest spectators experienced an element of danger. One needed to stay well clear of a person wielding a scythe. For example, in 1858 *The New York Times* recounts that "an Irishman is said to have insulted an American citizen while the latter was mowing in the ... town of Somerville [Mass.] whereupon the American citizen stabbed him so that he died and kept on mowing with the utmost *sang froid*, and was not arrested for some time."[29]

Modern day scything competitions are historical and infrequent. The most notable is held annually in Addison County, Vermont. They are relatively short affairs emphasizing speed and the skill of mowing a close and even swath. In drought years the contests are cancelled when there is not much of anything to scythe.

Occasionally competitions also offer a stoking event, that is, how to tie sheaves and stook (stand up) grain for drying in the field. Teams of mowers and stokers work together against the clock and judges appraise the quality of the job. One should not confuse modern day lawn mowing contests, or the annual and factitious Gross National Parade's "Lawn Mowers Precision Drill team" exhibition with 19th century mowing contests.

A Final Word

One can not underestimate the influence of Richard Fox's *National Police Gazette* in promoting many of the lesser known worker competitions during the last third of the 19th century. Fox understood that work, at least in America, was the key component of one's identity and he became a relentless sponsor of many sporting events. He offered championship belts, cups and trophies to the winners of many traditional sports and bestowed the designation "champion" on workers who displayed outstanding skills. He also ran contests for hairdressers, firemen, cakewalkers (dancers), barbers, bartenders, oyster openers, steeple climbers, dog trainers and practitioners of other occupations. This type of promotional activity was common among contemporary publishers.[30] His main sport was boxing but Fox became a sort of P.T. Barnum for occupational sports, and competitions in a number of these occupations continue to this day. Excellent examples would be modern contests for bartenders and barbers. Fox's overriding goal was to place a copy of his (sometimes) salacious pink paper in every saloon and barbershop in the nation and he was particularly keen on making minor celebrities out of barbers. *Gazette* historian Guy Reel reports that "one champion haircutter gave a professional haircut in 30 seconds, resulting in a frightened but satisfied customer."[31]

George Griffiths, an 18 year old employee of the Mutual District Messenger Company, was the champion messenger boy of New York City in 1882. He ran 95 miles, 65 yards in 23 hours and fifteen minutes at an indoor trial of endurance at the American Institute Indoor Hall in March, 1882 (*National Police Gazette*. April 15, 1882).

The *Gazette* was known for its ribald irreverence and some of Fox's competitions appear silly today. He overdid it by promoting such activities as

12. Obsolete Work-Sports

bridge jumping, one legged dancing, rat catching, drinking and worse. Because he awarded trophies for all sorts of sports and occupations, he attracted cranks, to his disdain. He told a rival publisher that he was thinking of starting a crank's carnival.

> One man wrote him from Chicago: "I propose to walk seven hundred (700) miles in one hundred and thirty four (134) hours, covering this distance by walking around an ordinary flour barrel four thousand, one hundred and ninety-eight (4,198) laps to a mile." All he asked from Fox was to pay the rent for Madison Square Garden for a week, plus $50. Fox said he was inclined to agree with this offer if the man walked inside instead of outside the barrel.[32]

Yet Fox understood that the working class needed an escape, even for a short time, from anonymity. He bestowed the term "champion" on many and became an organizer and publicizer.

Reports of many of Fox's worker competitions wound up on the pages of his newspaper. Yet most work-sports never got that far and subsequently died an early death.

13

Modern Work-Sports

What is the current status of the work-sports phenomenon? Many 19th century work-sports have survived in their original form. And new worker-competitions have materialized. Today U.S. work-sports are offered on four different planes.

Modern Spectator Work-Sport

Several work-sports have developed as public entertainment. These professional spectator work-sports are highly popular at the national level, have long standing television contracts, and encompass a cadre of specialists who make their living as worker-athletes. Rodeo, timber sports and some forms of firefighting fall into this category. Today rodeo is the most successful of all former work-sports. It is practiced in over 40 states and at every imaginable level. Almost 100 U.S. colleges sponsor a rodeo team and offer scholarships. Women enjoy professional cowgirl events. Rodeo events also focused on children, gays, high schoolers, native Americans, and African-Americans. Even prisons offer rodeo as a sport. Hundreds of low-key rodeos are held with country fairs and livestock shows. There are more than 10,000 professional cowboys who annually compete at the highest level in over 600 major league rodeos for more than 30 million dollars in prize money before 28 million spectators.

The *Professional Rodeo Cowboys Association* sets the standard for rodeo competition and offers a bi-monthly magazine and a website that rivals any collegiate athletic department site. Professional rodeo action consists of two types of events — roughstock competitions and timed events — and offers an all-around cowboy crown. Roughstock includes bareback riding, saddle bronc riding and bill riding. In timed events — steer wrestling, team roping, barrel racing, steer roping and tie-down roping — competitors race the clock.

13. Modern Work-Sports 161

Calf roping was a practical skill of the 19th century cowboy that was turned into a rodeo event. Several hundred hours of television coverage are devoted to rodeo events annually with another 50 or so to bull riding. Rodeo is contested at every conceivable level (stock photo-no restrictions, accessed October 19, 2011. http://geekphilosopher.com/geekphilosopher.com/gallery/gallery.aspx?aid=193).

A national finals rodeo, sponsored by Wrangler, is held each December, usually in Las Vegas. Bull riding has become so popular to spectators that it has been spun off into its own sport with a unique sponsoring federation.[1] Several hundred hours of network and cable television are devoted annually to rodeo. Add another 50 hours for bull riding.[2] Annual viewer-ship is estimated at 60 million.[3]

The numbers are only slightly less impressive for lumberjacking. The American Lumberjack Association (ALA), the United States Axemen's Association (USAA), and the American Birling Association (ABA) all set rules, sanction events, keep records and standardize the sport.

A national championship is held annually in 21 separate chopping, sawing and climbing events with significant prize money. A roaming band of professional lumberjacks (some from New Zealand and Australia) compete in the Stihl Timbersports Series and, until recently, ESPN's Great Outdoor Games. Today several hundred lumberjack competitions dot the regional American landscape, with particularly important ones in the traditional forestry states of New England, the upper Midwest and the far Northwest.

Thundering chainsaws, nimble footed birlers, amazingly strong choppers and sawyers, plus the remarkable quickness of pole climbers entertain and

Today fireman musters proliferate and the sport is older than baseball. Many modern musters display antiquated equipment but the real feature are the contests which underscore firefighting skills. At this 1975 muster in Walkersville, Maryland, the victorious Vigilant Hose Co. from Emmitsburg, Maryland (founded 1884), is victorious in a timed response and hook-up competition (Courtesy of Vigilant Hose Co, Emmitsburg, Maryland).

instruct millions. In 2012 several hundred timber sports competitions were conducted nationally with total live attendance estimated at 800,000 plus. Until 2010 the Stihl series of televised competitions, which included regional qualifying affairs, a national collegiate championship and a U.S. championship, drew an audience of over 20 million from 62 nations.[4]

The timbering occupation received a recent blast of notoriety. The History Channel's *Ax Men* series, the latest in a string of at-work reality shows, premiered in 2010 and explored the hardy and dangerous world of loggers.

The third leg of a trio of frequently televised worker competitions is a spinoff but a far cry from the oldest team work-sport in the books, firemen's musters. Extreme firefighters race to nozzle hoses, knock down doors, rescue heavy dummies, and put out fires in timed events. National finals are televised on very, very late night broadcasting. The occupation has also spawned a recent Sony playstation hero, Rosco McQueen Firefighter Extreme.

Chamber of Commerce Events

On another level, many work-athletes parade their skills at national events, regional and local festivals, state and county fairs, and trade shows and conventions. Here we are dealing with practitioners, not professional worker-athletes. Many of the work-sports are well over 100 years old: corn husking, oyster shucking, plowing, sheep shearing, hay loading, traditional firefighting, cotton picking, bartending, masonry and a variety of harvesting/picking contests too numerous to mention. These examples of modern work-sports are practiced at every level but each of the above named activities is conducted at a national championship level. Worker athletes do not make a living at these affairs, but they are fiercely competitive and offer an opportunity to display occupational skills. Many could be termed "chamber of commerce" events, sponsored to promote tourism, civic pride or fund-raising. A good example is the Abe Lincoln national rail splitting championship. Conducted by local civic groups, it has a 40-year history. Today many construction trades conduct national championships, including everything from bricklaying to shoveling to nail driving to carpentry. For example, the popular "Fastest Trowel in the West" masonry contest annually matches the nation's top bricklayers.[5] Most of these events are sponsored by trade associations and a conservative estimate puts participants at several hundred thousand annually. Some events are historic festivals, some are harvesting events while others are industry promotions. The list is almost endless, including bookbinding contests, welding and cutting games, cotton picking, Christmas tree baling, crab trap pulling, skillet tossing, fence and window painting, vine pruning, bootblacking, bartending, lei making (in Hawaii), machine tooling, cashiering — well, you get the picture. Most conduct a national championship.

And there are many more recent occupational sports. Window washers, grocery baggers, grave diggers (yes, there is a Cemetery Olympics), gift wrappers, chamber-maids, stenographers, truck drivers, tree climbers, lifeguards, knitters, telegraph linemen, taxidermists, and delivery bike couriers all conduct local and regional competitions and a national finals annually. In the most improbable of sports reporting outlets, *The Wall Street Journal*, from 1996 thru 2005 were 19 front page feature stories (usually 1500–2000 words) about modern American worker competitions. Nineteen! Front page! The incidence, variety and importance of worker competitions which have become sporting events in American culture is undeniable. A list of the stories with citations can be found in Appendix 5.

In the same time frame, in *The Wall Street Journal*, the National Football League accounted for just six stories; the National Basketball Association registered nine; Major League Baseball, fourteen. The era's most featured indi-

Each June downtown Kansas City, Missouri, is overrun by student worker-athletes competing in national Skills-USA (formerly known as VICA-Vocational Industrial Clubs of America, founded in 1965) final. The Kemper Arena and the city's Convention Center are sites of week-long competitions among American state champions in nearly 90 occupations. This 2009 scene of the Kemper Arena is indicative of the size and scope of the modern work-sport event (Skills USA).

viduals, also, were eclipsed by work-sports. Federal Reserve Chairman Alan Greenspan, himself a former work-sports participant, had ten feature stories in the same time period. President Bill Clinton came closest with sixteen.

It should also be noted that the *Journal* reserves front page space (previously column four, now bottom-center) for an entertaining feature and one must examine every story — 2,600 of them over the timeframe — to ascertain if they refer to work-sports. A few were judgment calls. The May 1998 *Journal* feature on "killer competitions," about professional snipers, was included as a worker competition.[6] This is what they did for a living, and the weekend competitions were both a rehearsal and preparation for actual work situations. On the other hand, I did not include the marksman competition under the auspices of the American Zoot Shooters Association. Mimicking gangsters, members compete while dressed in 1940s Zoot Suits. I concluded that this could only be a work-sport if they were actually members of the mob. Nor did I include frequent and meticulous scavenger contests, nor limbo relay races played by bored college kids at all-night Wal-Marts.

A recent *Journal* offering is an account about the Aeronautical Pentathlon, an obscure competition demonstrating the skills of downed pilots.[7]

Confined to an elite group of workers who have access to military aircraft, this pentathlon inexplicably has six events, and even for a work-sport has flown pretty much under the radar.

What is the future for work-sports? Indeed, the number of possible work-sports opportunities seems endless, limited only by the number of possible occupations and one's imagination. Because the nature of American work has changed, mostly into office jobs one would think that work-sports, defined here as physical activity on or about the job, would be stagnant. In actuality today, work-sports thrive. Most have websites. A conservative estimate finds more than half a million workers compete in worker competitions annually. The actual count could be three times that. And that's before we even get to students or trainees.

The Educational System and SkillsUSA

Attesting to their influence on productivity, some work-sports have become part of the educational process. For example, each June more than 4000 students, mostly from vocational-technical institutions, descend on downtown Kansas City, Missouri, for the SkillsUSA nationals, one of the nation's largest and longest work-sport events. The students, each a "state occupational champion," demonstrate speed, strength, endurance, planning and mental toughness by competing in time-honored contests against one another. Trade and union representatives assist in the organization and judging. What emerges are national champions in over ninety occupations. A chapter of SkillsUSA, a national nonprofit organization serving students who are preparing for careers in trade, technical and skilled service occupations, can be found in every vocational high school in the nation.

On a recent June day in downtown Kansas City, fifty student bricklayers, each given 500 bricks, unlimited cement, and identical instructions, were allotted six hours to simultaneously demonstrate their skill. The competition area, as big as four basketball courts, was roped off and surrounded by hundreds spectators, many of whom, it turns out, had a vested interest in the work competition. I sidled up to a heavy, gum-chewing man who was watching the Maryland entry, a skinny youth from the local vocational high school near my home. After a few minutes of chat I asked, "Why are you here?" "You see that kid," he replied, pointing to the same feverishly working youngster. "I own a construction company and I don't have anyone who's remotely as good as he is. I'd offer him forty-five [thousand dollars] to start tomorrow." This was, in a real sense, a job audition. And so it went, as potential employers roamed the competition sites searching for gems ... there were competitions in computer maintenance, carpentry, engine repair, commercial baking, architectural drafting, automotive refinishing, broadcast news production, cabinet making, plumbing, practical nursing, residential wiring, sheet metal working, welding, cosmetology and more. It was a work-sports junkie's heaven, with over 4000 occupational competitions in ninety-four competitions in a single week.

My favorite was the "TeamWorks" contest, where squads of four students were required to build a construction project over three days. One such project was to complete a slice of a house (parts of 4 rooms), using carpentry, electrical, plumbing and masonry skills while meeting "competition specified" building codes, and standards on safety and cleanliness. All of the building materials were delivered on day one and the work proceeded at a deliberate pace. I would go back every couple of hours to see how the work was coming and was dazzled by a Massachusetts team of students that attracted a large crowd of admirers. They never seemed to be in a hurry but they sure got the job done. After three days they had completed one-third of a house! They won easily.

Only the nation's best student occupational competitors make it to Kansas City. Qualifying rounds are held at the school, local, regional and state levels. Skills/USA, the national coordinating arm, estimates that annually 300,000 students (in more than 17,000 chapters) compete in occupational contests at some level in 54 states and territories.[8] Only the state champions qualify to compete in Kansas City which conducts the competitions at the adjacent downtown convention center and the Kemper Arena. Since the inception of Vocational Industrial Clubs of America (VICA) in 1965, more than 10.5 million students have competed at an occupational contest at some level or another. A national headquarters was built near Leesburg, Va., in 1977 and VICA's competitions went international in 1981 with the International Youth Skill Olympics. The name was changed in 1995 to SkillsUSA.

Today the contests are in skilled trade events and health occupation events, with another 25 in occupationally related or leadership events. And it doesn't end there. Annually a number of vocational national champions go on to compete at the World Skills Competition, a sort of occupational Olympics for high school students.

The contributions and competitions conducted by other well-known educational groups, like the Future Farmers of America (FFA) and 4-H clubs, are familiar enough to most of us. Combined membership of these two groups approaches 7 million nationwide in nearly 100,000 chapters.[9] Although competitions are not their primary function, they conduct many.

Trainee/Preparation Competitions

The final type of modern worker competitions are on-the-job contests. In nearly two centuries, American work-sports have come full circle. Many of today's competitions are now back where they started, on the job site, and not in a stadiums, parks or arenas. For example trade associations use competitions as part of the apprentice process. A good example would be tooling and machine contests conducted by the National Tooling and Machining Association. The NTMA oversees eleven training centers nationwide, seven of them on campuses of community colleges.

More work-related contests arise from state-mandated exercises. In West Virginia, for example, mine owners are required to manage rescue and EMT (emergency medical technicians) programs within their mines. Some owners have turned these into competitions, literally on-the-job work-sports.

A fine example of on-the-job training that has evolved into a large, standardized and trendy competition is the MacDonald's crew competition. Contests are conducted at the store, local, regional and national levels. Speed, accuracy and teamwork are emphasized for the functions related to providing fast-food. Several hundred thousand employees (the 2011 MacDonald's workforce numbered 1.3 million nationwide) compete in 29,000 restaurants.

Another work-sports trend has also emerged at the gym. Some personal trainers, gym proprietors and fitness gurus are designing workouts that closely resemble real work. Instead of using exercise machines, stationary bikes, barbells, dumbbells, or medicine balls in air-conditioned gyms, accountants, teachers and other assorted white-collar types are working out like laborers. They are hoisting beer kegs, rolling tractor tires and bench pressing wobbly PVC pipes filled with water.[10] For some, exercise routines replicate physical labor. The movement is relatively new.

Summary/Future

Today work-sports must be viewed in the larger context of all sporting activities, the big picture. There are more sports than ever with new additions daily. Sociologists who study the way civilization plays offer several explanations for the proliferation of sporting activities. First, it may be that sporting activities simply get stale and participants search for alternatives. Part of the surge may be simple American inventiveness. In the last generation tinkering with equipment has spawned mountain bikes, snowboards, rollerblades and their associated competitions. Add skateboarding, wind surfing, in-line skating, sky-surfing (skydiving on a snow board), and waterboarding. The list is extensive.

The U.S. sports inventory surge may be partially explained by ABC's 1960s show, "Wide World of Sports," which introduced an American audience to many novel activities, and by the 1979 debut of ESPN, the all-sports network and its name-alike counterparts, that opened up thousands of hours of programming time for sports other than the big four: baseball, basketball, football and ice hockey. So many new sports have been developed that new categories like "extreme sports were born." "Rarely does a day go by when a new sport proposal doesn't float past ESPN. Boomerang throwing, greased pole climbing, free-style rope jumping.... Many of the ideas are too offbeat, even for ESPN."[11] Indeed, it would be worrisome if ESPN did not continue to receive new sport proposals.

The number of worker competitions too has surged, but their creation comes for different reasons. Work-sports, by definition, are an outgrowth of occupational effort, that is, work. The changing nature of jobs has put more people in offices, often seated behind desks or in front of computers. Some of the additional sporting activity may be a reaction to the mundane features of office work. The attitude of Arden "Jamie" Cogar, a 253-pound trial attorney from West Hamlin, West Virginia, who spends his time in courts, offices and law libraries, sums up one conventional attitude and rationale for participation in a work-sport. "After a hard day at the office, nothing is more rewarding than going home, grabbing an axe, and beating the crap out of something that can't hit me back."[12] Cogar is acknowledged as one of America's top all-around lumberjacks and he reasons that worker competitions are a diversion.

Another explanation may be that Americans are now more inclined to celebrate historic work at the several thousand "heritage day" festivals events which now seem to dot every corner of the nation. The events include firemen's musters in Bath, Maine; shingle making in Thurmont, Maryland; carriage driving in Tunbridge, Vermont; woodcutting contests in Cullowhee, North Carolina; logging games in Greenville, Maine; black rodeo contests in Houston, Texas; and horseshoe making and butchering demonstrations at Intercourse, Pennsylvania. These games have become de facto, living history demonstrations.

There also seems to be an explosion of new, technologically driven competitions. For instance, there is now the two-person team LG Mobile World Cup in texting, where teenage girls with nimble fingers and lots of experience dominate. In 2010 a pair of Korean teenagers, Bae Young-Hoe, 17, and Ha Mok Min, 18, won $100,000 in an event requiring speed and accuracy and featuring competitors from a dozen counties. Sixteen-year-old Kate Moore, Des Moines, Iowa, and Morgan Dynda, 14, Pooler, Ga., took the $20,000 second prize.

These competitions do not meet my definition of work-sports, even though messages are processed *very* quickly. I have excluded them because the focus differs and because they do not involve much physical work. "My thumbs are up for the challenge," Moore announced before the recent world event in New York City. She averages 12,000 texts per month and has been timed at 3.5 characters per second.[13] Nor do I include any games played on or with computers. Computer hackers might be considered as work-sports competitors, for hacking may be job related. To my astonishment the activity fulfills many of Guttmann's characteristics of a modern sport. There are even two federations which keep records, offer clinics, promulgate guidelines and promote computer hacking.[14]

In spite of all of today's occupations which require being seated in front of a computer, work-sports thrive in America, as televised events, at local festivals, and in schools. Most of the sports or sponsoring organizations have websites. More than one and one-half million workers compete annually in U.S. worker-competitions. Work-sports have been around for more than 200 years, and as long as there are occupations which require strength, dexterity and speed, or even the memory of such physical jobs, there will be worker-competitions.

14

Work-Sports in Popular Culture

What I am calling work-sports includes labor and sport and has had an impact on American culture and folklore. Just look at team names: Cornhuskers, Lumberjacks, Miners, Cowboys, Packers and Boilermakers. These are not only the nicknames of prominent collegiate or professional sporting teams, they are also the occupations of nineteenth and early 20th century worker-athletes. A scan of collegiate and high school team names finds several hundred which have adopted occupational identities. For instance, each day I drive by a high school whose team is known as the "Canners," named for a local applesauce processing plant.

The evidence of this cultural phenomenon is everywhere. Work-sports show up in newpapers and magazines, in company histories, and in trade and technical journals. They also show up in our literature, theatre, music, art, movies, even our folklore. The evidence of work-sports surrounds us, envelops us. The cultural manifestations of work-sports in this chapter are not comprehensive. Rather, they are offered as examples of its wide range of influence. But the point is incontestable. As a society, we have recognized worker competitions as reasonably important and reported them as such and they are now a significant part of our culture. We have only failed to see the bigger picture.

Journalism

Our initial confirmation comes from 19th century sporting journalism.[1] In the ante-bellum and immediate post bellum periods work sports were directly aided by sporting journals (technically, weekly magazines in newspaper form). Many of the early 19th century worker-competitions were agricultural (e.g., plowing, sheepshearing, milking) and appeared in local news accounts of agricultural fairs. The young country's lone national agricultural publication in the early days of the 19th century was the *American Farmer* founded in 1819 by John F. Skinner of Baltimore. Skinner also established the *American Turf Register and Sporting Magazine* (1829). Both were published weekly. The former included the nation's first sports column, *Sporting Olio*. The latter was not devoted to the turf alone. It also featured material on outdoor sports, pedestrianism and, occasionally, worker-competitions.

The nation's first sporting newspapers, the *American Turf Register* and the *Spirit of the Times*, founded in 1831 by William Porter, also printed abundant reports on worker competitions sent by local enthusiasts.[2] For its initial thirty years, the *Spirit of the Times* focused on horse racing but also published frequent accounts (sometimes snippets and sometimes detailed) of worker-competitions. The entire collection of original issues of both papers is now in the hands of the National Sporting Library in Middleburg, Va.

By mid-century the weekly *New York Clipper*, founded in 1853 by Frank Queen, was a strong advocate of all sports, not just turf, boxing, pedestrianism and base-ball. It also published numerous, detailed accounts on musters as well as on reaping, plowing, mowing, tinkering, cradling, and pole climbing contests and more. The number of reported worker competitions in the *Clipper* is surprisingly high. For example, from 1856 to 1858, the *Clipper* published 135 accounts of competitions between and among workers. These normally included the date and location of the contest, a short description of the event, the names of the contestants and frequently the size of the wager.[3] John Rickards Betts reminded us that, in the 1850s and 60s, there was little to write about in the winter months. The organization of now traditional sports was still in its formative stages and Frank Queen may have been looking for material, unintentionally promoting work-sport.

After the Civil War the nation was seized by an athletic impulse, and work-sports went along for the ride.[4] It affected all classes. The working class was the target of a novel tabloid, the *National Police Gazette,* which had been taken over by a young Northern Ireland immigrant in 1877, Richard Kyle Fox. Prior to Fox's arrival the *Gazette* featured spicy stories, buxom showgirls, scandals and crime reports, all printed on pink paper. Fox rapidly invaded the world of sport, reduced subscription rates for barber shops (the *Gazette* was known as the "Barber's Bible"), saloons and hotels and began to sponsor and report boxing bouts. The *Gazette* soon reached into every corner of the nation with a weekly circulation of 150,000. The influence of Fox and the *Gazette* in promoting lesser known worker-competitions has been discussed earlier. During the 1870s the nation's big three, *Spirit of the Times*, *Clipper* and *National Police Gazette*, were a sports junkie's dream. Of lesser importance in promoting work-sports were the yellow rags of the 1880s and 1890s, led by the *New York World* (owned by Joseph Pulitzer) and *New York Sun* (edited by

Charles A. Dana). The popular monthly magazine *Outing* (founded in 1882) was eminently responsible for promoting all forms of respectable recreation, camping, outdoor life and travel but played no role in the work-sports narrative.

After 1894 the *New York Clipper* was folded into a theatrical journal (eventually becoming a segment of *Variety*) and the circulation of the *National Police Gazette* fell off rapidly. At the turn of the century work-sports were well established and accounts of them appeared in the regular press (often not as part of the sports pages, rather appearing in sections devoted to agriculture, style, culture or local activities). And accounts were also scattered among farming newspapers (e.g., *Wallace's Farmer, Prairie Farmer, Nebraska Farmer*); union reports (e.g., Reports of Local 6 of International Typographical Union); company annuals (e.g., Bethlehem Steel and the Edison Electric Co.);[5] rodeo journalism (e.g., *The Journal of the West* and *The Cattleman*); and trade journals (the earliest were the *Farmer's, Mechanic's, Manufacturer's and Sportsman's Magazine*, published 1826–27 and *The Plough, The Loom and the Anvil*, 1848–51). The history of work-sports is much like a mosaic and when one pieces all of the evidence together one finds a nation both at work and at play.

Literature

On occasion a non-fiction magazine piece uncovers a work-sports episode as a reminder of this 19th century labor tendency. For instance, Bil Gilbert's first-rate *Sports Illustrated* story, "A Turn on the Old Pike," about rock-breaking, takes us back to the early days of worker competitions.[6] The number of non-fiction magazine articles and books on rodeo and firemen's musters numbers in the hundreds.[7] There are three books on the history of corn husking and one on the history of the typesetting swifts, but there is much less collected and published information about other forms of work-sport.[8]

Fictional accounts of American work sports are also numerous. My favorite, "Blacksmith's Boy," by Edward W. O'Brien, a story about two midwest blacksmiths engaged in a horseshoe making contest, initially appeared in the November 2, 1940, edition of the *Saturday Evening Post*.[9] Some of America's top novelists have used work-sports as a backdrop. I recommend John P. Marquand's *The Late George Apley*, a 1938 Pulitzer prize-winning novel which is set among fireman's musters. A Web search lists several hundred novels about the rodeo.

Art

At the Dartmouth-Hitchcock Medical Center in Hanover, New Hampshire, at the phlebotomy center is a large and convincing oil painting of a hand-pumping contest at an early 20th century muster.[10] The artist claimed that he painted the scene entirely from his boyhood memory of New England musters.

Perhaps the most famous painting of a worker competition belongs to Norman Rockwell, whose *Blacksmith's Boy* accompanied O'Brien's fictional account of a horseshoe making contest in the *Saturday Evening Post*.

Rodeo art seems almost limitless. Rodeo rider sculptures dot skylines and private collections. Two of the most famous larger-than-life sculptures are *Bronco Buster* by Alexander Phimister Proctor, which adorns Civic Center Park in Denver, and *Ride High TC*, a sculpture of South Dakota bronco riding champ Travis Calvin Holloway, sculpted by western artist Tony Chytka and displayed in Deadwood, South Dakota.

Thousands, perhaps hundreds of thousands, of smaller, bronze rodeo statues, statuettes and figurines have found their way into American households. Three of the most famous are Frederic Remington's *Outlaw* bronze, Don Beck's *8 Seconds* bull rider, and *Cap and Necktie*, a bronze of Casey Tibbs and the bronc Necktie by Edd Hayes.

The rather angelic, ***The Little Fireman***, an 1857 Currier and Ives lithograph prepared by Louis Mauer, was a favorite 19th century portrait. Idealized portraits of young children in worker garb, produced by Currier and Ives, were a cultural phenomenon. They decorated the walls of America's bedrooms and nurseries in the 19th century. Here a young boy is in the role of a "Chief Engineer" at a fire (courtesy of the American Insurance Association).

Movies and Documentaries

Because of their historical ties and the element of danger, movies about rodeo cowboys, lumberjacks and firemen are common. There have been eighteen feature-length movies about rodeos. Perhaps the most popular was *8 Seconds*, with Luke Perry and Stephen Baldwin, the tragic life story of a

A 2009 U.S. postage stamp showing Abraham Lincoln as a rail splitter includes the earliest-known photograph of Lincoln, dated 1846, by N. H. Shepherd. The stamp depicts Lincoln as a youth splitting a log for a rail fence on what was then the American frontier. When he was a candidate for president in 1860, the image of Lincoln as a "rail-splitter" was used by the Republican Party to enhance his "workingman" appeal (http://www.djmcadam.com/lincoln-stamps.html, accessed September 9, 2011).

bull-riding icon, Lane Frost played by (Perry). Of the others, the most notable include *The Lusty Men* (1952), starring Robert Mitchum and Susan Hayward; *The Rounders* (1965), starring Glenn Ford, Henry Fonda and Casey Tibbs; *The Electric Horseman*, (1979) with Robert Redford and Jane Fonda; and *Colorado Cowboy: The Bruce Ford Story* (1994), an award-winning documentary on rodeo life featuring the first cowboy to win one million dollars in prize money.

Lumberjack contest movies include *Seven Brides for Seven Brothers*, a musical about seven lumberjack brothers who, like the Romans with their rape of the Sabine women, raid a nearby town, kidnapping future brides. *Gangs of New York*, directed by Martin Scorsese and starring Leonardo DiCaprio, featured scenes depicting 19th century firemen, but needed more research. By 2010, forty firefighting movies had grossed over five hundred million dollars.[11]

In 2001 an Academy Award finalist for short films featured the story of John Henry and was produced by the Walt Disney studio. The most recent worker competition DVD, by Heritage Documentaries, is *When Farmers Were Heroes: the Era of National Corn Husking Contests* (2009). It celebrates agrarian values and reminds the viewer that, during the Great Depression corn husking contests drew enormous crowds and buoyed the spirits of the American farming community.

Music

Song has always been part of American work. Work songs, often rhythmic, are frequently designed to accompany specific forms of work. And some work songs and lyrics are about work. Either way there seems to be an inordinately large number of songs related to work and a resulting spillover of work-sports related songs. For example there are over 50 songs about rodeo. "Rodeo" by Garth Brooks, "Bull ridin' Son of a Gun" by the Charlie Daniels Band and rodeo cowboy Chris Ledoux's "Bareback Jack" and "8 Second Ride" have been particularly popular. My personal favorite has always been Willie Nelson's "My Heroes Have Always Been Cowboys." An excellent example of a rhythmic work song, this one for the track layers who spiked rails to ties, is "Swing Boys Swing" by Aengus Finnan. It can be found in a contemporary North Wind album.

Many agricultural and harvesting work songs were rhythmic and sung by people working on a physical and repetitive task. The intention is to relieve boredom and enhance productivity. This was true for farms and ante-bellum plantations. The lyrics of the slave song "Shuck Dat Corn Before You Eat" reminded slaves of the reward for their effort.

So too lumberjacks and miners had their songs. Lumberjack songs from Maine and Minnesota have steadfast followings. Songs about John Henry dominated the work of rock drillers and miners. Scott Reynolds Nelson tells us that there are more songs about John Henry, more than 200, than about any other American individual.[12] Harry Belafonte, the Smothers Brothers, Bruce Springsteen, Woody Guthrie, Pete Seeger and Johnny Cash have all performed ballads about John Henry's contest with a mechanical drill.

Folklore

Many of the occupations discussed in this volume have developed fictional heroes who have become icons in American folklore. Some, like John Henry, even have a work-sports connection. And this is yet another reason to consider the importance of work-sports. Other sports had their heroes: Mike 'King" Kelley (baseball), Donald Dinnie (Caledonian Games) and John L. Sullivan (boxing) are a few late 19th century examples. In approximately the same era occupational heroes, real and mythical, proliferated.

The very first occupational icon was Ol' Mose or Mose the Bowery b'hoy, modeled after one Moses Humphrey, a New York fireboy on the Lady Washington engine number 40 and a notorious street brawler. Mose became a city legend when he became the subject of a Broadway play, *Scenes of New York*, one of the moist successful plays in Broadway history, before or since. Its sequels and spinoffs ran for years, making Ol Mose, in his shiny stovepipe hat (making him appear over 7 feet tall), bright red shirt and rolled up trousers, one of the most recognizable figures of the 19th century. Folklorist Richard Dorson calls the fireman "America's first urban folk hero."[13]

Others followed. Paul Bunyan (timbering),[14] John Henry (rock drilling), Pecos Bill (rodeo), Johnny Appleseed–John Chapman (farming), Casey Jones (railroads), Gib Morgan (oil fields), to name but a few.[15] Two, Ole Mose and Johnny Appleseed of the 1840s, actually predate any of the other American sporting heros. Worker athletes can even claim a presidential member in Abe Lincoln, a six-foot, four-inch, 216-pound rail splitter.[16]

Mose, the Fighting Fireman, may have been America's first worker icon. He loved to both put out fires and bully anyone in sight. One either loved or hated the guy, but everyone recognized him. This 1848 lithograph is of actor F.S. Chanfrau who played the character of "Ole Mose" on Broadway (Peter's Collection, National Museum of American History, Smithsonian Institution, Photo 600446-B).

In 1996, recognizing the importance of worker icons, the U.S. Postal Service issued a series of commerative "folk-hero" 32-cent postage stamps, which included a trio of worker icons from the late nineteenth and early 20th century: Paul Bunyan (timbering), John Henry (mining), and Pecos Bill (rodeo).[17] Two years earlier the Walt Disney Company released the regrettable

Tall Tale: The Unbelievable Adventures of Pecos Bill, a movie featuring a child befriended by Paul Bunyan, John Henry and Pecos Bill. *The New York Times* panned it, saying, "This is not the stuff of which legends are made."

Halls of Fame/Museums

Finally, in America we acknowledge the importance of a sporting activity by establishing halls of fame to recall both memorable feats and athletes. Have work-sports achieved a Cooperstown status? Are there worker competition halls of fame? Consider, there are seven national rodeo halls of fame. The ProRodeo Hall of Fame (Colorado Springs, Col.), and the Rodeo Hall of Fame (Oklahoma City, Okla.) vie for constituents and recognition as the sport's true center. There are at least four firefighter halls of fame and hundreds of state and local firemen's museums. The newest is located in my home town.[18] On a national scale, the Mining Hall of Fame is located in Leadville, Colo.; the Lumberjack Hall of Fame (Sponsored by Stihl) is in Pigeon Forge, Tenn.; the Blacksmith Hall of Fame is in Buena Vista, Minn.; the Plowing Hall of Fame is in Jefferson, Iowa; and the National Corn Huskers Hall of Fame makes its home in Kewanee, Il. In addition there are literally dozens of similar institutions on the state and regional level. The point is palpable. If a work-sport has a hall of fame, at the very least, *someone* has recognized it as a sport.

15

Why Work-Sports?

The common thread in this book is that American laborers participated in games or contests which replicated their work. Given the economic and cultural significance of this phenomenon it is important to conclude this work by addressing three important questions: first, why so many worker competitions occurred in the first place; second, whether work-sports participants are really athletes in the conventional sense of the term, and third, what was the economic impact of the contests? For this final chapter I draw upon much of my 2004 study published in the *Journal of Leisure Research*.[1] It is obvious that this U.S. labor/sporting phenomenon was neither scattered nor random. For approximately one hundred years American worker competitions were pervasive and an explanation is necessary.

But first, a brief note about work-sports and social status.[2] Individual worker-athletes never stood near the apex of the American social structure. That work-sports were for the working class should occasion no surprise. The dramatic sporting surge in England during the mid–19th century determinedly influenced American elites who followed the lead of the English upper classes in promoting cricket, lawn tennis, yachting, rowing and track and field. Horse racing was already well established. To *gentlemen,* work and play were discrete spheres of activity. But for the working class work and play morphed into one another. This may explain why much of 19th century work-sports was overlooked by the conventional media while socially elite sports grew in importance. Some sporting papers simply ignored anything but elite sports. For example, the popular monthly magazine *Outing* (1882–1923) completely disregarded worker competitions. Even baseball, going through its most important growth stage in the 1880s and 1890s, went ten years without warranting a mention in *Outing.*

The reporting of many sporting activities was class-specific after the Civil War and it was mainly up to the *Clipper* and the *National Police Gazette* to carry the ball by reporting work-sports that were not just local in scope. When both papers lost prominence in the waning days of the 19th century there was no national reporting mechanism. Although work-sports continued, even thrived during this period, they were overlooked by the national press and were sequestered in local newspapers — rarely on the sports page, but rather in sections dealing with community or farming news. And this goes a long way in explaining, even up to the present, why the movement has been overlooked by historians. The trend is easy enough to miss if there is no avenue for reporting and accounting for it. The last *Clipper Annual* which detailed many competition reports and work-sports records was published in 1899.[3]

Rationale

First, let us look at why worker-competitions happened in abundance. Social and economic theory may be helpful. One possible explanation for the emergence of work-sports may have been that workers were alienated on the job and responded by creating competitions. The century of American work-sport, roughly1840–1940, coincides with the early growth of capitalism, with its expansion of markets and where many workers toiled in a factory system. It may have been that the emphasis on mass production, national markets and the division of labor relegated workers to mundane, repetitive tasks.

In the 19th century Karl Marx argued that in a modern capitalist society, the worker lives an alienated and dehumanizing existence. Alienation was the historical product of the division of labor and capitalism. Marx explained that with estranged labor, "the worker does not fulfill himself in his work, but denies himself: has a feeling of misery rather than well being, does not develop freely his mental and physical energies but is physically exhausted and mentally debased. The worker, therefore, feels himself at home only during leisure time, whereas at work he feels homeless. His work is not voluntary, but imposed, forced labor."[4] Max Weber, a German sociologist and political economist, associated the development of capitalism with worker disenchantment, thereby extending Marx's argument. Weber contended that, in modern work, men could no longer engage in socially significant action unless they joined large scale organizations in which they were allocated specific tasks and to which they were admitted only upon condition that they sacrificed their personal desires and predilections to the impersonal goals and procedures that governed the whole. By doing so they would be cut off from a part of themselves, they would become alienated. For Weber, competition, either for the firm or the worker, had religious roots in the Protestant work ethic.[5]

Both Marx and Weber likely would have maintained that worker alienation pushed 19th century workers into competitive events. Yet, given the voluntary nature of most of the contests, this line of reasoning is unconvincing. For example, many of the earliest American work-sports were agricultural. It seems unlikely that alienated farmers would respond to alienation by playing on the job.

The experience of the 19th century racing typesetters, the swifts, offers insight into the attitude of many shop-floor athletes. There is no evidence that they were alienated. Rather, newspaper typesetters took their mundane task of setting endless lines of type and fashioned it into a timed contest. The initial contests, begun in the early 1870s, were both local and intramural. By 1885 they had become so popular that city, regional and national championships were held in dime museums and other public arenas. Rather than feel estranged, typesetters decided to put on a show.[6]

A second explanation, one offered by sporting historians to account for the explosion and interest of 19th century sporting activities, is simply that this was all made possible by increased leisure time. The additional leisure time, say historians, came about from labor-saving devices, economies of scale or negotiated reductions in working hours.

Are not work and play polarizations? Work, on one hand, is purposeful, necessary labor, whether physical or mental. Play, on the other hand, is a cultural phenomenon and is not seen as necessary. In his seminal work on play, *Homo Ludens,* R.J. Huizinga (1944) described play as having the following characteristics:

> a free activity standing quite consciously outside "ordinary" life as being "not serious," but at the same time absorbing the player intensely and utterly. It is an activity connected with no material interest, and no profit can be gained from it. It proceeds within its own proper boundaries of time and space according to fixed rules and in an orderly manner.[7]

To Huizinga, because of the polarity of a utilitarian necessity and a cultural phenomenon, worker-competitions were not a possibility. In spite of Huizinga's theory 19th century worker competitions were genuine sports that can possibly be explained as arising from the political/economic struggle to reduce the work week, industrialization and the nature of leisure.

Did the emergence of additional spare time make laborers want to take jobs from the workplace and make contests of them, in a sense, to make play of work, or, in effect, to *substitute* play for work? Did the additional free time allow this? It is true that the 19th century political and economic struggles of the working class brought shorter workdays and more time for recreation. Just how much additional time was there? Daniel Rodgers has noted that, after 1850, the American workday had been condensed by "squeezing periods of relaxation and amusement out of working hours, by trading long hours of casual work, for shorter, more concentrated workdays."[8]

Roy Rosenzweig gives us part of the answer: "In 1830 eleven hours per day or more was the standard at more than half the establishments surveyed in a U.S. Census Bureau study; by 1860 the figure had dropped to less than one-third."[9] He focused on the city of Worcester, Massachusetts, home to over 170 manufacturing establishments by 1860, whose population exceeded 100,000 before the end of the century. By 1900, Worcester was the 29th largest U.S. city, made up of a plethora of factories, churches, playgrounds, industrial neighborhoods, schools, and movie houses and one small Catholic college.[10] Rosenzweig focused on *where* the working class spent its leisure hours; at saloons, play and picnic grounds, fraternal lodges, nickelodeons and amusement parks. But he does not address the concept of playing at work.

By the 1850s the ten-hour day was common and in 1878 the Knights of Labor included the demand for an eight-hour day in its first constitution. The average work week in 1850 was nearly 70 hours. Historian David Nasaw has chronicled the rise of vaudeville, amusement parks, baseball games and amusement parks in the late 19th century and concludes that, for this era, "the fear of idle time as the devils workshop gave way to a reverence for play, promoted alike by middle-class reformers and working-class organizers."[11]

Workers used their increased leisure time in a wide variety of ways. The reduction in work time provided the opportunity for worker competitions. Susan Hirsch examined the free time of factory workers in the antebellum period and found that they tended to join leisure groups, most notably volunteer fire companies.[12] An earlier chapter has described just how prevalent and desired membership in local fire companies was in the immediate antebellum and postbellum periods, an era when volunteer firemen displayed their skills in numerous worker competitions. At the beginning of the 20th century, G.E. Bevans, in his Columbia University doctoral dissertation, confirmed that a small but significant amount of the spare time of tradesmen was used for athletic games.[13]

Yet the leisure time theory is unconvincing and a bit simplistic. Just because workers may have had additional time on their hands does not explain why worker competitions proliferated. We must look further.

Nineteenth-century industrialization also helps explain the emergence of worker-competitions. Factory and non-factory workers alike became increasingly time-conscious as mechanization dictated a day organized by the clock. Time not only separated work and leisure but became a way to judge the completion of tasks. Both David Brody and Gary Cross tell us that the more routine the job and the less vital craftsmanship became, the more essential time was. Jobs and most worker-competitions featured the element of time. For example, hand drilling had to be completed within 15 minutes; husking within 80 minutes; and laying rails within a 12-hour day.[14]

Many nineteenth century jobs, whether out-of-doors or on shop floors, whether skilled or not, were physically demanding, dull and routine. In this period of industrialization, efficiency-minded managers split up jobs into more productive but less complex tasks. Factory work was relentless and monotonous. One historian has observed, "There were often built within these jobs many of those things like camaraderie, competition, and entertainment that made their tasks pleasurable."[15]

We should not find it at all unusual that everyday workers in menial jobs find clever and creative ways to avoid becoming dehumanized. Barbara Garson maintains that when work is stripped of its inherent meaning and reduced to trivial, repetitive tasks, this necessarily eliminates some of the worker's humanity. Many of us want to work. Work is part of our nature. But we are not relentless industrial robots. One avenue to minimize the mindlessness of an inexorable task is to make a game out of work.[16] Again, the example of the typesetting swifts is insightful. Instead of rebelling against a piece rate system, long hours, and technological improvements that might hasten an occupational demise, the American typesetters of the 1870s and 1880s decided to celebrate their speed by displaying it in contests. Walter Rumble tells us that English and French compositors, similarly challenged, either boycotted or picketed. In the United States the typesetters raced.[17]

1860 presidential campaign poster for the Republican Party candidate, Abraham Lincoln, who relied on his reputation as a rail splitter, a practical occupation that became a work-sport. The intention was to appeal to the working class (www.retrocampaigns.com, accessed Sept.15, 2011).

It is possible that some of the explanation for worker-competitions is tied to masculinity, since most of our central characters were male. A large body of scholarly study concerns itself with the development and perception of masculinities, with years covering the late 19th and early 20th centuries seen by many historians as a watershed era, particularly in the history of men in the United States. By the end of the 19th century the typical American male was no longer a tough frontiersman or even a hardworking farmer; many were immigrants and lived in cities while working industrial jobs. Sixty percent of men were farmers in 1860; by 1920, only 33 percent were. In the same period men in manufacturing and construction—city jobs—rose from18 percent to 31 percent. The creation of a working-class man who was not bound to agriculture led to greater pursuit of sporting activity, both in leisure and in profession. This applied both to the working class as well as to the middle class. The upper class continued to be spectators.

In addition, craftsmen were threatened by a rapidly changing economy, including the creation of national markets and the evolution of mass production and distribution. Many men asserted a sense of personal autonomy, yet they were not independent when it came to their jobs.

Because in some occupations industrialization had de-emphasized physical strength, a myth about the "decadence" of masculinity developed. The responses were many and varied: a rise in physical training or physical culture which had been discouraged for generations; the creation of the Boy Scouts; the growth of taverns and barbershops as male-only domains; an enthusiasm for health and sports, especially college athletics; and, in due course, the development of worker-competitions.[18]

John Higham, in his influential 1970 essay, identified a cult of masculinity at the end of the 19th century and argued that beginning in the 1890s, America had an urge to be young, masculine and adventurous. It was a rejoinder against "the sheer dullness of urban industrial culture." Later, social historians Elizabeth Pleck and Joseph Pleck named the years 1861 to 1919 as the period of the "strenuous life" in America, one of four major periods of men's history in the United States. The others, according to Pleck and Pleck, were the years of "agrarian patriarchy" (1630–1820), the "commercial age" (1820–1860), and an era of "companionate providing" (1920–1965). The definition of periods of history is always somewhat arbitrary, but these authors argued that certain economic and political forces set apart the late nineteenth and early 20th centuries as especially important in the development of perception of masculinities. Many of those forces have been cited repeatedly by scholars and historians as key factors that contributed to beliefs, portrayals, actions and reactions that shaped what it meant to be a man in America.[19] This was not just reflected by the tabloids like the *National Police Gazette*, or by an interest in hiking or bodybuilding. A major result was the demonstration of job skills—work-sports contests.

In the 1860s, the middle class had seen the ideal male body as lean and wiry. By the 1890s, however, an ideal male body required physical bulk and well-defined muscles. The new fascination with muscularity allowed for powerful and brawny work-sports heroes such as Paul Bunyan and John Henry.

As the 19th century developed, and men tried to fulfill themselves through achievements in their professions and businesses, their competitive passions naturally grew. Rivalry, ambition, and aggression drove the new system of individual interest. Combativeness, toughness and self-made manhood were admired. In the market economy it was one's work that became key to identity. Work-sports competitions were a sphere in which workers could prove themselves. Some of them may seem silly today but these events helped address the working-class need for an escape from anonymity. It was possible for many to be occupational "champions." The work-sports competition tested men's skill or experience or endurance.

A final explanation for the emergence of work-sports is psychological. Most modern scholars recognize a link between work and leisure and most assume that the former has an effect on the latter. Steven Gelber argues that leisure either compensates people (compensatory hypothesis) for some shortcoming in their work experience, or models (congruent/spillover hypothesis) their work situation. Both arguments assume the job will determine leisure behavior, the question being whether the determinant is negative (compensatory) or positive (congruent/spillover).[20]

The lion's share of modern social science data supports the congruent or spillover theory. Gelber claims that "it is fairly obvious that people who have developed manual, mental, or social dexterity on the job will often seek pastimes that showcase these same abilities."[21] This theory is useful in explaining why someone who hand drilled rocks for 12 hours daily and all week long would give up his weekend to engage in a rock drilling contest. The compensatory hypothesis cannot explain this. The congruence theory does since it is based on the assumption that people do not reject their experience in the world of work. In other words, their choice of leisure activity reflects the environment of the workplace. A generation ago Mihaly Csikszentmihalyi, then head of the Psychology Department at the University of Chicago and noteworthy for his notion of flow as well as for his infamously difficult name, reminded us, "The more a job inherently resembles a game — with variety, appropriate and flexible challenges, clear goals and immediate feedback — the more enjoyable it will be regardless of the worker's level of development."[22]

For example, it is useful to recall that many farm games began as work sharings, then turned competitive as work was turned into play. Ted Ownby has explained why rural Southern men, aside from reasons of gambling and drinking, fashioned a recreational culture in the 19th century.[23] Workers, for example, took the same delight in completing, say, a husking chore in a certain amount of time or laying bricks smartly as they would in a husking or brick laying contest. For many nineteenth and early 20th century American laborers, work became a fulfilling activity, a means of self-creation.[24]

In summary, considering the nature of work within the framework of the congruence theory, an emerging industrial era and additional leisure time set the table for work-sports. Socially independent and vigorously competitive people did the rest.

Are Worker Athletes Really Athletes?

When discussing my research I occasionally get a response that goes something like this, "Well, there is no denying the work-sports experience but these guys were not real athletes, not like a Joe DiMaggio, or a Bruce Jenner or an Albert Pujols." And thus, the thought continues, work-sports are not true sports. Perhaps in the back of their minds is the image of an overweight muster fireman clomping down the street in unfastened boots attempting to nozzle a hose to a hydrant.[25] Can we really call him an athlete?

There is a pervasive notion that real athletes wouldn't get involved in worker competitions and, conversely, that worker-athletes couldn't handle real sports. This seems to be a common impression when I describe the work-sports experience. Nothing is further from the truth, for, in fact, many of the outstanding real athletes of established sports and the work-sports jocks have been the very same people. A few examples, in no particular order, should suffice.

In southern Ontario, summer firemen's musters are as common as they are in the New England states. Participants demonstrate skills by leaping into firemen's garb, racing hoses down the street, and putting out mock fires, all under the alert eye of the stopwatch. A few of the Ontario fireman realize that they are competing against Dave Steen, one of the world's great all-around athletes. It was the same Steen, a former University of California student, who won the bronze medal at the 1988 Seoul Olympic Games in the toughest sporting event on the books, the decathlon. For a decade before his retirement to the life of a professional fireman, Steen was acknowledged as one of the world's most elite athletes while medaling in the world's most important track meets. This fireman and modern work-sports jock is a better athlete than 99.9 percent of all of history's athletes.

In the 1990s Stacy Dragila, a student at Idaho State University, spent most of her free time training for rodeo events. At 5–7, 140 pounds, she became proficient at goat tying, breakaway roping and team roping and won a few prizes and accolades along the way. Yet it was not fulfilling enough and she opted to train for the pole vault, a track and field event that was, at the time, beginning to open to women. Previously the conventional wisdom was that females did not have the upper body strength or mental toughness to excel at the pole vault.

But in the early 1990s, as a move toward gender equity, the vault was made part of both the NCAA and USA championship meet agenda and became an overnight sensation, known in some circles as "Chicks with Sticks." Not only *could* Dragila and *did* Dragila out-vault 98 percent of all men, but when she became the first American female to vault 15 feet, then set seven world records and win three IAAF world championships and capture the event's first Olympic gold medal in Sydney in 2000, no one contended that she was not a real athlete. It was the same Stacy Dragila who roped in rodeos. Here was a work-sports star who could outperform all women and 98 percent of all men in an established sport.

Tris Speaker may have been the greatest center fielder in the history of major league baseball. Fans of Joe DiMaggio, Mickey Mantle and Willie Mays may disagree but Speaker out-hit them all. His playing career, in baseball's dead-ball era, spanned 22 seasons and his .345 lifetime batting average is still the fourth best ever. His record of 792 career doubles has never been approached. Yet Speaker was better known for his exploits in centerfield. He played so shallow that he is credited with 6 unassisted double plays. His playing style revolutionized the game before the lively ball era for he was literally a fifth infielder. He was, with Babe Ruth, Ty Cobb and Cy Young, in the first class (1937) elected to baseball's Hall of Fame.

Speaker is the subject of two biographies,[26] but he is less well known as a rodeo cowboy. Ballplayers normally used the winter months for second-income jobs. Speaker's highest pre–World War I salary was $18,000. He had tried rodeo as a teenager before turning to baseball and would return home to Hubbard, Texas, in the off season to compete in events like the Fort Worth Stock Show rodeo. As a roper, he has been referred to as a rodeo performer of "some distinction."[27] In December 1922, at age 34, he came within 3 seconds of the world record for roping and tying a calf at the Hillsboro, Texas, rodeo.[28] Few athletes ever jumped back and forth from a work-sport to an established sport with the success of Tris Speaker.

The 19th century saw the same versatility. Perhaps the greatest athlete of the 19th century was Scottish highlander Donald Dinnie (1837–1916), who toured America beginning in 1870 on three occasions. Not only did he take on all comers in Caledonian Games heavy events as well as wrestling and weightlifting, but he was also known to offer a work-sports challenge.[29] Dinnie, at 6–1, 220, was the physical specimen of the age. He was also a trained stonemason. One historian reminds us that Dinnie once issued a challenge to any mason in the world to compete against him in dressing and building with granite.[30] Dinnie's home of Aberdeen, Scotland, was known for its granite. A mercenary worker/athlete, he would occasionally put on "building demonstrations" with other strong men.

Bob Way was a champion professional jumpist (long, triple and high jumper) in the middle of the 19th century. He took on and responded to jumping challenges. He was also a skilled craftsman who made shingles, an important 19th century building product. In 1869 the *Clipper* reported that Way "lathed, saved, jointed and sorted into three qualities, 23,000 shingles in 12 hours at Westmore's Mill in Corydon, Ohio."[31] That works out to fashioning nearly 32 shingles every minute.

John Goldie, one of the nation's best athletes of the 19th century, was born in Scotland, worked the circus, and became a volunteer fireman with the Mutual Hose Company in New York City before the Civil War.[32] Successful at fireman's musters (no small thanks to Goldie), the Mutuals embraced a new game, base-ball and formed a club for the 1858 season. The Mutuals played their home games at Elysian Fields in Hoboken, N.J. with the New York Knickerbockers, before moving to the Union Grounds in Brooklyn immediately after the war. One of their stars was Goldie, a rangy, slugging first baseman. By 1861 the Mutuals were champions of all baseball. Goldie had uncommon success as a base-ballist, and by 1869, was the star for the Union Club of Morrisania, N.Y., acknowledged as the sport's top team. In 1869 the Unions relinquished the title to the newly professional Cincinnati Red Stockings, 13–12, in an early September game in which Goldie had four hits.

Yet base-ball and musters were not the end-all of Goldie's athletic career. The versatile Scot became, from 1858 through 1867, the nation's most noteworthy track and field performer. Before the advent of the amateur era, track and field was a professional sport, conducted mostly at regional Scottish Games and Goldie, as a "jumpist" and "heavy," was the sport's biggest star. In 1859, for example, he entered 12 of the 13 running, jumping and throwing events at the New York Caledonian Club annual, the nation's biggest and most important meet. He won five and placed in the top three in five more.[33]

When the New York Athletic Club conducted the first amateur track and field meet (frequently misreported as simply the nation's initial track meet) in 1867, they invited the New York Caledonian Club as opponents. Goldie and his club won the majority of the events. Goldie's younger brother, George, became better known as America's champion all-round athlete, and subsequently became a coach at Princeton College and the New York Athletic Club. But, for a decade, as in Canada a century later, the nation's best athlete, hands down, was a fireman.

I considered additional examples like Babe Didrickson Zaharias, declared by many as the greatest female athlete of the 20th century for her Olympic exploits and golfing prowess. Yet the reports that she was a champion typist before turning to track and field seem to have been apocryphal. But the point has been made. There is no way to judge and compare athletes in different sports. But many of the fine work-sports athletes had a foot in both camps. And no one can claim that individuals like Steen, Dragila, Speaker, Dinnie, Way and Goldie were not real athletes.

Productivity

There is the issue of whether worker productivity was enhanced by the use of work-sports. Frankly it is extremely difficult to gauge the economic impact of worker-competitions on 19th century labor productivity.[34] Work-sports is like the Industrial Recreation (IR) movement which was legitimized during World War II. The concept is well understood both at the national and firm levels. Hundreds of plants and factories provided recreational programs, facilities and equipment to wartime workers, emphasizing the importance of teamwork for the war effort.[35] A. Castle made repeated claims in 1950 that IR directly contributed to increased levels of productivity then and during the Korean War.[36] Although the inferences appear reasonable, no measurable evidence supports this contention.

It seems sound to treat worker-competitions in the same vein and as a subset of education and training. Noted economic historian Edward Denison argued that for much of the 20th century, education and training accounted for about 12 percent of U.S. growth.[37] What data we do have for 19th century industries in which work-sports were frequent, is notable. Mining, for example, experienced a 29.2 percent increase in productivity between 1880 and 1900, according to the U.S. Census Bureau.[38] Another well-known study by Professor Carroll Pursell of Case-Western University claims the productivity improvements in mining approached 50 percent in the same period.[39] Productivity increases in the building of railroads was even more impressive, improving 29.4 percent in just ten years, 1889 to 1899. In agriculture, as mentioned earlier, the gains were equally significant. For example we find that in 1800 it took 373 man-hours to produce 100 bushels of wheat. By 1840 that figure was reduced to 233 man-hours, and by 1900 it took but 108 man-hours. The data on corn are equally impressive. The significant savings in time could be devoted to more wheat or other tasks.[40]

Productivity is generally measured as a ratio of output to input, the latter measured either by time, unit labor costs, or energy.[41] The previous worker-competition samples demonstrate a number of ways in which worker competitions played a small part in these impressive productivity gains. First, work-sports demonstrated to participants and non-participants alike both the quality and quantity of work that could be accomplished. A counter-quality example may have been the building of the Transcontinental Railroad, which required higher-than-normal maintenance. We are reminded that when Henry A. Wallace formalized national corn husking, he felt they "would make an excellent sport for farm families." In addition, he predicted that "onlooking farmers could learn how to become better huskers themselves."[42]

Typesetting swifts provide us with all the evidence necessary on the impact of worker competitions on productivity. Throughout 19th century, production quotas were a recurrent issue that dominated the agenda of the International Typographical Union (ITU). By the mid 1880s typesetting swifts had raised the productivity standard to such a high level that "on May 9, 1886, the Board of Delegates of New York's local [ITU] No. 6, officially condemned typeracing," fearing management would raise production quotas.[43]

Every 3rd year a collegiate woodman's games are held on the historic Green at Dartmouth College, Hanover, New Hampshire. Sponsored by the Dartmouth College Outing Club and manufacturer STIHL, this bucolic event attracts hundreds of student athletes who make up lumberJack/Jill teams from several dozen eastern college and universities. The event has both a purity and innocence about it for it simply salutes a century old notion that workers are eager to display an occupational skill (courtesy of Dartmouth College Library).

Second, worker competitions facilitated the refinement of equipment. Such labor-saving devices explain the bulk of the productivity gains. For example, champion drillers pioneered new hammers and steel drills, resulting in an enhancement of industry-wide drilling performances.[44] Third, worker competitions verified the importance of planning and preparation as a means of increasing labor productivity. The Central Pacific's "Ten Mile Day" in 1869 demonstrated that substantial gains in laying rail could be produced when every worker movement was analyzed and supplies were within easy reach. The "Ten Mile Day" was an early example of time and motion studies.

In summary, much of the productivity improvement in typesetting, farming, mining and laying rails is explained by standard factors: technological advances, more capital and economies of scale. A minor part is explained by worker competitions. Sociologist Amitai Etzioni maintains that productivity is enhanced when people derive psychological, social and cultural rewards from work.[45] Labor historians normally interested in 19th century labor institutions, could do well to focus on laborer or occupational activity.

Conclusion

No written history of 19th century American labor is complete without an account of the worker-competition movement. These contests provided laborers with a challenge and diversion from routine work, an efficiency check, team building, and a boost to morale. They may have been beneficial to worker productivity, although empirical data supporting these benefits are lacking.

Worker-competitions were initially local or regional events which flourished on the farm or frontier, typically in an all-male environment like cattle drives and mining or lumber camps. This overlooked labor practice offers a new understanding of 19th century work. At the time, work-sports were accepted as genuine sporting events.

In pre–Civil War Pittsburgh, for example, silver cups, medals and money were bestowed on champions of annual mowing, reaping and plowing contests.[46] The new sporting journals like the *American Farmer*, the *Turf Register*, the *Spirit of the Times* and the *New York Clipper* all gave attention to worker-competitions in their publications. Additional investigations need to go beyond descriptive accounts to provide an understanding of the bond between work and play.

Today more than one and one-half million workers compete annually in work-sports. Some job-related sports have attained entertainment status, while technical educational institutions, recognizing the impact on productivity, have made the contests a standard part of the curriculum.

15. Why Work-Sports?

One of the fallacies of accepted U.S. sporting history is that most American sports came from our British relatives. In the case of worker competitions, of which there were many, nothing is further than the truth.[47] Four decades ago a seminal article on the origin of American sports by a leading authority simply disregarded work-sports, so that the entire category became a superfluous academic cast-off.[48]

Work-sports matured in a different environment. In America, worker-competitions enhanced everything the economic system promoted: efficiency, competition, goals, and success. They captured the spirit of the American experience and contributed to the grand scheme in a more productive or utilitarian sense.[49] This may explain why Americans, with exception of the Southern oligarchy, did not engage overwhelmingly in the deliberately stylized games of the British. Rather they invented their own.

An important dream of most men is to be seen as someone who knows his business.

Talent, craftsmanship, and competence are what we admire in others. Michael Dirda reminds us that "a man deeply defines himself, consciously or not, by the work that he does and how well he does it. Work is his validation."[50] To Americans there was something natural about making a game of work. And along the way, worker athletes helped build a nation. That nineteenth and early 20th century work-sports were genuine should be self-evident. Without them, life on the farm, in the new factory or office, in the mine or in the lumber camp would have passed through a never-ending pattern of habit and work. Life was more enjoyable for their existence.

Nineteenth century work-sports in America were as undeniable as they were inevitable. This book provides only of glimpse of the work-sports phenomenon and the rationale for the interplay of work, leisure and economics. So little academic work has been done on the subject that most of the labor on 19th century worker-competitions lies ahead in the twenty-first century.

Appendices

1—U.S. Workers in Common Work-Sports Occupations, 1900

In thousands of people, 14 years old and over[1]

Occupation	Number
Bartenders	89
Blacksmiths	220
Brick masons	154[2]
Carpenters	596
Farmers	10,888
Firemen	15
Lumberjacks	210
Meat cutters	33
Miners	660
Other construction trade[3]	204
Railroad laborers	107
Sawyers	18
Typographers	134
Total	13,328
Total Active Work Force	29,030
% of work force in occupations in which worker-competitions are common	45.9%

Adapted from census data, reported in series 233–682, "Detailed Occupations of Economically Active Population: 1900 to 1970," U.S. Census Bureau, *Historical Statistics of the Unites States: Colonial Times to 1970* (Washington, D.C.: U.S. Department of Commerces 1975), 140–145, and M.A. Conk, *The United States Census and Labor Force Change: A History of Occupation Statistics* (Ann Arbor: UMI Research Press, 1980). "Brick masons" includes an estimated 6,000 apprentices. "Other construction trade" includes blacksmiths, millers, paperhangers, plasterers, roofers, stonecutters, tinsmiths, and non-manufacturing construction.

2 — Sample Muster News Account

The following *New York Clipper* (October 17, 1857) coverage of an 1857 muster in Hartford, Connecticut, with nearly three dozen teams and over 2,000 firemen/athletes is typical.

Exciting Contest With Fire Engines
Hartford, Sept. 24

A very interesting and exciting trial of fire engines took place in Hartford, Conn. On the 21st of September, of which the following is a report:

The playing ground was admirably arranged and planned to give general satisfaction. Two large cisterns or tanks were sunk into the ground, which were filled with water from the hydrants, and kept supplied. Close by was the Engineer's stand. The hose from each engine was run in a straight line to the east 400 feet, to the framework where the pipe holders were to stand. The first stake marks 100 feet, the second 140 feet, and from that up to 210 feet, the feet and inches were marked on a long board platform or track, 5 feet wide.

Each company played through 400 feet hose, and were allowed 15 minutes from the time of arriving at the reservoir for the trial. The following is the order in which they played, beginning with No. 1.

No.		Ft. In.
1.	Cataract Number 6, Poughkeepsie, N.Y., Capt. Johnson, 75 Men, Button Tub, 9 inch cylinder, 8 inch stroke	160 00
2.	Pacific No. 1, Chicopee, Capt. Drake, 55 men, Button tub	186 09
3.	Washington No. 1, Williamsburg, N.Y., Capt. Gill, 34 men, Smith tub	153 00
4.	Protector No. 2, New London, Capt. Dodge, Van Ness tub	100 00
5.	Warren No. 4, Charlestown, Capt. Prescott, 50 men, Hunneman engine, 6 inch cylinder, 13 inch stroke	137 05
6.	Phoenix No. 6, New Haven, Capt. Tuttle, 70 men, Hunneman engine	138 06
7.	Waterbury No. 2, Waterbury, Capt. Wallace, Van Ness machine	138 00
8.	Protector No. 22, New York, Capt. Entwhistle, 50 men, Crane engine, 8 inch cylinder, 7 to 9 inch stroke	137 00
9.	Rough and ready No. 5, North Providence, Capt. Leonard, 40 men, Button machine	146 00
10.	Phoenix No. 12, Brooklyn, N.Y., Capt. Coggins, 56 men Hunneman machine	146 04
11.	Columbia No. 5, new Bedford, Mass, Capt. Hyde, 50 men, Button machine. 1-0 inch cylinder, 7½ inch stroke	133 00
12.	Fire King No. 2, Rockville, Capt. Crosby, 60 men, Smith machine	158 00
13.	Deluge No. 2, Northampton, Mass, capt _____, 50 men, Jeffer's machine, 9 inch cylinder, 5¼ to 9½ inch stroke	148 00
14.	Washington No. 2, Medford, Capt. Mitchell, 50 men, Hunneman machine	146 00
15.	Quinnepac, Fair Haven, Capt. Bradley, 50 men, Van Ness machine	142 00

Appendix 3 195

No.		*Ft . In.*
16.	Rippowam No. 1, Stamford, Capt. Meeker, 45 men, Button engine, 10 inch cylinder, 8 inch stroke	146 00
17.	Pantoosic No. 2, Pittsfield, Capt. Shepardson, 40 men, Waterman engine	142 00
18.	Washington No. 2, New Haven, Capt. Blakcalce, 82 men, Otzelman & Stockard engine	126 00
19.	Phoenix No. 1, Waterbury, Capt. Laird, 50 men, Van Ness machine, 7¾ inch cylinder, 9 inch stroke	147 03
20.	Niagra No. 8, Worcester, Capt. Hudson, 40 men, Hunneman machine	133 08
21.	Bristol No. 1, Bristol, Conn. Capt. Fleming, 60 men, Ronerts machine, 8 inch cylinder, 7 inch stroke	138 00
22.	Empire No. 9, Fair Haven, Capt. Holt, 69 men, Van Ness piano machine , 9 inch cylinder, 8½ stroke	146 00
23.	Neptune No. 6, New Haven, Capt. Madden, 30 men, Torboss machine	175 02

The 4th and 5th prizes were of equal value, and the winners decided by lot. After the trials the judges awarded the prizes to the following companies:

1st Prize, to Pacific No. 1, Chicopee, Mass, 186 feet, 9 inches
2nd ", to Mayflower No. 4, North Bridgewater, Mass, 180 feet, 4 inches
3rd ", to Neptune No. 6, New Haven, Conn, 175 feet, 2 inches
4th ", to Gaspen, No. 9, Providence, R.I., 166 feet
5th ", to Collinsville No. 1, Collinsville, CT, 165 feet
6th ", to Holyoke No. 1, Holyoke, Mass., 161 feet
7th ", to Barnicoat No. 11, Boston, Mass, 160 feet, 4 inches
8th ", to Cataract No. 6, Poughkeepsie, N.Y. 160 feet.

3 — Numbers of U.S. Work-Sports Athletes, 2010

Top Spectator Level	N
Rodeo	
Professional	10,000
Collegiate and other	4,000
Lumberjacks	7,000
Firefighters	9,000
Mid-Level	
approximately 90 occupational sports	700,000
Educational Level	
e.g., SkillsUSA	315,000
Trainee/Preparation Level	
e.g. McDonald's	400,000
Total	1,445,000

Adapted from information provided by Professional Rodeo Cowboy

Association, U.S. Lumberjack Association, National Fire Academy and Skills USA. A work-sports athlete is defined as someone who has competed in at least one local, regional or national worker-competition, in 2010. "Collegiate and other" includes numbers of the 96 colleges and universities who sponsor the sport, cowgirls in Women's Association, and prison participants. "Lumberjacking" also include axmen and birlers.

4 — U.S. Occupational Sports, 2010

National Championships

Bartenders (1)
Bike Couriers (2)
Broom Sweeping (3)
Cashiers (4)
Cemetery Workers (5)
Chambermaids (6)
Corn Husking (7)
Farriers (8)
Fast Food Crews (9)
Fence Painting (10)
Fireman's Combat (11)
Gift Wrapping (12)
Life-Guarding (13)
Lumberjacking (14)
   Ax Throwing
   Single Bucking
   Double Bucking
   Standing Bloc Chop
   Speed Stock Saw
   Springboard Chop
   Log Rolling (Birling)
   Tree Climbing
   Tree Topping
   Power Sawing
   All-Around
Masonry (15)
Mine Safety & Rescue (16)
Moving & Storage (17)
Naval Pentathlon (18)
Oyster Shucking (19)
Plowing (20)
Police Games (21)
Rodeo (22)
   Riding
   Bareback

Local/Regional Contests Only

Barb Wire Splicing (30)
Blacksmithing (31)
Canning (32)
Crab Picking (33)
Crab Trap Pulling (34)
Firemen's Musters (35)
Gold Panning (Mucking) (36)
Grape Stomping (37)
Hand Drilling (38)
Hay Loading (39)
Iron Column Climbing (40)
Lawn Mower Racing (41)
Milking (42)
Milling (43)
Nail Driving (44)
Picking/Harvesting
   Berry (45)
   Cotton (46)
   Peanut (47)
   Potato (48)
Pruning (49)
   Fruit Trees
   Grapevines
Rail Splitting (50)
Raking, Cranberry (51)
Search and Rescue (52)
Taxidermy (53)
Threshing (54)
Tomahawk Throwing (55)
Town Crier (56)
Whitewashing (57)

SkillsUSA (58)

Air Cooled Gasoline Engine Technology
Automotive Service
Aviation Maintenance
Building Maintenance
Cabinetmaking
Carpentry
Collision Repair
Diesel Equipment Repair
HVACR (Heating, Ventilation, Air Conditioning, Refrigeration)
Industrial Maintenance
Industrial Motor Control
Major Appliance Technology
Marine Service
Masonry
Motorcycle Service
Precision Maintenance
Residential Plumbing
Residential Wiring
Sheet Metal
Welding

Teams
Team Build

FFA and 4-H (59)
Ag Mechanics
Forestry Contests
Logging
Motors
Tractor Driving
Welding
Wiring
Woodworking

National Championships

(Rodeo, cont.)
  Saddle Bronc
  Bull
  Roping
  Calf
  Steer
  Goat Tying
  Team
  Steer Wrestling
  Barrel Wrestling
  All-Around
Sheep Shearing (23)
  Sheep-to-Shawl
Shoveling, World Contest (24)
Telephone Linemen (25)
Truck Backing/Parking (26)
Typing (27)
Waiters, Waitresses (28)
Welding, Cutting (29)

SkillsUSA
Apprentice (60)
  Machining
  Masonry
  Tooling

Information on occupational competitions provided by the following organizations: (1) Fastest Bartenders Association (FBA); (2) Cycle Messenger World Champs (CMWC); (3) National Broom Sweeping Contest, Ancola, IL; (4) Food 4 Less, Inc.; (5) National Cemetery Games, Denver, CO, *Only a Game,* National Public Radio; (6) Super 8 Motels National Bed-making Contest, Bloomington, MN; (7) National Cornhusking Championships, Iowa State Fair, Des Moines, IA; (8) American Farriers Association (AFA); (9) McDonald's, Inc.; (10) Tom Sawyer Fence Painting Contest, Hannibal, MO; (11) On Target Challenge, Inc., Burtonsville, MD; (12) Wrap-Off, Minnesota Mining & Manufacturing Co., St. Paul, MN; (13) U.S. Life Guard Association (USLA) National Championships, San Diego, CA; (14) U.S. Lumberjack Association, U.S. Axemen Association, and American Birling Association; (15) Mason Contractors Association of America (MCAA); (16) West Virginia Office of Miners, Health, Safety and Training, and Northern Mine Rescue Contest, Bruceton, CO; (17) American Moving & Storage Association (AMSA); (18) Consell International du Sports Militarie (CISM), Belgium; (19) National Oyster Shucking Championships, St. Mary's County, Leonardtown, MD; (20) International Plowing Match and Farm Machinery Show, Guelph, Ontario; (21) World Police and Fire Games; (22) Pro Rodeo Cowboy Association (PRCA), Work Ranch Cowboy Association (WRCA), and National Intercollegiate Rodeo Association (NIRA); (23) National Sheep Shearing Contest, Denver Western National Livestock Show, Denver, CO;

(24) Shovel Museum, Stonehill College, North Easton, MA; (25) The Lineman's Rodeo, Kansas City, MO; (26) Mack Truck, Inc., Hagerstown, MD; (27) Underwood, Inc., (28) e.g., Bastille Day Celebration, Washington, D.C.; (29) National Welding and Cutting Manufacturers; (30) Kansas Barbed Wire Museum, LaCrosse, KS; (31) Artist Blacksmith Association of North America (ABANA) magazines—*The Anvil Ring* and *Hammer Blow*; (32) National Pickle Festival, Berrien Springs, MI; (33) & (34) National Hard Crab Derby and Fair, Crisfield, MD; (35) National Fire Academy (NFA), Emmitsburg, MD; (36) U.S. National Gold Panning Championships, Columa, CA; (37) e.g., Brotherhood Winery, Washingtonville, NY; (38) International Intercollegiate Mining Competition, University of Nevada, Reno, NV; (39) e.g., Antelope Valley Fair and Alfalfa Festival, Lancaster, CA; (40) Iron Workers Union; (41) National Lawn Mower Races, Indianapolis, IN; (42) All American Dairy Show, Harrisburg, PA; (43) Montana State University, Bozeman, MT; (44) Old Miners Association, Bear Lake, CA; (45) The Blackberry Bulletin, NJ Agricultural Experiment Station, Mays Landing, NJ; (46) Cotton Picking Contest, Ridgeville, AL; (47) National Peanut Festival, AL; (48) Idaho State Fair; (49) California State University–Fresno FFA Field Day, Fresno, CA; (50) Abraham Lincoln National Rail Splitting Contest, Logan County, IL; (51) State Historical Society of Wisconsin, Contest-Berlin, WI; (52) Annual National Search and Rescue Competition (for Navy and Coast Guard Air Crewman), San Diego, CA; (53) Annual Eastern Sports Boat, Camping, Travel & Outdoor Show, Harrisburg, PA; (54) Annual Threshing Contest, McLean, VA; (55) e.g., Burnt Hole Mountain man Rendezvous, West Yellowstone, MT; (56) The American Guild of Town Criers; (57) Mark Twain Days, Hannibal, MO; (58) SkillsUSA–VICA, Leesburg, VA; (59) Future Farmers of America (FFA) and National 4-H Clubs; (60) National Tooling and Machining Association (NTMA).

5 — *Wall Street Journal* Front Page Work-Sports Stories, 1995–2005

April 18, 1996	"Fantasy Stylists Go Toe to Toe: and its Hair-Raising," by Angelo Henderson, pp A–1, A–8.
May 18, 1998	"Killer Competitions, or How Real Snipers Spend Their Weekend," by James Sterba, pp. A–1, 8.
Nov. 9, 1998	"The Blade Brothers Vie to Make the Cut in a Whack Attack," by Neal Templin, pp.A1, 15.
April 20, 1999	"Window Washing is a Dirty Business on the Pro Circuit," by Charles Fleming, pp. A–1, 11.
July 20, 1999	"Moving Ornery Ewes Is Not a Real Trial for Lots of Yanks," by Geraldine Brooks, pp. A1, 8.
Nov. ?, 1999	"How a Good Bull Can Buck the Trend to the Meat Market," by Robert Tomshow, pp. A–1, 10.

Appendix 5

March 9, 2001	"Americans Put On Oven Mitts to Duke it out in the Kitchen," by Puinwing Tam, pp A–1, 8
May 9, 2001	"Stiff Competition, Taxidermists Head for the Wild Side," by James Sterba, pp A–1, 12
July 31, 2002	"Malibu Left Turn Into the Grass: Get Off the Runway Now," by Scott McCartnen, pp. A–1, 6
March 7, 2003	"Waiting for War, Marines in Kuwait are Fighting for Real," by Michael W. Phillips, pp.A–1, 8.
May ?, 2003	"As Supermarkets Go Bag-Your-Own, A Throwback Excels," by Melanie Trottman, pp. A–1, 6.
Dec. 2, 2003	"Ready, Aim, Bake, Army Field Cooks Shoot for Honors," by Fasih Ahmed, pp. A–1, 12
May 25, 2004	"Bucking Tradition, Bull Riding Fans Cheers for the Beasts," by Ellen Byron, pp. A–1, 8
Nov. 17, 2004	"In This Profession Everyone Moves Up, Some Fall," by Almar Latour, p. A–1, 11
Feb. 28, 2005	"Stitches in Time: Knitting Whizzes Go for Speed Records," by Scott Miller, pp. A–1, 11.
July 21, 2005	"At 6, Koby Blunt is Retiring at the Top in Muttin Bustin," by Michael. M. Phillips, pp. A–1, 7.
Aug. 15, 2005	"Smelling Opportunity, Farming Towns Bet on Cow-Pie Throws," by Timothy Martin, pp. A–1, 6.
Aug. 25, 2005	"Aiming For the Top, Expert Tree Climbers Face Off in the Forest," by Susan Warren, pp. A–1, 5.
Oct. 29–30, 2005	"The Great Pumpkin Backyard Botanists Shoot for the 1 Ton Mark," by Susan Warren, p. A–1, 9.

Chapter Notes

Introduction

1. See Appendix 1. Adapted from census data, reported in series 233–682, "Detailed Occupations of Economically Active Population: 1900 to 1970," U.S. Census Bureau, *Historical Statistics of the United Startes: Colonial Times to 1970* (Washington, D.C.: U.S. Department of Commerce, 1975), pp. 140–145.
2. Bero Rigauer, *Sport and Work*, trans. A. Guttman (New York: Columbia University Press, 1971), p. 78.
3. John F. Skinner, "The Late Cattle Show," *American Farmer*, November 7, 1828, Vol. 10, p. 272. John F. Skinner, Baltimore, founded the *American Farmer* (1819) and the *American Turf Register and Sporting Magazine* (1829). Both were published weekly. The former included a sports column called "Sporting Olio." The latter was not devoted to the turf alone. It also featured material on outdoor sports, pedestrianism and, occasionally, worker-competitions. The *Spirit of the Times*, founded in 1831 in New York, is said to have been the first all-around sporting journal in the United States. From 1831 to 1861 it focused on horse racing but also published frequent accounts (sometimes detailed, sometimes not) of worker-competitions. The *New York Clipper*, founded in 1853 by Frank Queen, was a weekly. But it also reported on reaping, plowing, mowing, tinkering, cradling, pole climbing contests and more.
4. See, for example, Francis G. Couvares, *The Remaking of Pittsburgh: Class and Culture in an Industrializing City, 1877–1919* (Albany: State University of New York Press, 1984); J.T. Cumbler, *Working Class Community in Industrial America: Work, Leisure and the Struggle of Two Industrial Cities, 1888–1930* (Westport, CT: Greenwood Press, 1979); Elliot Gorn and Warren Goldstein, *The Manly Art: Bare Knuckle Prizefighting in America* (Ithaca: Cornell University Press, 1986); Katherine H. Harvey, *The Best Dressed Miners: Life and Labor in the Maryland Coal Region, 1835–1910* (Ithaca: Cornell University Press, 1969); Daniel Nelson, *Managers and Workers: Origins of the Twentieth Century Factory System in the United States, 1880–1920* (Madison: University of Wisconsin Press, 1975); Roy Rosenzweig, *Eight Hours for What We Will: Workers and Leisure in an Industrial City, 1870–1920* (Cambridge, U.K.: Cambridge University Press, 1983).
5. see Gerald Zahavi, *Workers, Managers and Welfare Capitalism: The Shoemakers and Tanners of Endicott Johnson, 1880–1950* (Urbana: University of Illinois Press, 1988).
6. http://www.census.gov/population/www/documentation/twps0027/tab09.txt.
7. Rigauer, p. 78.
8. Frank Zarnowski, *All-Around Men: Heroes of a Forgotten Sport* (Lanham, MD: Scarecrow Press, 2005), chapter 3.
9. M. Conk, *The United States Census and Labor Force Change: A History of Occupational Statistics, 1870–1940* (Ann Arbor: UMI Research Press, 1980).
10. Nineteenth-century American worker competitions were numerous and varied. Worksports are defined as contests in which laborers fashioned a game from their job. A more complete yet inexhaustive list of worker games, contests and sports would include plowing, spading, cradling, mowing, picking, raking, reaping, threshing, digging, packing, sheep shearing, milking, wheel barrowing, lifting and brick laying, as well as contests/challenges for mechanics, draymen, tinkers and blacksmiths.
11. M. Buraway, *Manufacturing Consent: Changes in the Labor Force Process Under Monopoly Capitalism* (Chicago: University of Chicago Press, 1979).
12. Regauer, p. 15.
13. *Ibid.*, p. 27.
14. See Appendix 1 for a list of occupations and estimates of U.S. workers in 1900.
15. Labor productivity data from the Bureau of Labor Statistics (BLS) dates only to 1949. National Bureau of Economic Research (NBER) data is available for an earlier period for some industries. Neither provides productivity data by occupation.
16. See, for example, M. Blatt and M. Norkunas, eds., *Work, Recreation and Culture: Essays in American Labor History* (New York: Garland, 1996), and J.R. Svhleppi, "It Pays: John Patterson and Industrial Recreation at the National Cash Register Company," *Journal of Sport History*, Vol. 6, 1985, pp. 20–28.
17. See Ames Castle, "How Sports Helps

America to Out-produce the World," *Industrial Sport Journal*, Vol. 11, pp. 6, 9, 34.

18. See Edward F. Denison, *Trends in American Economic Growth, 1929–1982* (Washington, D.C.: Brookings Institution, 1985).

19. U.S. Census Bureau, *Historical Statistics of the United States: Colonial Times to 1970* (Washington, D.C.: U.S. Department of Commerce, 1975).

20. See Carroll B. Pursell, *The Machine in America: A Social History of Technology* (Baltimore: Johns Hopkins University Press, 1995).

21. See Leonard J. Jacobs, "Kings of the Hill: Illini Huskers, 1924–1941," *Journal of the Illinois State Historical Society*, Vol. 76, Autumn 1976, p. 206.

22. See Walter Rumble, *The Swifts: Printers in the Age of Typesetting Races* (Charlottesville: University of Virginia Press, 2003), p. 148.

23. See A. A. Richie, "The Real Facts About Those Hand-drilling Contests," *Engineering and Mining Journal*, Vol. 152, November 1951, pp. 84–85.

24. See Amitai Etzioni, "The Socio-economics of Work," *Meaning of Work*, Frederick C. Ganst, ed. (Albany: State University of New York Press, 1995), pp. 251–258.

25. See Alan Guttmann, *From Ritual to Record: The Nature of Modern Sports* (New York: Columbia University Press, 1978), p. 13.

26. See, for example, John R. Betts, *America's Sporting Heritage: 1850–1950* (Reading, MA: Addison-Wesley, 1974); Foster R. Dulles, *A History of Recreation: America Learns to Play* (New York: D. Appleton-Century, 1965); and Benjamin G. Rader, *American Sports: From the Age of Folk Games to the Age of Spectators*, 2d ed. (Englewood Cliffs, N.J.: Prentice-Hall, 1990).

27. See Alan Guttmann, *A Whole New Ball Game: An Interpretation of American Sports* (Chapel Hill: University of North Carolina Press, 1988).

28. See *New York Clipper*, May 1, 1858.

29. Betts.

30. See Marvin H. Eyler, "Origins of Contemporary Sports," *Research Quarterly*, Vol. 32, December 1961, pp. 480–489.

Chapter 1

1. Merritt Ierley, *Traveling the National Road: Across the Centuries on America's First Highway* (Woodstock, N.Y.: Overlook Press, 1990), pp. 42–43.

2. *Ibid.*, p. 44.

3. Thomas B. Searight, *The Old Pike: A History of the National Road* (Uniontown, PA: Thomas B. Searight, 1894), p. 321, and reprinted for the Western Pennsylvania Genealogical Society (Berryville, VA: Marcus, 1983).

4. *Ibid.*

5. *Ibid.*

6. Ted Vincent, *The Rise and Fall of American Sport: Mudville's Revenge* (Lincoln: University of Nebraska Press, 1994), p 16.

7. Allen Guttmann offers criteria for the formality of sport. See Guttmann (1988), *A Whole New Ball Game: An Interpretation of American Sports*. Chapel Hill: University of North Carolina Press, 1988.

8. For a detailed description of this phenomenon see Walker Rumble, *The Swifts: Printers in the Age of Typesetting Races* (Charlottesville: University of Virginia Press, 2003).

9. The prevalent 19th century practice of hippdroming referred to collusion between managersn and/or contestants to prearrange the outcoume of contests in order to profit through betting.

Chapter 2

1. "Wm. W. Bush: One of America's Firemen," *National Police Gazette/New York Clipper*, January 16, 1858, p. 312.

2. *Ibid.*

3. Vincent P. McNally, " A History of Volunteers: Part II," *Firehouse*, June 1986, p. 82.

4. *Ibid.*

5. Robert S. Holzman, *The Romance of Firefighting* (New York: Bonanza, 1956), p. 16.

6. *Ibid.*, p. 35.

7. *Ibid.*, p. 46.

8. *Ibid.*, p. 62.

9. William A. Murray, *The Unheralded Heroes of Baltimore's Big Blazes* (Baltimore: E.G. Schmitz, 1968), p. 3.

10. Herbert Asbury, *Ye Olde Fire Laddies* (New York: Knopf, 1930), p. xvi.

11. *The Volunteer Fire Department of Old New York, 1790–1866* (New York: American Review, 1962), p. 21.

12. Amy S. Greenberg, *Cause for Alarm: The Volunteer Fire Department in the Nineteenth Century City* (Princeton: Princeton University Press, 1997).

13. *Ibid.*, p. 93. See also *Baltimore Sun*, September 9, 1856.

14. Figures provided by National Fire Academy and FEMA, Emmitsburg, MD.

15. Stan Dixon, "A Century of Musters," *Firehouse Magazine*, June 1978, p. 77.

16. Much of the information in this section can be found in Stan Dixon, *The Firemen's Muster: America's Sport* (Newburyport, MA: Stan Dixon, 2001).

17. "Grand Fireman's Muster," *Worcester Transcript*, September 10, 1858, p. 10.

18. John Rickards Betts, "Sporting Journalism in Nineteenth-Century America," *American Quarterly*, Vol. 5, No. 1 (Spring 1953), pp 39–56.

19. Frank Queen, "Time Table," *New York Clipper*, April 23, 1859, p. 1. There seem to be few copies of the *Clipper Almanacs* remaining, but a set can be accessed at the Library of Congress, Washington, D.C.

20. Scriptorium.lib.duke.edu/adacess/railshistory.html, July, 27, 2007.

21. "National Musters of Firemen-Toronto," *New York Clipper*, May 1, 1858, p. 10. For reasons unknown this affair never came off.

22. A search of the era's sporting newspapers, including the *New York Clipper*, finds the Mutual Engine Company participating in numerous musters. Typical musters of the day included racing the engines (manually pulling them over a set distance); coupling hoses; and pumping streams of water for height or distance.
23. *New York Clipper*, April 4, 1869.
24. *New York Clipper*, September 5, 1869, p. 173.
25. In the 19th century the term "jumpist" referred to a leaper in an athletic contest, for example, the long jump or high jump. The term "jumper" was reserved for those who leaped off of buildings or bridges, often as a stunt or for a wager.
26. *Scottish-American Journal*, September 16, 1865, p. 5.
27. *New York Times*, July 17, 1871.
28. Contrast this figure with the annual paid attendance for the first professional baseball league, the National Association of 1871. Attendance *for the entire season* did not approach firemen's muster attendance.
29. Dixon, "A Century of Musters," p. 30.
30. John P. Marquand, "When We Ran with the Old Machine," *Point of No Return* (Boston: Little, Brown, 1949). In fact, Marquand was a member of the Neptune V.F.A. of Newburyport, Massachusetts.
31. "Barred Chief Hale's Men," *Kansas City Star*, August 19, 1900, p. 1; "Won as Professionals," *Kansas City Star*, August 20, 1900, p. 1; "Our Firemen in Paris," *Kansas City Star*, August 21, 1900, p. 1. In reality, the Kansas City professional firemen were segregated from the volunteer departments in Paris, winning a "professional division."
32. Holzman, *The Romance of Firefighting*, p. 91.
33. Frank Sibley, "New England Troops Find Familiar Game in France," *Boston Globe*, August 3, 1918.

Chapter 3

1. *Abstract of the Returns of the 5th Census* [Document 269], Clerk of the House of Representatives, 22nd Congress, Washington, D.C., 1832, p. 47. The 1830 figure was just over 2 million. By 1860, when slaves were enumerated separately in the census, the figure had more than doubled for the 15 slave states. For an 1860 breakdown see www.slaveryinamerica.org/.
2. Ted Ownby, *Subduing Satan: Religion, Recreation and Manhood in the Rural South, 1865–1920* (Chapel Hill: University of North Carolina Press, 1990), pp. 90–91.
3. David Kenneth Wiggins, *Sport and Popular Pastimes in the Plantation Community: The Slave Experience*, PhD. Dissertation, University of Maryland, College Park, 1979, DAI-A, 41/02.
4. Eugene D. Genovese, *Roll, Jordan, Roll: The World the Slaves Made* (New York: Vintage, 1974), p. 310.
5. Josiah Henson, *Truth Stranger Than Fiction: Father Henson's Story of His Own Life (with an introduction by Harriet Beecher Stowe)*, 1858. Chapters II and III were reproduced in *Slavery in the South: First Hand Accounts of the Ante-Bellum American Southland from Northern & Southern Whites, Negroes, & Foreign Observers*, Harvey Wish, ed. (New York: Farrar, Straus and Co., 1964), p. 29.
6. Ira Berlin, *Generations of Captivity: A History of African-American Slaves* (Cambridge, MA: Harvard University Press, 2003), pp. 77–78.
7. Genovese, p. 307.
8. David R. Bigham, *Public Culture in the Early Republic* (Washington, D.C.: Smithsonian Institution Press, 1998), p. 272.
9. Ibid.
10. George Rawick, ed., *The American Slave: A Composite Autobiography* (Westport, CT: Greenwood Press, 1972). The initial completed project totaled 19 volumes. Two supplements, published in 1977 and 1979, added another 22 volumes.
11. Rawick, ed., *American Narrative*, VI, (I), p. 89.
12. David K. Wiggins, "Good Times on the Old Plantation; Popular Recreations of the Black Slave in Antebellum South, 1810–1860," *Journal of Sport History*, Vol. 4, No. 3, 1977, p 279.
13. Genovese, p. 314
14. Weymouth T. Jordan, *Hugh Davis and his Alabama Plantation* (Tuscaloosa: University of Alabama Press, 1948), p. 105.
15. Ibid., p. 106.
16. Ibid.
17. Kathryn T. Abbey, ed., "Documents Relating to El Destino and Chemonie Plantations, Middle Florida, 1828–1866," *Florida Historical Society Quarterly*, VII, January, 1929, pp. 195–96
18. Excerpted from his autobiography, Solomon Northrup, *Twelve Years a Slave*, Auburn, Buffalo, 1854, reprinted in *Slavery in the South*, noted in footnote 5, p. 40.
19. Mark Swearingen, "Thirty Years of a Mississippi Plantation: Charles Whitmore of 'Montpelier,'" *Journal of Southern History*, Vol. 1, No. 2, 1935, p 205.
20. "Cotton," *American Farmer*, January 18, 1826, p. 338.
21. David K. Wiggins, "Sport and Popular Pastimes; Shadow of the Slavequarter," *Canadian Journal of History of Sport and Physical Education*, Vol. 11, No. 1, 1980, p 65.
22. Frederick Law Olmstead, *A Journey in the Seaboard Slave States* (New York: Putman & Sons, 1856), p. 91.
23. Wiggins, "Good Times on the Old Plantation," pp. 260–284.
24. See, for example, travel.webshots.com/photo/2795123240074575920btnQoK.

Chapter 4

1. William C. Barnes, Joseph W. McCann, and Alexander Duguid, *Fast Typesetting* (New York: Concord Cooperative, 1887), pp. 140–142.

Also see Walker Rumble, "From the Shop Floor to the Show: Joseph W. McCann, Typesetting Races and Expressive Work in 19th Century America," *Journal of Popular Culture*, Vol. 32, Issue 2, Fall 1998, p. 87.
 2. Walker Rumble, "Ready, Go, Set," *Heritage*, Spring 2001, www.americanheritage.com/articles/magazine/it/2001/4/.
 3. *Ibid.*, p. 2.
 4. Walker Rumble, *The Swifts: Printers in the Age of Typesetting Races* (Charlottesville: University of Virginia Press, 2003), p. 105.
 5. "Copy All Out: The Globe as Usual Leads All Competitors," *Boston Globe*. February 21, 1886, p. 1.
 6. See Walker Rumble, "A Showdown of 'Swifts': Women Compositors, Dime Museums, and the Boston Typesetting Races of 1886," *The New England Quarterly*, Vol. 71, No. 4, December 1998, pp. 615–628.
 7. *Ibid.*, p. 623–625.
 8. Barnes et al., *Fast Typesetting*, p. 33.

Chapter 5

 1. *New York Clipper*, January 14, 1882
 2. Ernie Millette, "You Could Leap to Your Death," *Bandwagon*, May–June 1985, p. 20.
 3. Steve Gossard, "Frank Gardner and the Great Leapers," *Bandwagon*, July–August 1990, p. 12.
 4. Millette, "You Could Leap to Your Death," p. 22.
 5. *New York Clipper*, January 23, 1858.
 6. *New York Evening Post*, July 1, 1859.
 7. *New York Clipper*, August 31, 1872.
 8. *New York Clipper*, October 17, 1874, p. 232.
 9. *New York Clipper*, September 15, 1877; June 28, 1878, p. 107; August 3, 1878, p. 152.
 10. The information in this section was accumulated at the Circus World Museum, Baraboo, Wisconsin, in the summer of 2001 and Steve Gossard's earlier cited works. I also heavily relied upon William L. Stout's *Olympians of the Sawdust Circle: A Biographical Dictionary of the Nineteenth Century American Circus* (San Bernardino: Borgo Press, 1998), pp. 22, 28, 29, 72, 108, 112, 153–64, 158, 289, 334.

Chapter 6

 1. Judah did not live to see the culmination of his efforts.
 2. Because the Central Pacific had to slug its way through both the Sierras and Rockies, their subsidies, at times, were tripled.
 3. Bruce W. Rosenberg, *The Code of the West* (Bloomington: Indiana University Press, 1982), pp.150–151.
 4. The Credit Mobilier resulted in a financial scandal, and, although it made Durant rich beyond imagination, he would spend the later days of his life in court.
 5. Estimates of the Consumer Price Index for 1869 were made by Ethel D. Hoover and are available at the website of the Federal Reserve Bank of Minneapolis. The standard procedure: $10,000 x CPI 2011/CPI 1868 was employed. See http://www.minneapolisfed.org/community_education/teacher/calc/hist1800.cfm, accessed May 13, 2011.
 6. *Ibid.*, p. 154.
 7. Dee Alexander Brown, *Hear That Lonesome Whistle Blow* (New York: Holt, Rinehart and Winston, 1977), pp. 123–124.
 8. Edwin L. Sabin, *Building the Pacific Railway* (Philadelphia: J.B. Lippincott, 1919), p. 113.
 9. "Pacific Railroad," *Daily Alta California*, April 30, 1869, p. 1.
 10. *Ibid.*
 11. *Sacramento Daily Union*, April 30, 1860, p. 3.
 12. Brown, *Hear That Lonesome Whistle Blow*, p. 110.
 13. Stanford University was founded in 1891 by Leland Stanford, two years before his death.
 14. See the Central Pacific Railroad website, http://cprr.org/Museum/Done!.html, accessed May 12, 2011.
 15. *Frank Leslie's Illustrated Newspaper*, May 29, 1869, p. 162.
 16. Rosenberg, *The Code of the West*, p. 146.
 17. See Walter Licht, *Working for the Railroad: The Organization of Work in the Nineteenth Century* (Princeton: Princeton University Press, 1989), p. 1. Also see Robert Fogel, *Railroads and American Economic Growth: Essays in Econometric History* (Baltimore: Johns Hopkins University Press, 1970).

Chapter 7

 1. In 1923 the Norman Film Company of Jacksonville, Florida, did produce a movie, *The Bull-dogger*, which featured Pickett, referring to him as "The World's Colored Champion."
 2. Bill O'Neal, "Bulldoggin' Bill Pickett," *The West That Was*, Thomas W. Knowles and Joe R. Lansdale, eds. (New York: Wing, 1993), p. 309.
 3. Fred Gibson, *Fabulous Empire* (Boston: Houghton Mifflin, 1946), p. 226.
 4. Col. Billy C. Hanes, *Bill Pickett, Bulldogger: The Biography of a Black Cowboy* (Norman: University of Oklahoma Press, 1977), p. 10.
 5. *Ibid.*, p. 40. A glowing account, for example, appeared in *Harper's Weekly*.
 6. Wallis, *The Real Wild West*, p. 321.
 7. *Ibid.*, p. 323.
 8. Lee Sullinger, "The Longhorns," *The West That Was*, Thomas W. Knowles and Joe R. Lansdale, eds. (New York: Wing, 1993), p. 295.
 9. James F. Hoy, "The Origins and Originality of the Rodeo," *Journal of the West*, Vol. XVII, July 1978, p. 19.
 10. Thomas Saunders, "How the Word 'Rodeo' Originated as Applied to Western Events," *The Quarter Horse Journal*, June 1968, pp 28–29.

11. Glenn R. Vernam, *Men on Horseback* (New York: Harper and Row, 1964), pp. 396–98.
12. Zenas Leonard, *Adventures of Zenas Leonard, Fur Trader,* John C. Evers, ed. (Norman: University of Oklahoma Press, 1959), p. 132.
13. There are any number of other early references but the following are notable. See Zenas Leonard, *Adventures of Zenas Leonard Fur Trader,* John C. Evers, ed. (Norman: University of Oklahoma Press, 1959), p. 132; Mary Lou LeCompte, "The First Rodeo in Texas," paper presented to the North American Society for Sports History, Albuquerque, May 1980; and Billy C. Hanes, *Bill Pickett, Bulldogger: The Biography of a Black Cowboy* (Norman: University of Oklahoma Press, 1977), p. 6.
14. Mary Lou LeCompte, "The First American Rodeo Never Happened," *Journal of Sport History,* Vol. 9, No. 2, Summer 1982, pp. 89–96. LeCompte's exacting research has uncovered that Captain Mayne Reid's reported rodeo did occur, but in Santa Fe, in the Mexican state of Vera Cruz, and not in what is today Santa Fe, New Mexico. Even more disquieting from a historian's point of view is that three standard rodeo histories give Reid, an Irish novelist who at the time had enlisted in the American army, three different spellings of his first name: Mayne, Mdyne, and Myne.
15. Hanes, *Bill Pickett, Bulldogger,* p. 7.
16. Mary Lou LeCompte, "The Hispanic Influence of the History of the Rodeo, 1823–1922," *Journal of Sport History,* Vol. 12, No. 1, Spring 1985, p. 29.
17. Mody C. Boatright, "The American Rodeo," *American Quarterly,* Vol. 16, No. 2, Part I, Summer 1964, p. 195.
18. Michael Wallis, *The Real Wild West: The 101 Ranch and the Creation of the American West* (New York: St. Martin's Griffin, 1999), p. 260.
19. James F. Hoy, "The Origins and Originality of the Rodeo," *Journal of the West,* Vol. XVII, July 1978, p. 26.
20. *Ibid.,* pp. 24–32.
21. Hanes, *Bill Pickett, Bulldogger,* p. 155.
22. *Ibid.,* p. 145.
23. Wallis, *The Real Wild West,* pp. 332–33.
24. Hoy, "The Origins and Originality of the Rodeo," p. 9.
25. Mary Lou LeCompte, "Rodeo," *Encyclopedia of World Sport,* David Levinson and Karen Christensen, eds. (Santa Barbara: ABC-CLIO, 1996), Vol. II, p. 809.
26. Clair Atkinson, "An 8 Second Ride Lures Sponsors Beyond the Rodeo," *New York Times,* December 11, 2007.

Chapter 8

1. John I. 1. Bellaire, "Michigan's Lumberjacks," *Michigan History Magazine,* Vol. 26, Spring 1942, p. 185.
2. Robert R. Fries, "Founding the Lumber Industry in Wisconsin," *Wisconsin Magazine of History,* Vol. 26, No. 1, September 1942, pp. 23–24.
3. George B. Enberg, "Who Were the Lumberjacks?" *Michigan History,* Vol. 32, No. 3, July–December 1948, p. 243.
4. *Ibid.,* p. 244.
5. W.T. Orcutt, "The Minnesota Lumberjacks," *Minnesota History,* Vol. 15, No. 1, March 1925, p. 16.
6. Richard G. Wood, *A History of Lumbering in Maine, 1820–1861* (Orono: University of Maine Press, 1935), p. 234.
7. Willis Ward, "Reminiscences of Michigan's Logging Days," *Michigan History Magazine,* Vol. 20, Autumn 1936, p. 301.
8. Stewart H. Holbrook, *Holy Old Mackinaw: A Natural History of the American Lumberjack* (New York: Macmillan, 1938), pp. 104–105.
9. John E. Nelligan, as told to Charles Sheridan, "The Life of a Lumberman," *Wisconsin Magazine of History,* Vol. 13, Issue 1, 1929–1930, p. 243.
10. *Ibid.,* p. 245.
11. Orcutt, "The Minnesota Lumberjacks," p. 14.
12. Nelligan, "The Life of a Lumberman," p. 250.
13. Holbrook, *Holy Old Mackinaw,* pp. 127–28.
14. Nelligan, "The Life of a Lumberman," p. 177.
15. Carl Leech, "Lumbering Days," *Michigan History Magazine,* Vol. 18, Spring 1934, p. 137.
16. See Eben Lehman, "The Fall of Timber Sports?" *New York Times,* July 29, 2009.
17. See William H. Gillespie, "Lumberjack Contests," http://www.wvencyclopedia.org/articles/1464, accessed October 8, 2011.
18. An incomplete list would include American Birling Association (ABA), American Lumberjack Association (ALA), Lumberjack Sports International, Canadian Logger Sports Association, New York State Lumberjack Association (NYSLA), Fred Scheer's Lumberjack Shows, and the U.S. Logrolling Association.
19. The earliest published version of the myth of Paul Bunyan is traced to a series of stories by James MacGillivray, a Michigan newspaper reporter who expanded and embellished his collected stories and published then in the *Detroit News* and later in *The Round River Drive* (1910).

Chapter 9

1. Charles Tatum, "Wilbursaurus—New Dinosaur Fossil Discovered Near Old Main," University of Arizona College of Engineering website, April 1, 2011, http://www.engr.arizona.edu/news/story.php?id=270, accessed September 14, 2011.
2. Mark Twain, *The Innocents Abroad and Roughing It,* Guy Caldwell, ed. (New York: Library of America, 1984). Initially published Hart-

ford, CT: American Publishing Company, 1886 [first published in 1872], pp. 683–685.
  3. *Ibid.*, p. 684.
  4. Scott Reynolds Nelson, *Steel Drivin' Man: John Henry, the Untold Story of an American Legend* (Oxford: Oxford University Press, 2006).
  5. Labor Force Statistics from Current Population Survey, U.S. Bureau of Labor Statistics website, U.S. Department of Labor, accessed July 2008.
  6. In 1909 there were in excess of 1 million miners in all types of coal and metals mines and a non-farm male work forces of 35.6 million (see Table #3, Class by Sex and Farm Status, 1910 Workforce, 16–65: www.sp2.upenn.edu/america2000/wp4tab.pdf, accessed April 2011.). The current figure for non-farm males is approximately one out of every 300.
  7. Twain, *The Innocents Abroad and Roughing It*, p. 685.
  8. Otis E. Young, with technical assistance of Robert Lenon, *Black Powder and Hand Steel: Miners and Machines on the Western Frontier* (Norman: University of Oklahoma Press, 1976), p. 10.
  9. *Ibid.*, p. 23.
  10. *Ibid.*, p. 55.
  11. Today it is standard nationwide to use New Hampshire granite for all rock drilling contests.
  12. Atha Richie was a well-known driller in the first decade of the 20th century and in 1950 recalled his experiences. See Atha Albert Richie, "The Real Truth About Those Old Famous Hand Drilling Contests," *Engineering and Mining Journal*, Vol. CLII, No. 11, November 1951, pp. 84–85.
  13. Young, *Black Powder and Hand Steel*, pp. 55–56.
  14. Frank Crampton, *Deep Enough* (Norman: University of Oklahoma Press, 1956), p. 64.
  15. Young, *Black Powder and Hand Steel*, p. 52.
  16. Mrs. Hugh Brown, "Railroad Days: A Memoir of Tonopah, 1904," *The American West*, Vol. 5, No. 6, November 1968, p. 28.
  17. Richie, "The Real Truth About Those Old Famous Hand Drilling Contests," p. 84.
  18. Was there really a John Henry? Was he the world's strongest man or just am musical legend? Scott Reynolds Nelson makes a powerful argument that he has identified the "real" John Henry in his *Steel Drivin' Man: John Henry, the Untold Story of an American Legend* (Oxford: Oxford University Press, 2006).
  19. *Ibid.*, p. 39. The entry is referenced "Prison Register, Penitentiary Records, Department of Corrections, Library of Virginia, Richmond."
  20. It has long been thought that John Henry worked and died at the Big Bend (or Great Bend) Tunnel near Talcott, West Virginia. This has been discredited by recent research, yet a statue of John Henry sits outside the Big Bend Tunnel.
  21. Nelson, *Steel Drivin' Man*, p. 170.
  22. *Ibid.*, p. 132.
  23. On the Caledonian Track and Field circuit two classes of similar sledge hammers were used for throwing. The Caledonians considered a 12-pound hammer, the same weight as John Henry's implements, "light," and a 16-pound hammer "heavy." There were no 30-pound hammers.
  24. See Frank Zarnowski, *All Around Men: Heroes of a Forgotten Sport* (Lanham, MD: Scarecrow Press, 2005), pp. 39–51 for Dinnie's story. He drew 20,000 spectators at the 1870 New York Caledonian Games, 15,000 in Toronto, and thousands more in other smaller festivals. In fact, he outdrew the darlings of the 1870 sporting world, the newly-professional Cincinnati Red Stockings base-ball club. It is estimated that, over a lengthy career, somewhere between 3 and 5 *million* came to watch Dinnie compete.
  25. *Ibid.*, p. 39. Dinnie frequently wore flesh colored tights when competing. He was variously referred to in the press as the "world's greatest athlete," "world's strongest man," and "world champion wrestler."
  26. The play, *The Day John Henry Came to School*, opened at Imagination Stage, Washington, D.C., and was reviewed by Celia Wren in "Theater Review," *Washington Post*, April 25, 2011, p. C-3.
  27. "Miners Stage Rock Drilling Races," *Popular Science*, December 1934, p. 40.
  28. The Nevada Day Annual World Championships, in a casino parking lot, have attached the "world championship" appellation since 1974. Sierra White Granite is traditionally used and $2,000 goes to the single jack champion.

Chapter 10

  1. Earl Conrad, *Billy Rose: Manhattan Primitive* (Cleveland: World, 1968), p. 19.
  2. *New York Times*, all 1912: August 21, p. 6; August 22, p. 6; August 23, p 10; August 25, pt. 5, p. 14; November 13, p. 12; December 5, p. 6; December 16, p. 12.
  3. Conrad, *Bill Rose*, p. 8. William Rosenberg attended the High School of Commerce on West 65th Street, between Broadway and Amsterdam Avenue in New York City. He graduated in May 1917.
  4. www.officemuseum.com/typewriters.htm, accessed September 10, 2007.
  5. "Still Another Challenge," *The Typewriter Operator*, Vol. 1, No. 10, January 1888, p. 51; "The Challenge Accepted," *The Cosmopolitan Shorthander*, Vol. 9, No. 6, June 1888, p. 155.
  6. S.B. Nelson, *History of Cincinnati and Hamilton County, Ohio* (Cincinnati, 1894), pp. 736–737.
  7. Paul Krugman, *Peddling Prosperity* (New York: W.W. Norton, 1994), p. 235.
  8. Stanley J. Liebowitz and Stephen E. Margolis, "The Fable of the Keys," *Journal of Law and Economics*, Vol. XXXIII, April 1990, pp. 1–26.
  9. The story of the QWERTY keyboard can be found in two successful economics books written for laymen: Robert Frank and Philip Cook, *The Winner-Take-All Society* (New York: Penguin, 1996), and Paul Krugman, *Peddling Pros-*

perity (New York: W.W. Norton, 1994). In the latter an entire chapter is devoted to the economics of QWERTY.

10. L.A. Miller and J.C. Thomas, "Behavioral Issues in the Use of Interactive Systems: Part I. General Issues," *International Journal of Man-Machine Studies*, Vol. 9, Number 5, 1977, pp. 509–536.

11. "McGurrin vs. Traub," *The Cosmopolitan Shorthander*, Vol. 10, No. 2, February 1889, pp. 21–23.

12. Liebowitz and Margolis, "The Fable of the Keys," pp. 1–26.

13. "Typewriters Contest for Metropolitan Stenographers Association Prize," *New York Times*, August 2, 1888, p. 2.

14. Angel Kwokel-Folland, *Engendering Business: Men and Women in the Corporate Office, 1879–1930* (Baltimore: Johns Hopkins University Press, 1994), p. 30.

15. Jack Larkin, *Where We Worked: A Celebration of America's Workers and the Nation They Built* (Guilford, CT: Lyons Press, 2010), pp. 341–343.

16. See *http://en.wikipedia.org/wiki/Typing*, accessed September 18, 2011.

17. Alan Greenspan, *The Age of Turbulence: Adventures in a New World* (New York: Penguin, 2007), pp. 22, 48–49.

18. See *http://en.wikipedia.org/wiki/Morse_code*, accessed September 18, 2011.

19. Claudia Goldin and Lawrence Katz, "The Decline of Non-Competing Groups: Changes in the Premium to Education, 1890 to 1940," *National Bureau of Economic Research*, Working Paper No. 5202, August 1995, pp. 1–30.

20. Kwokel-Folland, *Engendering Business*, p. 4.

21. Susan E. Cayleff, *Babe: The Life and Legend of Babe Didrickson Zaharias* (Urbana: University of Illinois Press, 1996), p. 51.

Chapter 11

1. "Last Call for Husking Contest," *Wallaces' Farmer*, November 14, 1924, p. 1472.

2. H.A. Wallace, "Young Grimmius Finally Wins," *Wallaces' Farmer*, November 28, 1924, p. 1531.

3. H. A. Wallace, "Iowa Wins Mid-West Championship," *Wallaces' Farmer*, December 5, 1924, p. 1561.

4. "Here's How It All Started," *The Prairie Farmer*, October 18, 1941, p. 67

5. "Against Corn Husking Contest," *Wallaces' Farmer*, November 14, 1924., p. 1479.

6. "To Husking Contest Objectors," *Wallaces' Farmer*, December 5, 1924, p. 1562..

7. Gay, Alva, "Corn Husking Contest," *Wallaces' Farmer*, June 4, 1924, p. 12.

8. "Local Husking Contests," *Wallaces' Farmer*, December 12, 1924, p. 1593.

9. "Here's How It All Started," p. 67.

10. Leonard J. Jacobs, "Kings of the Hill: Illini Huskers, 1924–1941," *Journal of the Illinois State Historical Society*, Vol. 76, No. 3, Autumn 1983, p. 206.

11. James F. Evans, *Prairie Farmer and the WLS* (Urbana: University of Illinois Press, 1969), p. 209.

12. John Strohm, *Prairie Farmer*, Vol. 113, October 18, 1941, p. 76.

13. Evans, *Prairie Farmer and the WLS*, p. 208.

14. *Ibid.*, p. 210.

15. Jacobs, "King of the Hill," p. 210.

16. Evans, *Prairie Farmer and the WLS*, p. 210.

17. Jacobs, "King of the Hill," p. 212.

18. *Ibid.*

19. The U.S. Census Bureau reported that the population ranged from 106 million in 1920 to 132 million in 1940 and that 48 percent (1920) and 43 percent (1940) were rural.

20. In 1938 11 states held frequent competitions to determine their "nationals" representatives. Iowa alone held husking contests in most of its 99 counties. Major league baseball drew nine million from its 1223 games.

21. Evans, *Prairie Farmer and the WLS*, p. 211.

22. U.S. Census Bureau, Population: 1790–1990, Table 4, http://www.census.gov/population/www/censusdata/hiscendata.html, accessed May 20, 2011.

23. John Cunniff, "County Fairs Turn Into Big Business," *Milwaukee Journal*, October 12, 1967, p. 21.

24. J. Skinner, ed., "The Late Cattle Show," *American Farmer*, Vol. 10, November 7, 1828, p. 272.

25. See, for example, Applebaum, Herbert, "The Concept of Work in Western Thought," *Meanings of Work*, Frederick C. Ganst, ed. (Albany: State University of New York Press, 1995).

26. Lillian Krueger, "Social Life in Wisconsin: Pre-Territorial through the Mid-Sixties," *Wisconsin Magazine of History*, Vol. 22, No. 4, June 1939, p. 410.

27. See Soeren S. Brynn, "Some Sports in Pittsburgh During the National Period: 1775–1860," *Western Pennsylvania History*, Vol. 51, No. 4, October 1968, p. 67. Brynn uses newspaper account of plowing matches from the *Pittsburgh Daily Gazette*, *Pittsburg Daily Dispatch* and *Daily Morning Post*.

28. See Guide to Iowa, *http://iowaguide.org/iowa-attractions/iowa-state-fair/*, accessed May 17, 2011.

29. "Plowing and Spading Match," *New York Clipper*, November 8, 1856, p. 228.

30. "Challenge to Plough," *New York Clipper*, September 27, 1856, p. 178.

31. Mary Bellis, *History of Tractors*, in About.com Guide, *http://inventors.about.com/od/tstartinventions/a/tractors.htm*, accessed May 20, 2011.

32. "Plowing Contest Also Political," *Tri City Herald*, Tri City, WA, September 22, 1960, p. 4.

33. Williard W. Cochrane and Mary E. Ryan, *American Farm Policy: 1948–1973* (Minneapolis: University of Minnesota Press, 1976), p. 28.

34. Associated Press, "Ike and Adalai Will Talk at Plow Contest," *Gettysburg Times*, Gettysburg, PA, September 6, 1956, p. 19. See also *Chicago Daily Tribune*, September 7, 1952, and *Los Angeles Times*, September 20, 1955.
35. Cunniff, "County Fairs Turn Into Big Business," p. 21.
36. Gary S. Cross, ed., "Agricultural Fairs," *Encyclopedia of Recreation and Leisure in America* (New York: Scribner, 2004), p.12.
37. After his father died Custis went to live at Mount Vernon where he was raised by Martha and her second husband, George Washington, as their own son. See National Park Service, Arlington House in Alexandria, VA, http://www.nps.gov/museum/exhibits/arho/print.html, accessed May 17, 2001.
38. Krueger, "Social Life in Wisconsin," p. 411.
39. See *New York Times*, May 3, 1894, p. 8; November 29, 1895, p. 6; and November 24, 1896, p. 3 for accounts of sheep shearing at livestock shows at Madison Square Garden.
40. William James Beal, *History of Michigan Agricultural College and Biographical Sketches of Trustees and Professors* (East Lansing: Michigan Agricultural College, 1915), p. 110.
41. *American Sheep Breeder*, October 15, 1904.
42. See http://www.kfyrtv.com/News_Stories.asp?news=43604, accessed May 20, 2011.
43. See *Central Pennsylvania Gazette*, January 6, 2008, or http://centralpagazelle.blogspot.com/2008/01/sheep-to-shawl-replaced-by-horse-to.html, accessed May 17, 2011.
44. See "Sheep and Wool Festival," *The Bow Times*, May 1, 2008, p. A–6.
45. "Grange Picnic Draws Thousands," *Spokane Spokesman-Review*, July 7, 1908, p. 1, 8.
46. Robert Meyer, Jr., *Festivals: USA & Canada* (New York: Ives Washburn, 1967), p. 72.
47. "Agricultural Fairs," *New York Herald*, October 4, 1958, p. 4.
48. For examples of other reported farming work sports see *New York Clipper*, September 6, 1956, p. 157 (mowing); November 19, 1859 (butchering); July 11, 1857 (reaping); and February 6, 1858, April 4, 1860, and November 11, 1869 (blacksmithing).
49. "State and County Fairs for 1867," *New York Clipper*, September 14, 1967, p. 180.
50. Meyer, *Festivals*, p. 63. See also Charles Fish, *Blue Ribbons and Burlesque: A Book of Country Fairs* (Woodstock, VT: Countryman Press, 1998).
51. I counted 2337 county fairs listed at http://www.stepintoplaces.com/Fairs%20and%20Festivals/County%20Fairs%20Index.htm, accessed May 22, 2011.
52. The author, while researching this work, once lived in Stafford, Vermont, home of Senator Morrill. Today half a dozen universities in the United States still bear the label "A&M." For additional references to the Morrill Act see http://www.answers.com/topic/morrill-land-grant-colleges-act#ixzz1N7DKTclr, accessed May 22, 2011.
53. See Constitution; minutes, 1915; correspondence, 1915; contest scores and results, 1914; judging regulations, 1913–1916; treasurer's report, 1914–1915; and the records of the secretary and treasurer, 1907–1915. New England Federation of Agricultural Students, University of Massachusetts, Amherst.
54. Ted Ownby, *Subduing Satan: Religion, Recreation and Manhood in the Rural South, 1865–1920* (Chapel Hill: University of North Carolina Press, 1990), p. 182.

Chapter 12

1. The figure exceeded 7000 ten years later. http://inventors.about.com/od/pstartinventions/a/printing_4.htm, accessed June 30, 2011.
2. A Constant Reader, "Another Horse Shoe Feat," *New York Clipper*, February 6, 1858, p. 330.
3. "Quick Work: For Horse Shoes and Nails," *New York Clipper*, April 4, 1860, p. 7.
4. Edward W. O'Brien, "Blacksmith Boy—Heel and Toe," *Saturday Evening Post*, November 2, 1940, pp. 9–11, 90, 92.
5. "Novel Blacksmithing Match," *New York Clipper*, January 16, 1869, p. 319.
6. See *New York Clipper Annual*, 1885.
7. "Dressing a Bullock," *New York Clipper*, March 29, 1858.
8. "Butcherdom Has a New Sensation," *New York Clipper*, February 16, 1861, p. 346.
9. "Another Butchering Match," *New York Clipper*, March 2, 1861, p. 362.
10. "Sheep Slaughtering Challenge," *New York Clipper*, October 10, 1868, p. 211.
11. "The Butcher's Champion Tourney: A Chicagoan Wins the Belt," *New York Clipper*, June 12, 1869, p. 74.
12. "Top Butcher Competition at Whole Foods," part of http://blogs.westwood.com/cafesociety/2011/05/no_meat_in_trim_top_butche,php, accessed May 31, 2011.
13. As well, there is also a Bourbon Barrel Racing championship annually in Kentucky which involves stacking 300-pound barrels. Neither are similar to 19th century barrel making contests.
14. "Feat in Coopering," *New York Clipper*, February 1958.
15. Every summer weekend, for example, barrel making demonstrations occur at the Valentown Museum, Victor, New York, as part of a heritage craft demonstration series.
16. Katy Doran, "Hat Making in Colonial Times," http://www.ehow.com/way_5553179_-hat-making-colonial-times.html, accessed May 31, 2001.
17. "Challenge to Hatters," *New York Clipper*, June 15, 1867, p. 74.
18. Edwin Emery and Michael Emery, *The Press and America: An Interpretive History of the Mass Media*, 4th ed. (Englewood Cliffs, N.J.: Prentice-Hall, 1978), pp. 119–123.

19. See "Record Performances: Folding Newspapers," *New York Clipper Annual*, 1884.
20. "Picking Up Potatoes-Amsterdam, NY," *New York Clipper*, April 3, 1859, p. 394.
21. "Bowling on the Road," *New York Clipper*, August 27, 1859, p. 146.
22. See *Annual Reports of the American Institute of New York City* available online. See also "Plowing and Spading Match," *NewYork Clipper*, November 8, 1856, p. 228.
23. "Pole Climbing," *New York Clipper*, October 31, 1857, p. 223.
24. "Climbing Match: Who Is the Champion?" *New York Clipper*, March 30, 1861, p. 394.
25. "Sport Among the Tinkers," *New York Clipper*, November 25, 1859, p. 250.
26. "Novel Match in Frisco," *New York Clipper*, June 17, 1868, p. 79.
27. "Mowing Match," *New York Clipper*, September 6, 1956, p. 157.
28. Alfred Habegger, *My Wars Are Laid Away in Books: The Life of Emily Dickinson* (New York: Modern Library, 2001).
29. "Massachusetts; The Celebration of Independence Day ... Murder in Somerville," *New York Times*, July 10, 1858, p.1.
30. Guy Reel, *The National Police Gazette and the Making of the Modern Man: 1879–1906* (New York: Palgrave, 2006), p. 13.
31. *Ibid.*, p. 54.
32. *Ibid.*, p. 128.

Chapter 13

1. Professional Bull Riders, Inc. They maintain their own website, http://www.pbr, and magazine, *Pro Bull Riding*.
2. http://www.pbrnow.com/schedule/, accessed July 1, 2011.
3. Professional Rodeo Cowboy Association, personal communications, beginning in October 2001.
4. STIHL Timbersports website: http://www.stihltimbersports.us/.
5. Rachel A. Young, "MCAAs Masonry Showcase 2001," *Masonry*, 40, May 2001, pp. 30–36.
6. James Sterba, "Killer Competitions, or How Real Snipers Spend Their Weekend," *Wall Street Journal*, May 18, 1998, pp. A–1, 8.
7. Adam Thompson and John Lyons, "The Aeronautical Pentathlon Has Six Events—and Flying Doesn't Count, *Wall Street Journal*, August 8, 2011, pp. A–1, 12.
8. The SkillsUSA website is continually updated. See http://www.skillsusa.org/about/facts.shtml, accessed July 2, 2011.
9. See www.ffa.org/about/whoweare/Pages/Statistics (523,000 student members for 2011 in 7500 chapters for the FFA) and www.4-h.org/about/Youth/Development (6.5 million members, ages 5 to 19, in 90,000 clubs for 4-H).
10. John Luciew, "Workers Romp," *The Patriot-News* (Harrisburg, PA), August 13, 2011, pp. A–1, 2.
11. Roger Thurow, "Jocks of All Trades: In Sports, Americans Set the Pace in Inventing New Ones," *Wall Street Journal*, December 18, 1996, pp. A–1, 4.
12. http://www.stihltimbersports.us/ardencogar-jr.aspx.
13. Associated Press, "Teens (Surprise) Are World Texting Champs," (Hanover, NH) *Valley News*, January 16, 2010, p. C-3.
14. National Ethical Hackers Association (NEHA) and the Global Ethical Hackers Association (GEHA).

Chapter 14

1. The author relied heavily on John Rickards Betts' standard work, "Sporting Journalism in Nineteenth-Century America," *American Quarterly*, Vol. 5, Issue 1, Spring, 1953, pp. 39–56.
2. *Ibid.*, p.41.
3. Numerous American libraries have the *New York Clipper* on microfilm. I used Baker Library at Dartmouth College and examined each issue for the years 1856, 1857 and 1858,(156 issues, which normally had 8 to 12 pages apiece).
4. Betts, "Sporting Journalism in Nineteenth-Century America," p. 51, fn 42. Betts demonstrates the emergence of sports into popular American culture by accounting for the number of sporting magazines named in his study. One appeared in the 1810s, 3 in the 1820s, 2 in the 1830s, 3 in the 1840s, 4 in the 1850s, 9 in the 1860s, 18 in the 1870s, 30 in the 1880s, and 48 in the 1890s.
5. The Hagley Museum and Library in Wilmington, Delaware, holds extensive manuscripts and archives of hundreds of U.S. firms starting with the 18th century in their Center for the History of Business, Technology and Society.
6. Bil Gilbert, "A Turn on the Old Pike," *Sports Illustrated*, Number 44, June 21, 1976, pp. 64–76.
7. Listing them all would be pointless, but I recommend W.K. Stratton's *Chasing the Rodeo: On Wild Rides and Big Dreams, Broken Hearts and Broken Bones, and One Man's Search for the West* (New York: Harcourt, 2005), and Stan Dixon, "A Century of Musters: Since 1849 the Tradition Goes On," *Firehouse*, June 1978, pp. 77–92.
8. For the corn husking books, see Leonard Jacobs, *Huskers Digest*, Illinois Corn Husking Association, 1942; J. Mitchell Burns, *The National*, self-published, 1988, and William E. Gillen's *Warren County Battle of the Bangboards* (Des Moines: Wallace-Homestead, 1985). For a history of typesetting contests see Walker Rumble, *The Swifts: Printers in the Age of Typesetting Races* (Charlottesville: University of Virginia Press, 2003).

9. See Edward W. O'Brien, "Blacksmith's Boy," *Saturday Evening Post*, November 2, 1940, pp. 10–13.
10. Artist Sol Levenson was then 85 years old.
11. See the website *http://boxofficemojo.com/genres/chart/?id=fire.htm*, accessed July 11, 2011.
12. Scott Reynolds Nelson, *Steel Drivin' Man: John Henry, The Untold Story of an American Legend* (New York: Oxford University Press, 2008).
13. Richard R. Dorson, *America in Legend: Folklore from the Colonial Period to the Present* (New York: Pantheon, 1973), p. 99.
14. The annual Michigan/Michigan State football game is played for the Paul Bunyan trophy.
15. Occupational heroes flourished for ethnic groups as well. For example, a whole set of African American occupational heroes exist of the same period, including Kerosene Charlie (a migrating laborer); Old Pete (a Herculean stevedore); and Roy Tyle (an ace mechanic). See volume one in the American Folkways series: Stetson Kennedy, *Palmetto Country* (New York: Duell, Sloan & Pearce, pp. 121–145.
16. For a description of Lincoln's rail splitting accomplishments see Louis A. Warren, *Lincoln's Youth: Indiana Years: Seven to Twenty-one, 1816–1830*, New York: Appleton, Century, Crofts, 1959), pp. 142–145, and William E. Barringer, *Lincoln Day by Day: A Chronology, 1809–1865* (Washington, D.C., 1960), Vol. I, pp. 12–13.
17. The fourth mythical hero was baseball's "Mighty Casey," who struck out.
18. The Frederick County Fire and Rescue Museum, located in Emmitsburg, Maryland, opened in July 2011.

Chapter 15

1. See C. Frank Zarnowski, "Working at Play: The Phenomenon of 19th Century Worker-Competitions," *Journal of Leisure Research*, Vol. 36, Number 2, 2004, pp. 257–281.
2. See Benjamin Rader, "The Impact of the Social Elites on Sports," *Sports in Modern America*, William J. Baker and John M. Carroll, eds. (St. Louis: River City, 1981), pp. 16–26.
3. The full title of the annual was *Clipper Annual for [Year], containing Theatrical, Musical and Sporting Chronologies for [Year]; a list of American and Foreign deaths in the Amusement Professions; Aquatic and Athletic Performances, Billiard, Racing and Trotting records, Baseball data, etc, together with Records of Fastest Time and Best Performances in all departments of sport*. The price was 15 cents.
4. Erich Fromm, *Marx's Concept of Man* (New York: F. Ungar, 1961), p. 85.
5. Although Max Weber's *The Protestant Ethic and the Spirit of Capitalism*, originally published in 1905, is arduous reading, the above explanation is standard.
6. See Walter Rumble, *The Swifts: Printers in the Age of Typesetting Races* (Charlottesville: University of Virginia Press, 2003), for an explanation of the worker competitions among typesetters.
7. R.J. Huizinga, *Homo Ludens: A Study of the Play Element in Culture* (London: Routledge & Kegan Paul, 1944), p. 13.
8. Daniel T. Rodgers, *The Work Ethic in Industrial America: 1850–1920* (Chicago: University of Chicago Press, 1978), p. 108.
9. Roy Rosenzweig, *Eight Hours for What We Will: Workers and Leisure in an Industrial City, 1870–1920* (Cambridge, U.K.: Cambridge University Press, 1983), p. 39.
10. By 1900 the population of Worcester was 118,000. The school was The College of the Holy Cross.
11. David Nasaw, *Going Out: the Rise and Fall of Public Amusement* (New York: Basic, 1993), p. 4.
12. Susan E. Hirsch, *Roots of the American Working Class: The Industrialization of Crafts in Newark: 1800–1860* (Philadelphia: University of Pennsylvania Press, 1978).
13. G.E. Bevans, *How Workingmen Spend Their Spare Time*, unpublished doctoral dissertation, Columbia University, 1913, pp. 1–10.
14. See both Gary Cross, *A Social History of Leisure Time Since 1600* (State College, PA: Venture, 1990), and David Brody, "Time and Work During Early American Industrialism," *Journal of Labor History*, Vol. 30, Winter 1989, pp. 5–46.
15. D.K. Wiggins, "Work, Leisure and Sport in America: the British Traveler's Image, 1830–1860," *Canadian Journal of History of Sport*, Vol. 13, 1982, pp. 28–60.
16. Barbara Garson, *All the Livelong Day: The Meaning and Demeaning of Routine Work* (New York: Penguin, 1994), p. 35.
17. Rumble, *The Swifts*.
18. For an excellent treatment of the causes and effects of the "muscularity" issue, see E. Anthony Rotundo, *American Manhood* (New York: Basic, 1993).
19. I am indebted for an explanation about how masculinity shaped a newspaper and vice versa to Gary Reel, *The National Police Gazette and the Making of the Modern American Man, 1879–1906* (New York: Palgrave, 2006).
20. Steven M. Gelber, "Working at Play: the Culture of the Workplace and the Rise of Baseball," *Journal of Social History*, Vol. 16, Spring 1983, pp. 3–22.
21. *Ibid.*, p. 18.
22. Mihaly Csikszentmihalyi, *Flow: The Psychology of Optimal Experience* (New York: Harper, 1990), p. 22.
23. See, for example, Ted Ownby, *Subduing Satan: Religion, Recreation and Manhood in the Rural South* (Chapel Hill: University of North Carolina Press, 1990), for a detailed description of how informal farm work turned into formal competitions.
24. An excellent summery of the self-fulfilling issue can be found in the work of André Gorz, a social philosopher, in his *Critique of Economic Reason* (London: Verso, 1980), pp. 73–89.

25. I must admit that this was exactly my recollection of a worker-athlete when I started the research on this topic and went to my first firemen's muster in Salisbury, Maryland, in 1998.

26. For more on Speaker one can consult Timothy Gay, *Tris Speaker: The Rough and Tumble Life of a Baseball Legend* (Lincoln: University of Nebraska Press, 2006), or Charles C. Alexander, *Spoke: The Biography of Tris Speaker* (Dallas: SMU Press, 2007). Gay almost totally ignores Speaker's rodeo past. Alexander's is more instructive. Speaker's career (1907–1928) roughly coincided with that of Ty Cobb and the first decade of that of Babe Ruth.

27. www.uta.edu/english/tim/lection/080201.html, accessed July 3, 2011. Speaker's hometown of Hubbard, Texas, also sponsors the Tris Speaker Sports Museum.

28. His performance was so notable that the feat was reported on the national wires. His time of 21 seconds was 8 seconds faster that of star cowboy roper Tommy Kirnan. "Tris Speaker Easily Defeats Star Roper in Texas Rodeo," *New York Times*, December 3, 1922.

29. Standard heavy events at Highland/Caledonian Games included putting the stone, throwing the hammer, tossing the 56-pound weight and tossing the caber.

30. See D.P. Webster, *Donald Dinnie: The First Sporting Superstar* (Glasgow: Ardo, 1999), p. 98.

31. See *New York Clipper*, April 17, 1869, p. 11.

32. For a short biography on John Goldie, see *New York Clipper*, April 3, 1869, p. 413, which claims that Goldie was so busy that he occasionally had to choose between baseball and Caledonian contests. Perhaps because of ethnic considerations or because prize money was involved, the latter won out.

33. Frank Zarnowski, *All-Around Men: Heroes of a Forgotten Sport* (Lanhan, MD: Scarecrow Press, 2005), pp. 6, 25, 28, 68.

34. Labor productivity data from the Bureau of Labor Statistics (BLS) dates only to 1949. National Bureau of Economic Research (NBER) data is available for an earlier period for some industries. Neither provides productivity data by occupation.

35. For the productivity impact at the national level see Martin Blatt and Martha Norkunas, eds., *Work, Recreation and Culture: Essays in American Labor History* (New York: Garland, 1996). An excellent source which explains the impact of productivity at the firm/plant level can be found in John R. Schleppi, "It Pays: John Patterson and Industrial Recreation at the National Cash Register Company," *Journal of Sport History*, Vol. 6, Spring 1985, pp. 20–28.

36. A. Castle, "How Sports Help America to Out-Produce the World," *Industrial Sport Journal*, 1950, Vol. 11, No. 2, 1950.

37. E.F. Denison, *Trends in American Economic Growth, 1929–1982* (Washington, D.C.: The Brookings Institution, 1985).

38. U.S. Census Bureau, *Historical Statistics of the United States: Colonial Times to 1970* (Washington, D.C.: U.S. Department of Commerce, 1975).

39. Carroll Pursell, *The Machine in America: A Social History of Technology* (Baltimore: Johns Hopkins University Press, 1995).

40. U.S. Census Bureau, *Historical Statistics of the United States: Colonial Times to 1970*.

41. An explanation of how productivity is measured can be found in K. Davis, *Human Behavior at Work*, 4th ed. (New York: McGraw-Hill, 1977).

42. Leonard J. Jacobs, "Kings of the Hill: Illini Huskers, 1924–1941," *Journal of Illinois State Historical Society*, Vol. 76, Autumn 1983, p. 206.

43. Rumble, *The Swifts*, p. 148.

44. Richie, "The Real Facts About Those Hand-Drilling Contests," pp. 84–85.

45. Amitai Etzioni, "The Socio-economics of Work," *The Meaning of Work*, Frederick C. Ganst, ed. (Albany: State University of New York Press, 1995), pp. 251–258.

46. S.S. Brynn, "Some Sports in Pittsburgh during the National Period, 1775–1860." *Western Pennsylvania Historical Magazine*, October 1968, pp, 51–52.

47. For a standard yet faulty understanding on this issue, see Jennie Holliman, *American Sports, 1735–1835* (Durham: Seeman Press, 1931).

48. See Marvin Eyler, "Origins of Contemporary Sports," *Research Quarterly*, Vol. 32, December 1961, pp. 480–89. Of the 95 sports covered Eyler concluded that "six came from work activities (examples: rodeo and birling)," and then turned a blind eye to them, simply ignoring the entire concept of worker competitions. Eyler admits that he deliberately cut out "sport-work activities or contests such as woodchopping, plowing, axethrowing, and tree climbing," but does not admit that he simply ignored many others in spite of the fact that they were well known and popular American sports. Two other highly-regarded sports historians have recognized work-sports and their work should be a starting point for any serious scholarship. See Benjamin Rader, *American Sports: From the Age of Folk Games to the Age of Spectators* (Englewood, N.J.: Prentice-Hall, 1983), and G.B. Kirsch, ed., *Sports in North America: A Documentary History* (Gulf Breeze, FL: Academic International Press, 1992), Vol. 5.

49. Wiggins, "Work, Leisure and Sport in America: the British Traveler's Image: 1830–1860," pp. 28–60.

50. See Michael Dirda, "How Three Damaged Men Work Their Way to Redemption," *Washington Post Book World*, June 3, 2007, p. 10.

Bibliography

Books

Alexander, Charles C. *Spoke: The Biography of Tris Speaker*. Dallas: SMU Press, 2007.

Altherr, Thomas L., et al. *Sports in North America: A Documentary History*. Gulf Breeze, FL: Academic International Press, 1995.

Baker, William J., and John M. Carroll, eds. *Sports in Modern America*. St. Louis: River City, 1981.

Baringer, W.E. *Lincoln Day by Day: A Chronology, 1809–1865*, Vol. 1. Washington, D.C.: Lincoln Sesquicentennial Commission, 1960.

Barnes, William C., Joseph W. McCann, and Alexander Duguid. *Fast Typesetting*. New York: Concord Cooperative Printing, 1887.

Beal, William James. *History of Michigan Agricultural College and Biographical Sketches of Trustees and Professors*. East Lansing: Michigan Agricultural College, 1915.

Berlin, Ira. *Generations of Captivity: A History of African-American Slaves*. Cambridge, MA: Harvard University Press, 2003.

Betts, John Rickards. *America's Sporting Heritage, 1850–1950*. Reading, MA: Addison-Wesley. 1974.

Blatt, Martin, and Martha Norkunas, eds. *Work, Recreation and Culture: Essays in American Labor History*. New York: Garland, 1996.

Bradley, Harriet, et al. *Myths at Work*. Cambridge, U.K: Polity Press, 2000.

Brigham, David R. *Public Culture in the Early Republic: Peale's Museum and its Audience*. Washington, D.C.: Smithsonian Institution Press, 1995.

Brown, Dee. *Hear That Lonesome Whistle Blow*. New York: Holt, Rinehart & Winston, 1997.

Burawoy, Michael. *Manufacturing Consent: Changes in the Labor Process Under Monopoly Capitalism*. Chicago: University of Chicago Press, 1979.

Burns, Mitchell. *The National*. Brookfield, MO: Mitchell Burns, 2000.

Cayleff, Susan E. *Babe: The Life and Legend of Babe Didrickson Zaharias*. Urbana: University of Illinois Press, 1996.

Cochrane, William W., and Mary E. Ryan. *American Farm Policy: 1948–1973*. Minneapolis: University of Minnesota Press, 1976.

Conk, Anderson. *The United States Census and Labor Force Change: A History of Occupational Statistics, 1870–1940*. Ann Arbor: UMI Research Press, 1980.

Conrad, Earl. *Billy Rose: Manhattan Primitive*. Cleveland: World, 1968.

Couvares, Francis G. *The Remaking of Pittsburgh: Class and Culture in an Industrializing City, 1877–1919*. Albany: State University of New York Press, 1984.

Crampton, Frank A. *Deep Enough: A Working Stiff in the Western Mine Camps*. Norman: University of Oklahoma Press, 1982.

Cross, Gary. *A Social History of Leisure since 1600*. State College, PA: Venture, 1990.

Csikszentmihalyi, Mihaly. *Flow: The Psychology of Optimal Experience*. New York: Harper, 1990.

Cumbler, John T. *Working Class Community in Industrial America: Work, Leisure and the Struggle in Two Industrial

Cities, 1888–1930. Westport, CT: Greenwood Press, 1979.
Davis, K. *Human Behavior at Work*. New York: McGraw-Hill, 1977.
Denison, Edward F. *Trends in American Economic Growth, 1929–1982*. Washington, D.C.: The Brookings Institution, 1985.
Dixon, Stan. *The Firemen's Muster: America's Sport*. Newburyport, MA: Stan Dixon, 2001.
Dorson, Richard M. *America in Legend: Folklore from the Colonial Period to the Present*. New York: Pantheon, 1973.
Dulles, Foster R. *A History of Recreation: America Learns to Play*. New York: D. Appleton-Century, 1965.
Emery, Edwin, and Michael Emery. *The Press and America: An Interpretive History of the Mass Media*, 4th ed. Englewood Cliffs, N.J.: Prentice-Hall, 1978.
Etzioni, Amitai. *The Moral Dimension*. New York: Free Press, 1988.
Evans, John. F. *Prairie Farmer and the WLS*. Urbana: University of Illinois Press, 1969.
Evers, John C., ed. *Adventures of Zenas Leonard, Fur Trader*. Norman: University of Oklahoma Press, 1959.
Fogel, Robert. *Railroads and American Economic Growth: Essays in Econometric History*. Baltimore: Johns Hopkins University Press, 1970.
Frank, Robert, and Philip Cook. *The Winner-Take-All Society*. New York: Penguin, 1996.
Gay, Timothy. *Tris Speaker: The Rough and Tumble Life of a Baseball Legend*. Lincoln: University of Nebraska Press, 2006.
Gamst, Frederick C., ed. *Meanings of Work*. Albany: State University of New York Press, 1995.
Garson, Barbara. *All the Livelong Day: The Meaning and Demeaning of Routine Work*. New York: Penguin, 1994.
Gelber, Steven. M. *Hobbies: Leisure and the Culture of Work in America*. New York: Columbia University Press, 1999.
Genovese, Eugene D. *Roll, Jordan, Roll: The World the Slaves Made*. New York: Vintage, 1974.
Gibson, Fred. *Fabulous Empire*. Boston: Houghton Mifflin, 1946.
Gillen, William E. *Warren County Battle of the Bangboards*. Des Moines: Wallace-Homestead, 1985.
Gorn, Elliot. *The Manly Art: Bare-knuckle Prize Fighting in America*. Ithaca: Cornell University Press, 1986.
Gorz, Andre. *Critique of Economic Reason*. London: Verso, 1989.
Greenburg, Amy S. *Cause for Alarm: The Volunteer Fire Department in the 19th Century City*. Princeton: Princeton University Press, 1991.
Greenspan, Alan. *The Age of Turbulence: Adventures in a New World*. New York: Penguin, 2007.
Guttmann, Allen. *From Ritual to Record: The Nature of Modern Sports*. New York: Columbia University Press, 1978.
_____. *Whole New Ball Game: An Interpretation of American Sports*. Chapel Hill: University of North Carolina Press, 1988.
Habeggar, Alfred. *My Wars Are Laid Away in Books: The Life of Emily Dickinson*. New York: Modern Library, 2001.
Hanes, Col. Billy C. *Bill Pickett, Bulldogger: The Biography of a Black Cowboy*. Norman: University of Oklahoma Press, 1977.
Harvey, Katherine A. *The Best Dressed Miners: Life and Labor in the Maryland Coal Region, 1835–1910*. Ithaca: Cornell University Press, 1969.
Hirsch, Susan E. *Roots of the American Working Class: The Industrialization of Crafts in Newark, 1800–1860*. Philadelphia: University of Pennsylvania Press, 1978.
Holbrook, Stewart H. *Holy Old Mackinaw: A Natural History of the American Lumberjack*. New York: Macmillan, 1938.
Holliman, Jennie. *American Sports, 1785–1835*. Durham: Seeman Press, 1931.
Holzman, Robert S. *The Romance of Firefighting*. New York: Bonanza, 1956.
Huizinga, Johan. *Homo Ludens: A Study of the Play Element in Culture*. London: Routledge & Kegan Paul, 1944.
Ierley, Merritt. *Traveling the National Road: Across the Centuries on America's First

Highway. Woodstock, N.Y.: Overlook Press, 1990.

Jacobs, Leonard. *Huskers Digest*. Illinois Corn Husking Association, 1942.

Kando, Thomas M. *Leisure and Popular Culture in Transition*, 2d ed. St. Louis: Mosby, 1980.

Kennedy, Stetson. *Palmetto Country*. New York: Duell, Sloan & Pearce, 1942.

Knowles, Thomas W., and Joe R. Lansdale, eds. *The West That Was*. New York: Wing, 1993.

Krugman, Paul. *Peddling Prosperity*. New York: W.W. Norton, 1994.

Kwokel-Folland, Angel. *Engendering Business: Men and Women in the Corporate Office, 1879–1930*. Baltimore: Johns Hopkins University Press, 1994.

Lankton, Larry. *Cradle to Grave: Life, Work and Death in the Lake Superior Copper Mines*. New York: Oxford University Press, 1981.

Larkin, Jack. *Where We Worked: A Celebration of America's Workers and the Nation They Built*. Guilford, CT: Lyons Press, 2010.

Licht, Walter. *Working for the Railroad: The Organization of Work in the Nineteenth Century*, Princeton: Princeton University Press, 1989.

Marquand, John P. *Point of No Return*. Boston: Little Brown, 1949.

Meyer, Robert, Jr. *Festivals: USA and Canada*. New York: Ives Washburn, 1967.

Mrozek, Donald J. *Sport and American Mentality*. Knoxville: University of Tennessee Press, 1983.

Murray, William A. *The Unheralded Heroes of Baltimore's Big Blazes*. Baltimore: E.G. Schmitz, 1968.

Nasaw, David. *Going Out: The Rise and Fall of Public Amusements*. New York: Basic, 1993.

Nelson, Daniel. *Managers and Workers: Origins of the Twentieth Century Factory System in the United States, 1880–1920*. Madison: University of Wisconsin Press, 1985.

Nelson, S.B. *History of Cincinnati and Hamilton County, Ohio*. Cincinnati: Nelson, 1894.

Nelson, Scott Reynolds. *Steel Drivin' Man: John Henry, the Untold Story of an American Legend*. Oxford: Oxford University Press, 2006.

Northrup, Solomon. *Twelve Years a Slave*. New York: Miller, Orton and Mulligan, 1855.

Olmsted, Frederick Law. *A Journey in the Seaboard Slave States*. New York: Putnam & Sons, 1856.

Ownby, Ted. *Subduing Satan: Religion, Recreation and Manhood in the Rural South*. Chapel Hill: University of North Carolina Press, 1990.

Pursell, Carroll B. *The Machine in America: A Social History of Technology*. Baltimore: Johns Hopkins University Press, 1995.

Rader, Benjamin G. *American Sports: From the Age of Folk Games to the Age of Spectators*, 2d ed. Englewood Cliffs, N.J.: Prentice-Hall, 1990.

Raitz, Karl, ed. *A Guide to the National Road*. Baltimore: Johns Hopkins University Press, 1996.

Rawick, George, ed. *The American Slave: A Composite Autobiography*. Westport, CT: Greenwood pRESS, 1972.

Reel, Guy. *The National Police Gazette and the Making of the Modern Man: 1879–1906*. New York: Palgrave, 2006.

Rigauer, Bero. *Sport and Work*. Trans. A. Guttman. New York: Columbia University Press, 1971.

Ritzer, G., and D. Walczak. *Working Conflict and Change*. Englewood Cliffs, N.J.: Prentice-Hall, 1986.

Rodgers, Daniel T. *The Work Ethic in Industrial America, 1850–1920*. Chicago: University of Chicago Press, 1978.

Rosenberg, Bruce A. *The Code of the West*. Bloomington: Indiana University Press, 1982.

Rosenzweig, Roy. *Eight Hours for What We Will: Workers and Leisure in an Industrial City, 1870–1920*. Cambridge, U.K.: Cambridge University Press, 1983.

Ross, S.J. *Workers on the Edge: Work, Leisure and Politics in Industrializing Cincinnati, 1788–1890*. New York: Columbia University Press, 1985.

Rotundo, E. Anthony. *American Manhood*. New York: Basic, 1993.

Rumble, Walker. *The Swifts: Printers in the Age of Typesetting Races.* Charlottesville: University of Virginia Press, 2003.

Sabin, Edwin L. *Building the Pacific Railroad.* Philadelphia: J.B. Lippincott, 1919.

Searight, Thomas B. *The Old Pike: A History of the National Road, with Incidents, Accidents and Anecdotes.* Uniontown, PA: Thomas B. Searight, 1894.

Smith, Duane A. *Rocky Mountain Mining Camps: The Urban Frontier.* Bloomington: Indiana University Press, 1967.

Stout, William L. *Olympians of the Sawdust Circle: A Biographical Dictionary of the Nineteenth Century American Circus.* San Bernardino: Borgo Press, 1998.

Stratton, W. *Chasing the Rodeo: On Wild Rides and Big Dreams, Broken Hearts and Broken Bones, and One Man's Search for the West.* New York: Harcourt, 2005.

Thompson, Edward P. *The Making of the British Working Class.* New York: Pantheon, 1963.

Twain, Mark. *The Innocents Abroad* and *Roughing It.* New York: Viking Press, 1984.

United States Census Bureau. *Abstract of the Returns of the 5th Census.* Washington, D.C., 1832.

_____. *Historical Statistics of the United States: Colonial Times to 1970.* Washington, D.C: U.S. Department of Commerce, 1975.

United States Department of Labor. *Occupational Outlook Handbook: 1998–99 Edition.* Washington, D.C.: U.S. Government Printing Office, 1998.

Vernam, Glenn R. *Men on Horseback.* New York: Harper and Row, 1964.

Vincent, Ted. *The Rise and Fall of American Sport: Mudville's Revenge.* Lincoln: University of Nebraska Press, 1994.

The Volunteer Fire Department of Old New York, 1790–1866. Scotia, N.Y: Americana Review, 1962.

Wallis, Michael. *The Real Wild West: The 101 Ranch and the Creation of the American West.* New York: St. Martin's Griffin, 1999.

Warren, Louis A. *Lincoln's Youth: Indiana Years, Seven to Twenty-one, 1816–1830.* New York: Appleton, Century, Crofts, 1959.

Weber, Max. *The Protestant Ethic and the Spirit of Capitalism.* Trans. Peter Baehr and Gordon C. Wells. Reprint of 1905 edition. New York: Penguin, 2002.

Webster, D.P. *Donald Dinnie: The First Sporting Superstar.* Glasgow: Ardo, 1999.

Weymouth, T. Jordan. *Hugh Davis and his Alabama Plantation.* Tuscaloosa: University of Alabama Press, 1948.

Wish, Harvey, ed. *Slavery in the South: First Hand Accounts of the Ante-Bellum American Southland from Northern & Southern Whites, Negroes, & Foreign Observers.* New York: Farrar, Straus and Co., 1964.

Wood, Richard G. *A History of Lumbering in Maine, 1820–1861.* Orono: University of Maine, 1935.

Young, Otis E. *Black Powder and Hand Steel: Miners and Machines on the Old Western Frontier.* Norman: University of Oklahoma Press, 1976.

Zahavi, Gerald. *Workers, Managers and Welfare Capitalism: The Shoemakers and Tanners of Endicott Johnson, 1890–1950.* Urbana: University of Illinois Press, 1988.

Zarnowski, Frank. *All-Around Men: Heroes of a Forgotten Sport.* Lanham, MD: Scarecrow Press, 2005.

Articles

Abbey, Kathryn T., ed. "Documents Relating to El Destino and Chemonie Plantations, Middle Florida, 1828–1866." *Florida Historical Society Quarterly* 7 (1929): 195–96.

Bellaire, John L. "Michigan Lumber-jacks." *Michigan History Magazine* 26 (Spring 1942): 173–187.

Betts, John Rickards. "Sporting Journalism in 19th Century America." *American Quarterly* 5 (1953): 39–56.

Boatright, Mody C. "The American Rodeo." *American Quarterly* 16, No. 2 (Summer 1964): 195.

Brody, David. "Time and Work During Early American Industrialism." *Journal of Labor History* 30 (Winter 1989): 5–46.

Brown, Mrs. Hugh. "Railroad Days: A Memoir of Tonopah, 1904." *The American West* 5 (November 1968).

Brynn, Soeren S. "Some Sports in Pittsburgh During the National Period, 1775–1860." *Western Pennsylvania Historical Magazine* (October 1968, January 1969): 51–52, 345–363, 57–79.

Castle, Ames. "How Sports Helps America to Out-Produce the World." *Industrial Sport Journal* 11 (September, October 1950): 9; 6, 34.

"The Challenge Accepted." *The Cosmopolitan Shorthander* 9, No. 6 (June 1888): 155.

Dill, Dorothy. "Lumberjack Stories." *Michigan History* 41 (September 1957): 327–334.

Dixon, Stan. "A Century of Musters: Since 1849 the Tradition Goes On." *Firehouse* (June 1978): 77–78, 92.

Enberg, George B. "Who Were the Lumberjacks?" *Michigan History* 32, No. 3 (July–December 1948) 243.

Eyler, Marvin H. "Origins of Contemporary Sports." *Research Quarterly* 32 (December 1961): 480–489.

Fries, R. F. "The Founding of the Lumber Industry in Wisconsin." *Wisconsin Magazine of History* 26 (September 1942): 23–35.

Gelber, Steven. M. "Working at Play: The Culture of the Workplace and the Rise of Baseball." *Journal of Social History* 16 (Spring 1983): 3–22.

Gilbert, Bil. "A Turn on the Old Pike." *Sports Illustrated* 44 (June 21, 1976): 64–76.

Ginsberg, Stephen F. "Above the Law: Volunteer Fireman in New York City, 1836–1837." *New York History* 50 (April 1969): 165–186.

Gossard, Steve. "Frank Gardner and the Great Leapers." *Bandwagon*, July–August 1990, 12.

Heilala, John J., "In an Upper Michigan Lumber Camp." *Michigan History* 6 (March 1962): 55–79.

Hoy, James F. "The Origins and Originality of the Rodeo." *Journal of the West*, Vol. XVII (July 1978): 19.

Jacobs, Leonard J. "Kings of the Hill: Illini Huskers, 1924–1941." *Journal of the Illinois State Historical Society* 76 (Autumn 1983): 205–212.

Kreuger, Lilian. "Social Lives in Wisconsin." *Wisconsin Historical Magazine* 22 (March, July 1939): 312–328, 396–426.

LeCompte, Mary Lou. "The First American Rodeo Never Happened." *Journal of Sport History*, Vol. 9, No. 2 (Summer 1982): 89–96.

———. "The Hispanic Influence of the History of the Rodeo, 1823–1922." *Journal of Sport History*, Vol. 12, No. 1 (Spring 1985): 29.

Leech, Carl. "Lumbering Days." *Michigan History Magazine* 18 (Spring 1934): 135–142.

Liebowitz, Stanley J., and Stephen E. Margolis. "The Fable of the Keys." *Journal of Law and Economics*, Vol, XXXIII (April 1990): 1–26.

MacDonald, M. "Kid Foss and the Birth of the Rodeo," *Montana* 1 (Summer 1971): 58–63.

McNally, Vincent P. "A History of Volunteers." *Firehouse* (May 1986): 43.

"McGurrin vs. Traub." *The Cosmopolitan Shorthander*, Vol. 10, No. 2 (February 1889): 21–23.

Miller, Lance A., and John C. Thomas. "Behavioral Issues in the Use of Interactive Systems: Part I. General Issues." *International Journal of Man-Machine Studies*, Vol. 9, No. 5 (1977): 509–536.

Millette, Ernie. "You Could Leap to Your Death." *Bandwagon*, May–June 1985, p. 20.

"Miners Stage Rock Drilling Races." *Popular Science*, December 1934, p. 40.

Nelligan, John E. "The Life of a Lumberman." *Wisconsin Magazine of History* 13 (September, December 1929): 3–65, 131–185.

O'Brien, Edward W. "Blacksmith's Boy — Heel and Toe." *Saturday Evening Post*, November 2, 1940, 9–11, 90, 92.

Orcutt, Wright T. "The Minnesota Lumberjacks." *Minnesota History* 15 (March 1925): 3–19.

Porter, Willard H. "The American Rodeo: Sport and Spectacle." *The American West* 8 (July 1971): 40–47.
Raney, William F. "Pine Lumbering in Wisconsin." *Wisconsin Magazine of History* 19 (September 1935): 71–90.
Richie, Atha. A. "The Real Facts about those Hand-Drilling Contests." *Engineering and Mining Journal* 152 (November 1951): 84–85.
Rumble, Walker. "From the Shop Floor to the Show: Joseph W. McCann, Typesetting Races and Expressive Work in 19th Century America." *Journal of Popular Culture*, Vol. 32, Issue 2 (Fall 1998): 87.
_____. "Ready, Go, Set." *Heritage*, Spring 2001.
_____. "A Showdown of 'Swifts': Women Compositors, Dime Museums, and the Boston Typesetting Races of 1886." *The New England Quarterly*, Vol.71, No. 4 (December 1998): 615–628.
Saunders, Thomas. "How the Word 'Rodeo' Originated as Applied to Western Events." *The Quarter Horse Journal*, June 1968, 28–29.
Schleppi, John R. "It Pays: John Patterson and Industrial Recreation at the National Cash Register Company." *Journal of Sport History* 6 (Spring 1985): 20–28.
"Still Another Challenge." *The Typewriter Operator*, Vol. 1, No. 10 (January 1888): 51.
Swearingen, Mark. "Thirty Years of a Mississippi Plantation: Charles Whitmore of Montpelier." *Journal of Southern History*, Vol. 1, No. 2 (1935): p. 205.
Tomlins, Christopher. "Why Wait for Industrialization? Work, Legal, Culture and the Example of Early America—A Historiographical Argument." *Journal of Labor History* 40 (1999): 5–34.
Ward, Willis C. "Reminiscences of Michigan's Logging Days." *Michigan History Magazine* 20 (Autumn 1936): 301–312.
Wiggins, David Kenneth. "Good Times on the Old Plantation: Popular Recreations of the Black Slave in Antebellum South, 1810–1860." *Journal of Sport History*, Vol. 4, No. 3 (1977): 279.
_____. "Sport and Popular Pastimes: Shadow of the Slavequarter." *Canadian Journal of History of Sport and Physical Education*, Vol. 11, No. 1 (1980): 65.
_____. "Work, Leisure and Sport in America: The British Traveler's Image, 1830–1860." *Canadian Journal of History of Sport* 13 (1982): 28–60.
Young, Rachel. "MCAAs Masonry Showcase, 2001." *Masonry* 40 (May 2001): 30–36.
Zarnowski, C. Frank. "Working at Play: The Phenomenon of 19th Century Worker-Competitions." *Journal of Leisure Research*, Vol. 36, No. 2 (2004): 257–281.

Newspaper Accounts (by paper)

New York Clipper
"Another Butchering Match." March 2, 1861, p. 362.
"Another Type-Setting Feat." March 26, 1870, p. 402.
"Bowling on the Road." August 27, 1859, p. 146.
"Butcherdom Has a New Sensation." February 16, 1861, p. 346.
"The Butcher's Champion Tourney." May 12, 1869, p.74.
"The Butcher's Champion Tourney: A Chicagoan Wins the Belt." June 12, 1869, p. 74.
"Challenge to Hatters," June 15, 1867, p. 74.
"Challenge to Plough," September 27, 1856, p. 178.
"Champion Fireman of America," January 16, 1858, p. 312.
"Climbing Match: Who Is the Champion?" March 30, 1861, p. 394.
A Constant Reader. "Another Horse Shoe Feat." February 6, 1858, p. 330.
"Dressing a Bullock." March 29, 1858.
"Feat in Coopering." February 1958.
"Firemen Playing." September 12, 1857, p. 163.
"Mowing Match," September 6, 1956, p. 157.
"National Musters of Firemen-Toronto." May 1, 1858, p. 10.
"Novel Blacksmithing Match." January 16, 1869, p. 319.
"Novel Match in Frisco." June 17, 1868, p. 79.
"Picking Up Potatoes—Amsterdam, NY." April 3, 1859, p. 394.

Bibliography

"Plowing and Spading Match." November 8, 1856, p. 228.
"Pole Climbing." October 31, 1857, p. 223.
"Quick Work: For Horse Shoes and Nails." April 4, 1860, p. 7.
"Sheep Slaughtering Challenge." October 10, 1868, p. 211.
"Sport Among the Tinkers." November 25, 1859, p. 250.
"State and County Fairs for 1867." September 14, 1967, p. 180.
"Wm. W. Bush: One of America's Firemen." January 16, 1858, p. 312.

New York Times
Atkinson, Clair. "An 8 Second Ride Lures Sponsors Beyond the Rodeo." December 11, 2007.
Lehman, Eben. "The Fall of Timber Sports?" July 29, 2009.
"Massachusetts: The Celebration of Independence Day ... Murder in Somerville." July 10, 1858, p. 1.
"Tris Speaker Easily Defeats Star Roper in Texas Rodeo." December 3, 1922.
"Typewriters Contest for Metropolitan Stenographers Association Prize." August 2, 1888, p. 2.

Wallace's Farmer
"Against Corn Husking Contest." November 14, 1924, p. 1479.
Gay, Alva. "Corn Husking Contest." June 4, 1924, p. 12.
"Last Call For Husking Contest." November 14, 1924, p. 1472.
"Local Husking Contests." December 12, 1924, p. 1593.
"To Husking Contest Objectors." December 5, 1924, p. 1562.
Wallace, H.A. "Iowa Wins Mid-West Championship." December 5, 1924, p. 1561.
_____. "Young Grimmius Finally Wins." November 28, 1924, p. 1531.

Other Newspapers
"Agricultural Fairs." *New York Herald*, October 4, 1958, p. 4.
"Barred Chief Hale's Men." *Kansas City Star*, August 19, 1900, p. 1.
"Copy All Out: The Globe as Usual, Leads All Competitors." *Boston Globe*, February 21, 1886, p. 1.
"Cotton." *American Farmer*, January 18, 1826, p. 338.
Cunniff, John. "County Fairs Turn into Big Business." *Milwaukee Journal*, October 12, 1967, p. 21.
Dirda, Michael. "How Three Damaged Men Work Their Way to Redemption." *Washington Post Bork World*, June 3, 2007, p. 10.
"Grand Fireman's Muster." *Worcester Transcript*, September 10, 1858, p. 10.
"Grange Picnic Draws Thousands." *Spokane Spokesman-Review*, July 7, 1908, p. 1, 8.
"Greatest Track Laying Feat of the Age — Ten Miles of Rail Laid by the Central Pacific — Their Competitors Give Up." *Daily Alta California*, April 29, 1869, p. 1.
"Here's How It All Started." *The Prairie Farmer*, October 18, 1941, p. 67.
"Ike and Adalai Will Talk at Plow Contest." Associated Press in the *Gettysburg Times* (Gettysburg, PA), September 6, 1956, p. 19.
Luciew, John. "Workers Romp." *The Patriot-News* (Harrisburg, PA), August 13, 2011, pp. A 1–2.
"Our Firemen in Paris." *Kansas City Star*, August 21, 1900. p. 1.
"Pacific Railroad." *Daily Alta California*, April 30, 1869, p. 1.
"Plowing Contest Also Political." *Tri City Herald* (Tri City, WA), September 22, 1960, p. 4.
"Sheep and Wool Festival." *The Bow Times* (Contocook, NH), May 1, 2008, p. A–6.
Sibley, Frank. "New England Troops Find Familiar Game in France." *Boston Globe*, August 3, 1918.
Skinner, J., ed. "The Late Cattle Show." *American Farmer*, November 7, 1828, p. 272.
Sterba, James. "Killer Competitions, or How Real Snipers Spend Their Weekend." *Wall Street Journal*, May 18, 1998.
"Teens (Surprise) Are World Texting Champs." Associated Press in (Hanover,

NH) *Valley News*, January 16, 2010, p. C-3.
Thompson, Adam, and John Lyons. "The Aeronautical Pentathlon Has Six Events—and Flying Doesn't Count." *Wall Street Journal*, August 8, 2011, pp. A–1, 12.
Thurow, Roger. "Jocks of All Trades: In Sports, Americans Set the Pace in Inventing New Ones." *Wall Street Journal*, December 18, 1996, pp. A–1, 4.
"Trial of Steam Fire Engines." *Boston Post*, September 1–2, 1858, p. 1, 1.
"Won as Professionals." *Kansas City Star*, August 20, 1900, p. 1.
Wren, Celia. "The Day John Henry Came to School-Theater Review." *Washington Post*, April 25, 2011, p. C-3.

Other Sources

Bevans, G. E. *How Workingmen Spend Their Spare Time*. Unpublished doctoral dissertation, Columbia University, New York, 1913.
Cross, Gary S., ed. "Agricultural Fairs." *Encyclopedia of Recreation and Leisure in America*. New York: Scribner, 2004.
Goldin, Claudia, and Lawrence Katz. "The Decline of Non-Competing Groups: Changes in the Premium to Education, 1890 to 1940." *National Bureau of Economic Research*, Working Paper No. 5202, August 1995.
LeCompte, Mary Lou. "The First Rodeo in Texas." Paper presented to the North American Society for Sports History, Albuquerque, May 1980.
_____. "Rodeo." *Encyclopedia of World Sport*, Vol. II, eds. David Levinson and Karen Christensen. Santa Barbara: ABC-CLIO, 1996.
New York Clipper 1887 Annual. New York: Frank Queen, 1888.
SkillsUSA. *2000 SkillsUSA—VICA, The Year in Review*. Leesburg, VA: SkillsUSA—VICA, 2001.
United States Census Bureau. *Historical Statistics of the United States: Colonial Times to 1970*. Washington, D.C.: U.S. Department of Labor, 1975.
Wiggins, David Kenneth. *Sport and Popular Pastimes in the Plantation Community: The Slave Experience*. Ph.D. Dissertation, University of Maryland, College Park, 1979, DAI-A, 41/02.

Index

Aberdeen, Scotland 186
Academy Award 174
Academy of Natural Sciences 105
Adam Forepaugh Circus 72
Addison County, VT 157
Adventures of Zenas Leonard, Fur Trader 89
Aeronautical Pentathlon 164
Afghans 92
agricultural fairs 30, 141–42, 170
Albany, NY 142
Alberta, Canada 85, 90
alienation 17
All Sports Record Book 132
Allegheny, CA 115
Allegheny Mountains 23
Alleman, IA 128
American Birling Association (ABA) 161
American Engine Company Number 6 (NYC) 32
American Expeditionary Forces (AEF, WWI) 47
American Farmer 53, 135, 171, 190
American Fireman Series 34
American Institute 137, 154–55
American Institute Annual 155
American Institute Indoor Hall (NYC) 158
American Lumberjack Association (ALA) 161
American Revolution 141
American Sewing Guild 156
American Turf Register and Sporting Magazine 21, 41, 135, 171
American Zoot Shooters Association 164
Americus Six 33
Ames, IA 127
Amsterdam, NY 153–54
Annual Clipper Almanac 41

antebellum period 28
antelopes 131
Appalachia coal regions 106
Appalachian Mountains 112, 113
Applebaum, Herbert 135
Appleseed, Johnny 176
architectural drafting 165
Arensberg, George 57, 60
Argentine gauchos 92
Arizona 107
Arlington, RI 45
Arlington, VA 138
Arnesberg, Richard 73
Asheville, NC 125
Ashland, MA 40
Ashland, WI 102
asparagus eating contests 142
Associated Press 126
Athol, MA 46
Atlantic Ocean 2
Audubon 5
Austin, TX 84
Austin and Stone's Dime Museum (Boston) 60–61
Australia 104, 161
automotive refinishing 165
average workweek 18
Ax Men 162
axe throwing 103

Babe (blue ox) 104
Bae Young-Hoe 168
Baker-Berry Library (Dartmouth) 11
Baldwin, Stephen 173
baling 141
Ball, Mr. 157
Baltimore, MD 35, 38–39, 124, 135, 150, 171
Baltimore Sun 39, 65
Banta, San 37
Baraboo, WI 11
"Barber's Bible" 171
"Bareback Jack" 175
Barnes, William C. 55, 57–62, 64

Barnesville, MN 142
Barnum, P.T. 35, 58, 158
bartending 163
Bartlett, E.S. 139
Baruch, Bernard 117
baseball 175, 178
base-ball, baseball 43
Baseball Hall of Fame 186
Batcheller, George 71, 73
Batcheller, William 66, 70, 71–73
Bath, ME 40, 168
batoute (springboard) 66, 676
Battery (NYC) 58
Battle Creek, MI 45
Bayou Boeuf 53
Beatty, William 155
Beaver Bend plantation, AL 51
Beck, Don 173
Belafonte, Harry 175
Belmond, IA 138
Bend, OR 102
Bengal Tiger 35
Berbers 92
Berkshire Museum 14
Bethlehem Steel Co. 172
betting 55
Betts, John 40
Bevans, G.E. 181
Bicknell, James 138
Bienvenida 85
bike couriers 163
birling 48, 50–51, 97, 101–102
Bisbee, AZ 108, 115
Bison, SD 139
Black Codes 113
Black Hawk War 99
black rodeo contests 168
Blackburn, Barbara 124
blacksmith 115
Blacksmith Hall of Fame 177
blacksmithing 29, 141
"Blacksmith's Boy" 14, 147, 172–73
Blondin *see* Garvelet, Emile
blueberry picking contests 142

221

Bluemont, VA 142
Blytheville, Arkansas 54
Boatright, Mody C. 90
Boilermakers 170
Bonds, Barry 37
bookbinding contests 163
boot-blacking 163
Boston 33
Boston Globe 58, 59, 60
Boulder, CO 115
boxing 175
Brice, Fannie 120
brick pull, Fairfield, PA 3–5
bricklaying 165
Bridgeport, IL 149
British Museum 59
broadcast news production 165
Broadway 119, 176
Brockton, MA 46
Brody, David 181
bronc riding: bareback 91; saddle 91
Bronco Buster 173
Brooklyn, NY 123, 146, 187
Brooklyn Bridge 68
Brooks, Garth 175
Brown, Dee 79
Brown, Mrs. Hugh 110
Buena Vista, MN 177
Buffalo Bill *see* Cody, William F.
Buffalo, NY 46, 138, 151
Bugeaters 131
The Bull-Dogger 94
bull penis-to-keychain contest 140
bull riding 91, 92, 161
bulldogging 83–85, 87
bullfighting 85
"Bullridin' Son of a Gun" 175
Bunyan, Paul 38, 103–4, 114, 176–77, 184
Burawoy, Michael 17
Burdick, KS 85
bureaucracies 21
Burlieghy cotton plantation (MS) 50
Burnett, Prof. L.C. 127
Burton's patent (sewing) machine 156
Bush, William W. 31, 33, 45
butchering demonstrations 168
butchering rules 149
Butcher's Championships 149
Butte, Montana 107, 108

cabbage bowling contests 143
cabinet making 166
Caledonian Games 43–44, 68, 114, 175, 186
calf roping 161
Calgary Stampede 90
California 88, 150; gold rush 106
California Spirit of the Times 41
caligraph machines 121, 123
Caligraph No. 2 121
Cambridge, MA 45, 46
Campbell, Alexander 24
Campbell, Milt 115
camping 172
Canada 97–98, 136, 138
Canfield, OH 143
"Canners" 170
Cap and Necktie 173
carpentry 165–66
carriage driving 168
Carson's Nevada Days 115
Carter, Patsy 11
Carthage, IL 71
Case-Western University 188
Cash, Johnny 115, 175
cashiering 163
Castle, A. 188
The Cattleman 172
Cattleman's Carnival (Garden City, KS) 93
Cemetery Olympics 163
Census Bureau, U.S. 19, 181, 188
Central Pacific Railroad 9, 20, 74–78, 190
Chadwick, Henry 129
chamber-maids 153
Chamberlain and Make 109, 112
Champion Bronco Buster of the Plains 89
champion leaper of the world 72
Chanfrau, Frank 37–38
Chanfrau, Henry 37–38
Chanfrau, Joseph 37–38
Chanfrau, Peter 37–38
Chapman, John *see* Johnny Appleseed
Charles County, MD 48
Charleston, WV 104, 113
Charlie Daniels Band 175
Charlottesville, VA 113
charreria 88
charro 89
Chatsworth, IL 70
Cherokee 83–84
Chesapeake & Ohio Railroad 103, 113
Chesterton, MD 154
Cheyenne, WY 84, 89, 95
Cheyenne Bill 85
Cheyenne tribe 80
Chicago 63, 71, 100, 124, 147–50, 156, 159
Chicago Butcher Society 149
Chicago Cubs 134
Chicago Evening Journal 62
Chicago Roundup 93
Chicago White Sox 134
Chicago World's Fair (1893) 140
"Chicks with Sticks" 186
chili pepper toss 143
Chinamen 77
Christmas tree baling 163
Chytka, Tony 173
Cincinnati, OH 39, 58, 121, 123, 151
Cincinnati Enquirer 62
Cincinnati Red Stockings 39, 43, 187
circus season 66
Circus World Museum 11
Civic Center Park (Denver) 173
Civil War 16, 18, 28, 30, 40–41, 43–45, 55, 66, 69–70, 75, 99, 105, 106, 120, 125, 135, 141, 154, 171
Clemens, Samuel Longhorne *see* Twain, Mark
Clemson University 35
clerk population 125
Cleveland, OH 151
Clinton, Bill 164
Clinton, Harry 147
Clinton, MA 137
Cloverdale Farms 140
coal mining 106
Cobb, Ty 186
Cody, William F. (Buffalo Bill) 90, 91
Coe, Pete 11
Coeur d'Alene, ID 108
coffee bean picking contests 142
Cogar, Arden "Jamie" 104, 168
Colorado Cowboy: The Bruce Ford Story 174
Colorado Springs, CO 177
Columbia University 181
Columbus Day 45
Colz, William 148
Comish, John 72
Commerce High School (Brooklyn) 117
commercial baking 165
Commerford, Irish Jack 110

Index

compensatory hypothesis 184
compositors 55, 62
computer games 169
computer maintenance 165
Comstock Lode 74, 106
Conestoga wagons 23
congruent/spillover hypothesis 184
Connecticut 58
Contoocook, NH 140
Convention Center, Kansas City 164
Cookson, Frank 96, 97
Cooperstown, NY 177
copper mining 107
corn shuckings 48, 50
corn thinning 51
cornhusking 131, 163, 170
Cornwall 106, 115
Corydon, OH 187
cosmetology 166
Cosmopolitan Shorthander 121
cotton picking 50, 54, 142, 163
County, Orange 37
Cousin Jacks 106, 110
Cow Palace, San Francisco 140–41
cowboys 95, 170
Cowboys Turtle Association (CTA) 94
crab trap pulling 163
cradling 141, 171
Crampton, Frank 110
Cranston, RI 45
Credit Mobilier of America 76
Creevy, William 64
cricket 43, 178
Criollo 87
Criss, Howard Paul, Jr. 103
Crocker, Charles 74, 76–78
Cross, Gary 181
crow's feet 147
Csikszentmihalyi, Mihaly 184
Cullowhee, NC 168
Cumberland, MD 23
Cumberland Pike 23
Curley, Louis 129
Currier, Nathaniel 34
Custis, Daniel 138
Custis, George Washington Parke 138

Dabney, Thomas 50
Dailey 78
Daily Alta California 77
Daily Herald (Chicago) 59
Daily News (Chicago) 59
Daily Union (Sacramento) 78

Daily Whig and Courier (Bangor, ME) 99
Dan Rice Paris Pavilion Circus 71
Dana, Charles A. 172
Danbury, CT 151
Dartmouth College 7–8, 10–11, 172, 189
Daugherty, Duffy 139
Davenport, IA 148
Davis, Hugh 51
Davis, J.R. 58–60, 62
Dawkins, Richard 2
Dayton, OH 41
Dead Rabbits gang 37
Deadwood, Dakota Territory 42
Deadwood, SD 173
decathlon 185
Deer Trail, Colorado Territory 89
Deere, John 136
Defender Co (East Weymouth, MA) 45
Democratic Party 24–25, 138
Denham, John 35
Denison, Edward 188
Dennison, Walter 147
Denver, CO 173
Department of Interior 80
Des Moines, IA 127, 128, 137, 168
Detroit, MI 35
Detroit Publishing Co. 97
Detroit Tigers 2
Dewey, Thomas 137
Dexter, IA 137
Díaz, Porfirio 86
Di Caprio, Leonardo 174
Dickinson, Emily 157
Didrikson-Zaharias, Mildred (Babe) 126, 187–88
Dillon, MR. 154
DiMaggio, Joe 185–86
dime museums 29, 59, 63
Dinnie, Donald 114, 175, 186–88
dinosaur 105
Dirda, Michael 191
Dirdo, Michael 191
Discover 5
Disney, Walt 174, 176
Dockrill & Leon's Circus and Hippodrome 66, 72
Dodge, Grenville 74, 76, 78
Dorsey, Peter 11
Dorson, Richard 176
"double-jack" drilling 107–109, 111, 113
Dover, NH 154
Doyle 100–101

Dragila, Stacy 93, 185, 188
Dublin, Ireland 57
Du Bois, W.E.B. 48
Duguid, Alexander 61–63
Dunbar, Fayette County, PA 24, 30
Durant, Thomas C. 75, 76, 78–79
"Dusky Demon" 83, 84, 86, 93
Dvorak, August 123
Dynda, Morgan 168

Eau Clair, WI 72, 102
economic forces 63
economic growth, US 81, 188
Edenton, NC 53
Edison Electric Co. 172
"8 Second Ride" 175
8 Seconds (art) 173
8 Seconds (movie) 173
Eisenhower, Dwight D. 138
Elastic Skin Man 62
The Electric Horseman 174
electrical skills 166
elephants 67, 69, 70
Elizabeth, NJ 112
Elliot 78
Ellison, George 148
El Paso, TX 109
Elysian Fields (Hoboken, NJ) 187
Employers Casualty Insurance Company (Dallas, TX) 126
EMT programs 167
Engine Company Number 15 (NYC) 35
engine repair 165
equality 21
equipment (of work sports) 190
Erie Canal 99
Erie County, NY 138
ESPN 10, 47, 94, 104, 167–68
Essex Agricultural Society 141
Etzioni, Amitai 20, 190
Europeans 98
Evening Journal (Chicago) 59, 62
Evening Mail (Chicago) 64
extreme sports 167
Eyler, Marvin H. 21

"Fable of the Keys" 121
Facing the Enemy 34
Fairfield, PA 3
Fairlee, VT 7
Farm Show Arena, Harrisburg, PA 139–40

Farmer's, Mechanic's, Manufacturer's and Sportsman's Magazine 172
Fast Eddie 119
Fast Typesetting 61
Fastest Trowel in the West 163
Fayette County, PA 24, 30
Federal Highway Act of 1956 30
Federal Highway Administration 27
Federal Reserve Board of Governors 125
fence painting 163
Finnan, Aengus 175
Firefighter Combat Challenge 47
Firefighter Halls of Fame 177
firefighting 160, 162
The Fireman's Journal 40, 41
First American Macadam Road 27
Fischel, Bill 11
Fitzpatrick, Andrew 137
Florida 48, 52
Flynn, Charles 152
fodder pulling 51
Fogel, Robert 81
Fonda, Henry 174
Fonda, Jane 174
Ford, Glenn 174
Ford, Henry 137
Forepaugh & Sells Brothers Circus 67
Fort Dodge, IA 127, 133
Fort Leavenworth, KS 133
Fort Worth Stock Show 186
Forty Thieves gang 37
Fosbury, Dick 72
Fosbury Flop 73
Foster, George 146
4-H clubs 166
Fox, Richard Kyle 41, 158–59, 171
Fox Brothers Shop 147
Fox River 96
Frank Leslie's Illustrated Newspaper 49, 52, 80, 95
Franklin, Benjamin 32
French-Canadians 98
Friendship (Fire) Co., Alexandria, VA 32
Fries, Robert 97
Frijoles Chiquitos 86
Fritz, Rose L. 124
frolics 52
"Frontier Days" 88–90; Cheyenne 89; Prescott, AZ 90
Frost, Lane 174

Furey, Sean 8, 11
Future Farmers of America (FFA) 166

Galamb, Joseph 137
Galesburg, IL 70, 71, 73
Gangs of New York 174
Gardenshire, Emilnie 89
Gardner, Frank 66, 70, 71, 73
Gardner, MA 45
Garson, Barbara 182
Garvelet, Emile (Blondin) 69
Gauchos, Argentine 92
Gay, Alva 130
Gelber, Stephen 184
General Mills 134
Germans 98
Geronimo 84, 93
Gettysburg, PA 3, 11
Gibson, Hoot 93
gift wrappers 163
Gilbert, Bil 1, 10–11, 89, 172
Gilmore, Capt. Elias 24–26, 30
A Glance at New York 37–38
Glens Falls, NY 70, 71, 73
Goddard, Steven 69
gold mining 107
Golden Spike ceremony 76, 79
Goldfield, NV 112
Goldie, George 44, 68, 187
Goldie, John 43–44, 68, 187–88
Good Intent Line 24
goose pull 2
Gorman, Roger 148
Gosnell, AR 142
Grabill, John C.H. 42
Graham, George 57, 60, 61
Grand Detour, IL 136
Grand National Livestock Exposition 140
Grant, M.C. 123
grape stomping contests 143
Grass Valley, CA 110
grave diggers 163
"graybacks" 103
Great Basin 106
Great Depression 91, 134, 137
Great Lakes region 97, 99, 100, 102
Great Outdoor Games (ESPN) 104, 161
Great Plains 80
Great Salt Lake 76
Greeley, Horace 16, 64
Green, John 155–56
Greenberg, Amy 38
Greenspan, Alan 125–26, 164

Greenville, ME 168
Gregg, John Robert 118–19
Griffiths, George 158
Grimmius, Ben 127
grocery baggers 163
Gross National Parade 158
Grundy County, IA 127
Guinness Book of World Records 41, 124
Gunn, Johnny 116
Gunnison granite 111
Guthrie, Woody 115, 175
Guttmann, Allen 20–21, 169

Ha Mok Min 168
Hagley Museum 11
Hall, Mr. C.H. 137
handsetting 65
Hanover, NH 11, 172
Harding, Warren 129
Harlem 136–37, 155
Harper's New Monthly Magazine 49
Harper's Weekly 16, 30
harvests 51
Hatch Valley, NM 143
Havana 66, 72
hay loading 163
hay stacking 141
Hayes, Ed 173
Hays, Jack Coffee 89
Hayward, Susan 174
Hayward, WI 104
Hearst, William Randolph 152
Henriele, Charles L. 151
Henry, John 28, 38, 73, 105–6, 112–15, 127, 174–77, 184
Henson, Josiah 48–50
Heritage documentaries 174
Heritage Foundation 134
Hero of Niagara 69
Higham, John 183
Hillsboro, TX 186
Hillsgrove, RI 46
"Hindoo Princess" 61–62
Hinds, Carol 11
Hinds, MS 50
hippodroming 29
Hirak, Kory 11
History Channel 162
Hoboken, NJ 187
hog killings 48, 50, 51
Hogsett, Robert 24
Holloway, Travis Calvin 173
Holm, Eleanor 120
Holman Brothers, Ltd 115
Holzman, Robert 33
Homer 135
Homer, Winslow 49
Homo Ludens 180

Index 225

Honolulu 38
Hood College 11
hoolihaning 93
Hoover, Herbert 133
Hope, AR 142
Hopkins, Mark 74
horse pulling 134
horse racing 178
Horse-to-Glue contest 139–40
horseshoe making 168, 173
Houston, TX 168
Howe, Elias 156
Howe's Great London Circus 70
Hoy, James F. 88
Hoyl, Emmit 115
Hubbard, TX 186
huckleberry homesteader pentathlon 143
Hudson, Joseph 64
Huizinga, R.J. 180
Humphrey, Moses (Old Mose) 37–38, 73, 176
Hun-and-Hub race 42
Huns 92
Huntington, Collis 74
Hyde, Arthur M. 133

IAAF World T&F championships 186
ice-getting 51
Idaho Springs, CO 115
Idaho State University 185
Illinois 106, 128, 131–34, 136, 139
Indiana 131
Indiana State Fair 121
Indianapolis 63
Industrial Recreation (IR) movement 19, 188
Industrial Revolution 17
Inland Printer Magazine 56
in-line skating 167
Intercourse, PA 168
International Amateur Athletic Federation (IAAF) 73
International Amateur Radio Union (IARU) 125
International Business Show 124
International Exposition and Olympic Games (1900) 47
International Fire Congress (Paris, 1900)
International Plowing Match and Rural Exhibition 138
International Sheep Shearing Festival Association 139
International Typographical Union (ITU) 19, 57, 61–63, 189
International Youth Skill Olympics 166
Inter-Ocean (Chicago) 59
INTERSTENO 119
Iowa 136
Ireland 106
Ireland, George 153
Irish 98
Ives, James Merritt 34

James T. Johnson Circus 70
Jamestown, Colony at 32
Jefferson, IA 177
Jenner, Bruce 73, 185
Jennings Clothing Store fire, 36
Jeroloman, Jim 37–38
Jewell, Milt Construction Co. 7
Johnson, Curt 11
Johnson, Earvin "Magic" 139
Johnson, Rafer 115
Jones, Buck 93
Jones, Casey 176
Jones, George Noble 52
Jordan, Weymouth T. 51
Journal of Law and Economics 121
Journal of Leisure Research 11, 178
Journal of the West 172
journalism 170–72
Joyce 78
Judah, Theodore (Crazy Ted) 74
July 4th 4, 108
Jumbo 58
"jumper" 68
"jumpist" 68
The Jungle 150

Kansas 88, 133
Kansas City Fire Department 47
Kansas City, MO 164–66
Kansas City, MO, Convention Center 15
Kasson, MN 138
Kelley, Mike 'King" 175
Kelley, Peter 24
Kellogg, ID 108
Kelly, George M. 70
Kelly, J.F. 148
Kemper Arena, Kansas City 15, 164, 166
Kennbec #1 40
Kennedy 78
Kennedy, John F. 138
Kenney, Miss 61
Kenney, Mr. 154
Keokuk, IA 148
Kerrigan's Hall (NYC) 148
Kewanee, IL 177
Killeen 78
killer competitions 164
King, Thomas 69
Kirkland, C.D. 95
Kitten-to-Mitten contest 140
Knights of Labor 62, 181
Knights of the Anvil 147
"Knights of the Wax and Thread" 156
knitters 163
Know Nothing Party 24
Knox, Jennie 11
Kohl and Middleton (dime museums) 58, 60, 62
Kona, HI 142
Kopren, Wade 139
Korean War 188
Kreitz, Denton 11
Krugman, Paul 121

Labor Day 102, 108, 112
La Crosse, WI 72
Lady Washington Engine Company Number #40 15, 37–38
Lake Erie 31
Lake George, NY 119
Lalors Slaughterhouse (NYC) 148
Lanesboro, MN 142
Larivee, John 11
Las Vegas, NV 94, 161
LaSalle County, IL 134
The Late George Apley 172
Laurel Hill, PA 27
lawn mower precision drill team 158
lawn tennis 178
Lawrence, Edward 148
Leaden, R.J. 146
Leadville (CO) Boom Days 115, 177
leapers 66–68, 70–72
leaping line 67
LeCompte, Mary Lou 88, 89
Ledoux, Chris 175
Lee County, IA 129
Leech, Carl 103
Leesburg, VA 166
lei making (in Hawaii) 163
leisure time 180–81
Lentill & H.W. Barnes 156
Leonard, Zenas 88–89
Leon's Amphitheatre (Havana)

Index

Leslie, Mr. 137
Levy, Thomas C. 62
Lewis Tunnel (VA-WV) 113
Lexington Market (Baltimore) 39
Leyden, Charles 149
LG Mobile World Cup 168
Library of Congress, Washington, DC 11
Liebowitz, Stanley 121–23
life-guards 163
Life magazine 5
light cotton 52
Lincoln, Abraham 3, 142, 163, 174, 176, 182
Lincoln, NE 131
linotype machine 56
literature 172
Little Falls, MN 101
Local 6 of International Typographical Union 172
Lockport, NY 31, 33, 45
Lodge, Joseph P. 155
log rolling 48, 50, 51; see also birling
logging 168
Londergas, John 150–51
London Zoo 58
longhorn steers 83, 87, 88
Longley's Shorthand and Typewriting Institute (Cincinnati, OH) 121
Louis, Joe 115
Louisiana State University 35
Lucy (slave) 51–52
lumber camps 96, 99–101
lumber industry 97–99, 103
lumber sports 103–4
lumberjacks 97, 98, 168, 170; contest movies 174; Hall of Fame 177; World Championships 104
The Lusty Men 174

MacDonalds 98; crew competition 167
machine shorthand writers (stenotypists) 119
machine tooling 163
Mackay School of Mines 116
Macomb, George "Darby" 148
Macomb, IL 70
Madison, WI 10
Madison Square Garden (NYC) 58, 91, 139, 159
Mahoney, Jack 102
Maine 96–98, 157, 175
Major League Baseball 163
Malone, John 147
Manchester, NH 45

Mantle, Mickey 186
Marblehead, MA 46
Margolis, Stephen 121–23
Markwyn, Abby 11
Marlinton, WV 143
Marquand, John P. 44, 172
Marx, Karl 17, 64, 179
Maryland 48, 135, 164
Maryland plowing match 14
masculinity 182–83
Mason-Dixon Line 1
masonry contests 163, 166
Massachusetts 166
Master Frank, Little Horseman 71
Mather, Cotton 3
Matthews, Joyce 120
Maynard, Ken 93
Mays, Willie 186
McCann, Joseph W. 55, 57–62, 64
McCleester, Johnny 37
McCluskey, Country 37
McCullum, Alexander 155
McDowell, Robert S. 24–26, 30
McElroy, Ted R. 125
McGurrin, Frank E. 121–23
McKinley, Pres. William 46
McNamara 78
McQueen, Roscoe (firefighter extreme) 162
McVane, D. 155
Mergenthaler linotype machine 56
Merrimack Square, Manchester, NH 44
Methuen, MA 8
Mexican-American War (1844) 89, 139
Mexico 88, 92
Mexico City 85, 87; Olympic games (1968) 72
Meyer, Robert 142
Michigan 96–98, 100, 106–7
Michigan Agricultural College (now Michigan State University) 139
micromucking 108
Middleburg, VA 11, 171
Mid-West Corn Husking 131
milking 134, 170
Mill Iron Ranch 89
Miller, Charles 156
Miller, Zach 83, 85, 86
Miller Brothers 101 Wild West Show 83, 87, 90, 91, 93
Millette, Ernie 68
Milwaukee County, WI 135, 148

mining 170, 188; Hall of Fame 177
mining camps 107–108
Minnesota 98, 130, 175
Mississippi River 75, 101
Missouri 131, 133
Mitchum, Robert 174
Mix, Tom 91, 93
Model T 127
Mongols 92
Monoma County, IA 128–29
Montpelier, VT 150
Montreal 58
Moore, Kate 168
Moors 92
Morgan, Gib 176
Morrill, Sen. Justin S. 142
Morrisania, NY 187
Morse, Samuel F.B. 124
Morse Code competitions 124–25
Mose of the Bowery B'hoy 37, 175
Mossburg, Cora 73
Mott Haven, NY 155
Mount St. Mary's College (University) 1, 10
Mount Washington, PA 24
mountain bikes 167
mowing 16, 141, 157–58, 171
Moxley, D.N. 52
muckers 107
Mulhall, Lucille 93
Munn, Asa B. 137
music 175
musters 40–46; New England 172–73; sample news account 194–95
Mutual District Messenger Co. (NY) 158
Mutual Engine Company (NYC) (Mutuals) 43, 187
"My Heroes Have Always Been Cowboys" 175

Nala Damjanta 62
Nasaw, David 181
NASCAR 5, 110
National Association of Base-Ball Players (NABA) 43
National Basketball Association 163
National Corn Huskers Hall of Fame 177
National Corn Husking Association 131, 135
National Finals Rodeo 94
National Fireman's Musters Association (NFMA) 43
National Football League 163

National Police Gazette 41, 136, 145, 153, 158, 171–72, 178, 183
National Road 23–27, 30
National Rodeo Cowboy Hall of Fame 94
National Shorthand Reporters Association-NSRA 118
National speed contests for stenographers 119
National Sporting Library 11, 171
National Tooling and Machining Association (NTMA) 167
Native Americans of the Plains 92
NBC 133
NCAA 115, 186
Nebraska ("Cornhusker" state) 128, 131
Nebraska Farmer 128, 172
Nelligan, John 100, 102
Nelson, George 140
Nelson, Scott Reynolds 106, 112, 175
Nelson, Willie 175
Nestor Estate Logging Company(MI) 100
Nevada 116
New Amsterdam 32
New Brunswick, CAN 97
New Brunswick, NJ 156
New England 14, 98, 136, 140–41, 161, 185
New England Federation of Agricultural Students 142
New Hampshire 7, 11; Sheep & Wool Festival 140
New Market Fire Company (MD) 39
New York 130, 139
New York Athletic Club 44, 187
New York Caledonian Club 187
New York City 31, 32, 34–37, 55–63, 117–18, 124, 154, 169, 187
New York Clipper 18, 21, 31, 33, 40, 41, 43, 44, 69, 70, 71, 72, 135–37, 142, 145–49, 151–54, 156, 171–72, 179, 190
New York Engine #5 36
New York Evening Post 69
New York Herald 55, 58, 59, 62, 64, 141
New York Sportsman 41, 136, 145

New York Stampede 93
New York State Agricultural Society 136, 142
New York State Fair 138, 140
New York Sun 152, 171
New York Times 5, 118, 123, 153, 177
New York Tribune 36, 64
New York World 55, 61, 62, 64, 171
New Zealand 104, 161
Newburgh, NY 148, 154
Newburyport, MA 45
newspaper folding 152–53
Newton, IA 138
Niblo's Garden (New York) 69
Nixon, Richard M. 138
Nobel Prize in economics 81
Nolan, Jim 146
North American United Caledonian Association (NAUCA) 43
North Wind album 175
Northrup, Solomon 52
Norway pine 99
Norwich, NY 146

O'Brien, Edward W. 147, 172
O'Brien, Fred 70, 71, 72
O'Brien, Patrick 148
occupational sports, 2101 196–98
O'Connor, Roger 155
O'Neal Shaquille 115
O'Neil's, Martin (Chicago) 149
Ogden Charles 137
Ohio 106, 131
Ohiopyle, PA 24
Oklahoma City, OK 177
Old Gold Knights 131
"Old Maid" Engine 35, 37–38
Old Pike 23, 30
Oliver, Tom 102
Olmstead, Frederick Law 53
Olson, Walter 134
Olympic games: Los Angeles (1932) 126; Mexico City (1968) 73; Seoul (1988) 47, 185
Olympic Theatre (NYC) 37
Olympic Trials, U.S. 5
Omaha, NE 79
Ontario, CAN 185
Ontario, OR 129–30
Ontario Plowmen Association 138
Orange, NJ 137
orange picking contests 142

Orcutt, W.T. 99, 101
Oregon State University 72
Orlando, FL 142
Orr, Miss May 123
Osborne, Thomas 123
outdoor life 172
Outing 172, 178
Outing Club (Dartmouth College) 189
Outlaw 173
Oval Office 117
Ownby, Ted 142, 184
oyster shucking 163
Ozarks 106

Pacific Northwest 97
Packers 170
Paddies 106
palm hook 132
Pan-American Exposition (1901 World's Fair) 45
Paris 46
"path dependence" 121
Pathé-Frères (Motion Picture Co.) 87
Patsey (slave) 53
Pearl Harbor 134
peavies (pike poles) 103
Peck, Ira 137
Pecos Bill 114, 176–77
pedestrianism 171
peg (hook) 132
Pennsylvania 88, 106, 131, 136, 139
Perry, Luke 173
Perry County, AL 51
Pershing, General John B. 47
personal trainers 167
Petersburg, VA 113
Philadelphia 31–32, 39, 41, 62–63, 155
Phillips, H. 153
Phillips, L.E. 133
Phillips Petroleum Co. 133
Pickens, Big Jim 109
Pickens and Page 111–12
Pickett, Bill 9, 73, 83–89, 92, 93–95
Pickett, Con 139
picking (cotton) standards 53
Pigeon Forge, TN 177
"Pike boy" 24
El Pincharino 86
Pitman, Sir Isaac 117–19
Pittsburgh 63
Pittsfield, MA 14, 135, 141
Plambeck, Herb 137
Plaza El Toreo bull ring 86
Pleck, Elizabeth 183

Index

Pleck, Joseph 183
The Plough, the Loom and the Anvil 172
ploughing 135
plowing 134–38, 163, 170–71
Plowing Hall of Fame 177
plumbing 166
Point of No Return 44
pole climbing 103, 171
pole vault 186
Polk, James K. 139
Polk County, IA 129
Polley, Percy 3–4
Ponca City, OK 94
Pooler, GA 168
Porter, William T. 41, 171
Portsmouth, NH 45
Portuguese 92
potato peeling contests 142
Prairie Farmer 128, 129, 131, 132, 134, 172
Prescott, AZ 90
presidential campaign poster (1860) 182
Princeton College (University) 44, 117, 187
Pro Rodeo Hall of Fame 177
Proctor, Alexander Phimister 173
productivity 188–90; labor 19, 109
Professional Bull Riders 94
Professional Rodeo Cowboys Association (PRCA) 94, 160
Promontory Summit, Utah Territory 74–76
Protestant work ethic 179
Providence, RI 45
Pujols, Albert 185
Pulitzer, Joseph 171
Pulitzer prize 172
pumpers 33, 47
Pure Food and Drug Act (1906) 150
Pursell, Carroll 188

Quaker Oats Company 134
quantification 21
Quebec 58
Queen, Frank 41, 146, 155–56, 171
quiltings 48, 50
Quirk, Patrick 71, 73
quota competitions 52, 53
QWERTY keyboard 120–21, 123

R&N Construction Co. 8
Rae, Fred 60
rail-splitter 174, 182
rail splitting national championships 163
Railroad Day 108
railroad industry, US 78
Rakeman, Carl 27
Rambo, Thomas 146
rationalization 21
Rattlesnake Boys 131
Ravel and Martinette circus 69
Rawick, George 50
reaping 135, 141, 171
Red Jacket Company (Cambridge, MA) 46
Redford, Robert 174
Reel, Guy 158
Reid, Whitelow 64
Reid and Sherwin Packing House 149
Remington, Frederic 173
Remington and Sons, E. 118, 120–21, 124
Republican Party 25, 137–38, 174
residential wiring 166
Rheinhart, Sam 70
rhubarb stalk throwing contests 142
Richie, Atha 109, 111, 112
Richmond (VA) Penitentiary 113
Ride High TC 173
Riley's saloon (NYC)
Rio, Illinois 134
Ripley, Addison 157
Roach Guards gang 37
road bowling 154
Roberts, Robin 139
Robinson, Brooks 140
Robson, Paul 115
Rochester, NH 46
Rochester, NY 46, 123
rock drilling 108–112, 115, 135
Rockwell, Norman 14, 147, 173
Rocky Mountain range, silver deposits 106
rodeo 87, 90, 160–61, 185; all-around 160; art 173; Hall of Fame 177; journalism 171–72; "Rodeo" (song) 175; roughstock competitions 91, 160; timed events 160
Rodgers, Daniel 180
Rogers, Will 84, 93
rollerblades 167
Rollinsville, CO 115
Roman Empire 23
Roosevelt, Franklin D. 128
Roosevelt, Theodore 90
Rose, Billy *see* Rosenberg, William
Rosenberg, Bruce 76
Rosenberg, William 11, 117, 119–20, 126
Rosenzweig, Roy 181
Ross, John 96
The Rounders 174
roundups 88; at Pendleton, OR 90
rowing 178
Rumble, Walter 29, 57, 182
Rush, Hilda Rush 30
Rush, Sebastian "Boss" 25
Rutgers University 115
Ruth, Babe 186

Sabin, Edwin 76
Sacramento, CA 74
Saginaw, MI 101
St. Louis 38, 72
St. Louis Cardinals 2
St. Louis World's Fair (1904) 139–40
St. Monday 15
Salisbury, MD 47
Salt Lake City, UT 115, 121
San Antonio 88, 89
Sandburg, Carl 73
Sandwich Islands 38
San Francisco 38, 69, 88, 156–57
San Francisco Examiner 152
Santa Clara Mission 88
Santa Fe, NM 89
Saturday Evening Post 14, 147, 172
Savannah, GA 156; campaign 74
Scandinavians 98
Scenes of New York 175
Schofield, E.M. 156
Schumpeter, Joseph 64
Scorsese, Martin 174
Scotsmen 98
scything 141
Seattle 91
Seeger, Pete 115, 175
Sellers, O.P. 156
Seney, MI 96
Seven Brides for Seven Brothers 174
Shay 78
sheep-to-shawl contests 139–40
sheepshearing 138–140, 163, 170

Index

sheet metal 166
Shelbyville, TN 70
Shepherd, N.H. 174
Sherman, Charles S. (Cy) 131
Sherman, William Tecumseh 74
Sherman Anti-Trust Act 152
shingle making 168
shoeing (horse) 141
Sholes, Christopher Latham 120
shorthand 117–18
shovel toss 7
"Shuck Dat Corn Before You Eat" 175
Siegrist, August 69
Sierra Nevada silver deposits 106
Silver Creek, NY 142
silver mining 106–7
Silverton, CO 115
Simmons, Charles 155
Sinclair, Upton 150
Singer, Isaac 156
single-jack drilling 103, 107–109, 111, 113
Sioux Falls, SD 138
Sioux tribe 80
Six Mile, SC 142
skateboarding 167
skillet tossing 163
SkillsUSA 164–65
Skinner, John S. 41, 135, 171
sky-surfing 167
Slap Shot 37
slavery 48
slugcasting 65
Smith, Bubba 139
Smith, Mr. Jas. 137
Smithsonian 5
Smithsonian Institute 105
Smothers Brothers 175
snowboards 167
social status 178
Somers, Ira 58
Somerville, MA 157
Sommerfeld, PA 24
SONY playstation 162
South Boston, VA 70
South Dakota 131, 173
South Side Dime Museum (Chicago) 59, 64
South Weymouth, MA 45
Southern plantations 48
spading 141, 154–55
Spain 108
"Spanish Tramplin" 69
Speaker, Tris 93, 186, 188
specialization 21
speed writing 118–20

Spirit of the Times 11, 21, 41, 135–36, 145, 153, 171, 190
Sporting Life 41
Sporting Olio 135, 171
Sports Illustrated 5, 172
Spradley 83, 86, 87
Springfield, MA 45
Springsteen, Bruce 175
Stafford, VT 142
stampedes 88
standing block chop 103
Stanek, Fred 127, 128, 131, 133–34
Stanford, Leland 74, 79
State Agricultural Society, IA 136
State Agricultural Society, NY 136
Staten Island, NY 154
Steen, Dave 47, 185, 188
stenographers 121, 163; contests 117–19
Stevenson, Adlai 138
Stewart, Jim 102
Stickney, Robert 66, 70
STIHL 104, 177, 189; Timbersports Series 162
Stockton, CA 142
Stowe, Harriet Beecher 48
strawberry picking contests 142
Strobridge, James 76–77
Strohm, John 131
Stubbs, William H. 65
Sturgis, John P. 24
Stuyvesant, Peter 32
Sullivan, John L. 175
Sullivan, Patrick 148
Sullivan, Yankee 37
swampers 100
Swearigen, Mark 53
"swifts" (typesetters) 19, 55, 57–59, 60, 119, 180–82, 189
Swing Boys Swing 175
Sydney Olympic Games (2000) 186
Syracuse, NY 142

Tall Tale: The Unbelievable Adventures of Pecos Bill 177
Tammany Hall 32, 35, 37
Tartars 92
Taunton, MA 46
taxidermists 163
Taylor, Frederick W. 112
"TeamWorks" 166
technological forces 55, 63, 64
telegraph 124; linemen 163
telegraph pole climbing 155–56

Telluride, CO 111
"Ten Mile Day" 20, 76, 80–81, 190
Texas 48, 83–84, 88, 90
texting competitions 168
Thayer and Noyes circus 70
threshing 141
Thurmont, MD 168
Tibbs, Casey 173–74
tick (landing area) 66
Tidewater region 113
timber sports 104, 160
Timber Sports Collegiate Series Events 104
Time magazine 5, 134
tinkering 156, 171
Tombstone, AZ 115
Tonopah, NV 108, 110–12
Top Butcher Competition 150
Topsfield (MA) Fair 141
Toronto, Quebec 58
Tousey's Printing Office 55
track & field (athletics) 21, 178
trade journals 172
tramping 57
transcontinental railroad 76, 80, 189
trapshooting 134
Traub, Louis 121–23
Travis County, TX 83
tree climbers 163
tree cutting 135
tree falling 103
Tribune (Chicago) 59, 64
triple somersault 68–69
Trout Creek, MT 143
Troy, NY 40
truck drivers 163
True Californian 157
Truman, Harry S. 137
Tucson, AZ 105
Tunbridge, VT 168
The Turf Register 190
"A Turn on the Old Pike" 172
Turner, Harry 125
Twain, Mark 90, 105–106, 109
Tweed, William March "Boss" 32–33, 35, 37
two person crosscut saw 103
typesetters *see* swifts
"typestick" 55–57
typewriter 120
The Typewriter Operator 121
typing contests 120, 123

Uncle Tom 48
underhand chop 103

Index

Underwood Company 123
Union Club (Morrisania, NY) 187
Union Grounds (Brooklyn) 187
Union Pacific Railroad 9, 74–76, 79–80
Unions (Morrisiana) 43
Uniontown, PA 23–24
United States Axemen's Association (USAA) 161
U.S. Postal Service 176
U.S. Supreme Court 152
University of Arizona 105
University of California 47, 185
University of Chicago 184
University of Massachusetts (Amherst) 142
University of Missouri 35
University of Nebraska 131
University of Nevada–Reno 116
University of Washington 123
University of Wisconsin 10–11
US Route 40 30
USA Ploughing Organization (USAPO) 138
Utah Territory 76
Utica, NY 40

Vallejo, CA 157
Van Amburgh Circus (Carthage, IL) 71
Vance, James 155
Vancouver, Captain 88
Vandalia, Illinois 30
Varallo, J. Edward 119–20
Variety 172
Velocipede (George Arensberg) 60
Vermont 7, 136, 157
Vermont Patriot 150
Vernon, Buffalo 89
Veteran's Fireman's League 46
vice president 128
Vigilant Hose Co (Emmitsburg, MD) 162
vine pruning 163
Virginia 106, 112–114
Vocational Clubs of America (VICA) 166
volunteer fire companies 31–39

Wales 106
Walker, Joe 88
Walkersville, MD 162
Wall Street Journal 10, 22, 163–64; 1995–2005 front page stories 198–99
Wallace, Henry A. (Secretary of Agriculture) 19, 128–31, 189
Wallace, Henry C. 129
Wallace, John P. 128
Wallaces' Farmer 128, 130, 131, 172
Wallin, Carl 7, 11
Wal-Mart 164
Walsworth, Robert 146
"washed" 35, 38
Washington (state) 98
Washington, George 32, 138
Washington, Martha 138
Washington, DC 115, 124
waterboarding 167
watermelon tossing contests 142
Watson, Big Bill 115
Way, Bob 187–88
Weadick, Guy 85
Weaver, Bill 147
Weber, Max 17, 179
Webster County, IA 127
Webster County, WV 103
welding and cutting games 163, 166
West Hamlin, WV 168
West Virginia 106, 167
Westchester County, NY 155
Westmore's Mill (OH) 187
Weyerhaeuser North Wisconsin Lumber Co. 104
Wharton Iron Works, Philadelphia 147
wheat threshing 51
Wheaties 134
Wheeler & Blakes (New Orleans) 156
Wheeling, WV 71, 73
When Farmers Were Heroes: The Era of National Corn Husking Contests 134, 174
White House 18
White Roses (York, PA) 140
White Sulphur Springs, WV 113
Whitewater, WI 139
Whitman County Grange and Livestock Show 140

WHO (radio, Des Moines) 137
Whole Foods 150
"Wide World of Sports" (ABC) 167
Wiggins, David 48, 51, 53
Wilbursaurus 105
Wild West shows 84, 87, 90–91
Williamstown, Ireland 59
Willis, Joseph P. 152
Wilmington, DE 11
Wilson, Woodrow T. 117, 126
wind surfing 167
window painting 163
window washers 163
Windsor, ONT 119
Winter, Charles 156
Wisconsin 98, 99, 131
WLS (of Chicago) 133
Wolff, Dennis 140
woodcutting contests 168
Worcester, MA 40, 136, 181
work (term) 16
worker's sports 14
Worland, John 72
World Championship of Cotton Picking 54
World Rock Drilling Contests 115
World Skills Competition 166
World War I 47, 91, 117, 122
World War II 10–11, 19, 130, 134, 141, 188
World's Fair, Chicago, 1893 98, 100
Wrangler 94, 161
Wyatt 78

yachting 178
Yockey, Fred F. 112
York, NE 30
York, PA 140
Young, Cy 186
Young, Otis 108, 110
Yukon Exp[osition 91
YWCA 123

Zaharias, Babe Didrikson 126, 187–88
zinc mining 106

www.ingramcontent.com/pod-product-compliance
Ingram Content Group UK Ltd.
Pitfield, Milton Keynes, MK11 3LW, UK
UKHW041944140426
5217IPUK00014B/652